Finding Mecca in America

Finding Mecca in America

How Islam Is Becoming an American Religion

MUCAHIT BILICI

The University of Chicago Press   Chicago and London

Mucahit Bilici is assistant professor of sociology at John Jay College, City University of New York.

The University of Chicago Press, Chicago 60637
The University of Chicago Press, Ltd., London
© 2012 by The University of Chicago
All rights reserved. Published 2012.
Printed in the United States of America

21 20 19 18 17 16 15 14 13 12   1 2 3 4 5

ISBN-13: 978-0-226-04956-4 (cloth)
ISBN-13: 978-0-226-04957-1 (paper)
ISBN-13: 978-0-226-92287-4 (e-book)
ISBN-10: 0-226-04956-6 (cloth)
ISBN-10: 0-226-04957-4 (paper)
ISBN-10: 0-226-92287-1 (e-book)

Library of Congress Cataloging-in-Publication Data

Bilici, Mucahit, 1973– author.
   Finding Mecca in America : How Islam is becoming an American religion / Mucahit Bilici.
       pages cm
   Includes bibliographical references and index.
   ISBN-13: 978-0-226-04956-4 (cloth : alkaline paper)
   ISBN-10: 0-226-04956-6 (cloth : alkaline paper)
   ISBN-13: 978-0-226-04957-1 (paperback : alkaline paper)
   ISBN-10: 0-226-04957-4 (paperback : alkaline paper)   1. Muslims—United States—Social conditions—21st century. 2. Islam—United States.   I. Title.
   E184.M88B55 2012
   305.6'97073—dc23

                                                    2012004825

♾ This paper meets the requirements of ANSI/NISO Z39.48-1992 (Permanence of Paper).

tuba lil ghuraba

Contents

Illustrations

Acknowledgments

This book began its journey in Ann Arbor, Michigan, where it was written as a doctoral dissertation. My mentor, Fatma Müge Göçek, provided me with the best support and guidance. I shall forever be grateful to her for her confidence in me. While she gave me necessary direction, she always allowed me to be myself. I am also thankful to Geneviève Zubrzycki, Margaret Somers, and Michael Kennedy, who enriched me with their teaching, advice, and collegiality. In addition to these brilliant Michigan sociologists, I am indebted to an anthropologist at Michigan: Andrew Shryock. I was fortunate to be part of the Building Islam in Detroit Project initiated by him and Sally Howell. Both Sally and Andrew were invaluable sources of local knowledge and field know-how. My research experience with Andrew in and around Detroit sharpened my ethnographic eye. Among many memorable experiences I had with him was the day we were driving along, deep in conversation, when my car was suddenly engulfed by one of Detroit's notorious potholes. Our collaboration has thus extended both to research and to changing tires.

During my time as a graduate student at Michigan, I enjoyed the camaraderie of Baris Buyukokutan, Asli Gur, Asli Igsiz, Burcak Keskin-Kozat, Cihan Tugal, Serkan Turhal, Mohammad Hassan Khalil, Esra Ozyurek, Marc Baer, Atef Said, Hiro Saito, Dave Dobbie, Claire Decoteau, Kim Greenwell, Besnik Pula, Camilo Leslie, and many others.

I am also grateful to the members of the Muslim community who have generously opened their hearts and minds to me. I thank Nihad Awad and the other staff members of the

Council on American-Islamic Relations in Washington, DC. And in the Detroit area, among the many community members and spokespeople who generously helped me in this project, I want especially to thank Ihor Debryn, Eide Alawan, Najah Bazzy, Achmat Salie, and Dawud Walid.

I also benefited from the advice and encouragement of Christian Smith, José Casanova, Robert Wuthnow, Bryan S. Turner, Ahmet Kuru, Peter Mandaville, and especially Robert Zussman. I am grateful to them all.

This book took its final shape after I moved to New York. My colleagues in the Department of Sociology at John Jay College, City University of New York, have been very supportive. I thank Maria Volpe, Dave Brotherton, Amy Adamczyk, Bob Garot, Gail Garfield, Barry Spunt, Susan Opotow, Jayne Mooney, Rosemary Barberet, and Andrew Karmen.

I have had the privilege of working with a famed editor, Douglas Mitchell, who is both a book connoisseur and a drum virtuoso. He and his excellent assistant, Tim McGovern, have been uncommonly gracious in shepherding this book into existence.

My parents and my siblings—Murat abi, Fatma abla, Zeliha, Nermin, Esra (and Balkan and Zeynep)—have been supportive and loving throughout, despite my occasional disappearances into the academic wilderness. Of many friends in Turkey whose moral support has sustained me from afar, I would like to mention Samet Demir, Halim Bilici, Ahmet Nazli, and Aydin Ugur.

My final and deepest gratitude goes to my wife, Rachel. Without her editorial touch, my ideas would feel very shy in their poor clothes. And without her warm support and intellectual critique, this work would not have been possible.

Muslim Life and American Forms

You are, in many ways, strangers in a strange land. The Messenger of Allah said that the conditions of the stranger are blessed conditions: "they have paradise" for bearing the burden of alienation. An Arab proverb says, "O stranger in a strange land, be a man of courtesy and cultivation."

These are the words of a North African shaikh speaking in 1999 to a group of Muslims in the Bay Area. He was invited by the Zaytuna Institute, a neotraditional center of Islamic learning in Hayward, California. At that time, many in the audience (including some American-born converts) would have agreed with the depiction of themselves as "strangers in a strange land." Today, however, the language of the stranger has been replaced with that of the citizen. And in keeping with the Arab proverb, the leaders of the institution that hosted the speech have managed to turn a modest community center into America's first Muslim college, Zaytuna College.

Zaytuna College is just one of the many new institutions that have emerged as part of a growing Muslim community in America. Strangers are settling and becoming inhabitants of the land. What is the nature of this settlement process? How do strangers cultivate familiarity and aliens become citizens? What are some of the objective obstacles that these particular subjects have had to overcome in order no longer to feel like strangers here? In short, how have Muslim strangers come to inhabit this land and make "peace" between America and Islam?

1

Islam enters the American imagination as a "strange" thing. It appears as a distant thing that has been brought near. It causes anxiety and fear. Apart from their shocking physical toll, acts of terrorism have come as violent assaults on the national psyche, intensifying that fear and causing Islam to be seen as an intruder. Though Americans do recognize that Islam is something more than acts of terrorism, its status has not been fully established. Some feel so threatened that they ask if Islam is even a religion. Many think that even if it is a religion, it is a foreign one.

The terrorist acts of September 11, 2001 (henceforth 9/11), intensified the estrangement of Muslims. Islam became something monstrous. The Muslims most Americans knew were *jihadis*, those who had declared war on America. Even as the fog of war and terror dissipates, Islam and Muslims are still characterized by a motif of foreignness. Do Islam and Muslims belong to America? Can they really be(come) Americans? Most of the controversies surrounding Muslims "in" America seem to revolve around such questions. "American" and "Muslim" are seen as distinct, distant, and even opposing identities. An immigrant Muslim choosing to become American—and an American choosing to become Muslim— often face the question: can a Muslim be American; and an American, Muslim? No wonder the anxiety that gives rise to this question clusters around the assimilability of the immigrant (and the idea that they are unlike other immigrant groups) and the loyalty of the convert (who is often seen as cultural traitor). Asked from either direction, this question implies a sharp boundary and a vast distance between the two categories. The challenge, especially for the immigrant, is to overcome the distance. As they are brought closer, a union is established between the two categories. This process of linking, in its American narrative, usually culminates in a "hyphen," which serves as a bridge uniting the ethnic "heritage" and the American "dream."

America, unlike most European countries, is a nation of immigrants (a hyphen-nation). Though it is made of hyphenated bricks, it is still a building, a solid structure. By calling itself a nation of immigrants, it recognizes the multiplicity but remains a nation nonetheless. It allows every stone to preserve its original color but demands that they take the shape of a brick. It demands submission in the form of solidarity. The stone needs to be made subject to a new form. And like an ill-shaped rock tossed into the roadbed from who knows where, Islam appears to America as an obstinate and obscure object. It thwarts America by draining her attention and resources. Similarly, for many Muslims, their American habitat poses a considerable challenge. One might think, as many do, that Muslims and America are at war with each other. But are they really so distant?

The distance between Islam and America can be traced in the "representation" of Islam in American newspapers. Here I am not so much interested in the accuracy of the representation as its cartography.

Imagine that you are reading today's *New York Times*. As you begin to turn the pages, you notice that a great many of the stories have to do with Islam or Muslims. The reason Muslims get so much coverage these days is obvious. What is not immediately apparent, however, is that there are in fact two kinds of stories. The first has to do with Muslims overseas, who mostly enter the American public's imagination in the context of war and terror, or, to use the now-defunct official nomenclature, "the war on terror." For many years, this type of news dominated the pages of the *Times*. Totally unknown places like Basra, Fallujah, Kabul, and Kandahar became part of everyday American consciousness. In these stories Muslims appear as enemies, as troublemakers, or at best as friendly natives. (The recent Arab Spring has somewhat altered the character of stories about Muslims, though the elements of chaos, instability, and danger remain prominent.) These news stories deal with Muslims and Islam in their externality to American culture and geography and therefore appear under the rubric of foreign news.

You also come across stories belonging to a new genre of news about Muslims. These articles, still rather infrequent in comparison with the first type, are of an entirely different quality: they are stories about Muslims *in* America. The Muslims in these pieces appear either as suspects of terrorism (which puts them back into the first category) or—more often— as victims of the violation of rights. The members of this second group of Muslims are generally represented as next-door neighbors or decent Americans, people who are struggling for their civil rights and are in need of empathy, understanding, and respect. They are domestic Muslims.

In 2006, the *New York Times* assigned its first-ever correspondent for American Muslim affairs. As reported by National Public Radio on April 13, 2006, Neil MacFarquhar, a veteran foreign correspondent reporting on the Muslim world, moved from Cairo to San Francisco to begin covering the affairs of domestic Muslims. Then in 2007 Andrea Elliott, another *Times* reporter, won a Pulitzer Prize for her three-part series "An Imam in America." Published in March 2006, the articles in the series each covered more than two pages of the paper and were enthusiastically welcomed by the Muslim community. On April 17, 2007, the *Times* itself reported that the series received wide acclaim both inside and outside the Muslim community.

Curiosity about Muslims in the United States is not limited to the pages of the *New York Times*. It is shared by neighbors and coworkers, as well as by the FBI and the Department of Homeland Security. This interest is a mixture of fear and fascination. For a whole range of reasons, people wonder what it is like to be Muslim in America. The events of 9/11 had a deep impact on American society but an even deeper one on the Muslims living within it. Once practically invisible, they suddenly found themselves overexposed. Muslim membership in American society became more complicated. Are they terrorists? Should they be allowed to build their mosque in our neighborhood? Is Islamic law really compatible with American culture? Today such questions are asked constantly, explicitly or implicitly, in everyday encounters, in policy circles, and in government agencies. America has, perhaps unwillingly, stumbled across Islam. It is still an obscure cultural object that requires careful handling, whether in terms of homeland security, cultural diversity, religious freedom, or neighborly courtesy. This encounter—imposed on both sides, at least initially, by terrorist acts—is possible because of a confrontation that demands attention. This outbreak of alienation paradoxically brings with it an unplanned *care* in the form of *concern* between Muslims and America. Muslims are incorporated, perhaps for the first time explicitly, into the American imagination as strangers. Even when Muslims do not see themselves as strangers, they have to deal with Americans who do see them as such. There are at least some Muslims who see America as an un-Islamic strange place and some Americans who see Muslims as un-American strangers. Both assume a certain distance and alterity. The challenge for Muslims is to overcome the distance between themselves and America and between America and themselves. This book explores the transition from being *Muslim* in America to becoming an *American* Muslim. In other words, how does "American" become a property of Muslim identity? Becoming an inhabitant of America is a laborious process of cultivation. Completing this process of settlement has become all the more complex and urgent with the tragic interference of 9/11.

The Nation and the Alien: A Gulf Opens

The traumatic events of 9/11 (Foner 2005; Smelser 2004; Alexander 2004) brought death, fear, and terror. They destabilized the nation's sense of security and homeliness. They resulted in the release of collective psychosocial energies—patriotism and nativism. One of the major consequences was the inauguration of institutions intended to restore security and homeliness. This was the job of the Department of Homeland Security. The multifaceted response included a new emphasis on flags, the English

4

language, and border security. The nation's borders, both internal and external, were redeployed: they were "tightened" and "hardened." Growing concern and solidarity minimized the distances between members of the body. Both socially and mentally, people reached for each other and felt closer: "united we stand" was the motto. Meanwhile, Muslims appeared, more than ever before, as aliens within the body of the nation. Whether they were immigrants, American born, or even converts, 9/11 only intensified their stranger status. Until then invisible strangers, they became extremely visible strangers. In a diverse nation, they were the group that shared a religion with the terrorists. This alien part within was, rightly or wrongly, chastised for failing to keep up with the rhythms of solidarity. Muslims were accused of not partaking in the psychic and political work of the nation. No matter what they did, almost all Muslim organizations and individuals were criticized (wrongly but persistently) for "not denouncing terrorism." An overall sense of Durkheimian *collective effervescence* gave rise to nationalism in general and Islamophobia in particular. A gap emerged between the nation and an alien part within it.

This heightened sense of "one nation under threat," reinforced in the ensuing years by government policies (Cole 2005; Howell and Shryock 2003), created a disjuncture between the state and the nation—or, to put it differently, a withdrawal from *demos* to *ethnos* (Balibar 2004, 9; Habermas 1998, 129). Muslims were aliens because they were seen as standing outside the nation while they remained inside the state. True solidarity, at least for some time, required the suspension of the classificatory power of the law. Certain distinctions between the public and private spheres evaporated. Even resistance to the erosions of civil rights had to be formulated in the language of patriotism, as attested by the common bumper sticker "Dissent is patriotic!"

The formal and inclusive character of the state with respect to its domestic inhabitants gave way to the emotional and exclusive mood of the nation.[1] Rules and regulations that had been directed outward—and from which the nation's interior had been mostly exempt—now entered domestic space. As a result, during the Bush administration, the instruments of security once part of the exterior of the state were turned inward. Post-9/11 America witnessed the establishment of the Department of Homeland Security, the Patriot Acts, and the merging of agencies of domestic and foreign intelligence. Spying became internal surveillance, defense became security, kidnapping became detention, and arbitrary acts became "executive decisions" beyond the reach of law, justified by such terms as "security risk" and "national security." The state was cleansed of those outside the nation by means of denationalization, deportation,

I.1 Muslims at the airport. Cartoon by Khalil Bendib (*Muslim Observer*, August 31–September 6, 2006).

and rendition. The interests of the nation took priority over the law of the state. What happened was, in the words of Hannah Arendt, "the transformation of the state from an instrument of the law into an instrument of the nation . . . the nation had conquered the state" (1973, 275).

The crisis and ensuing backlash (Bakalian and Bozorgmehr 2009; Baker and Shryock 2009; Cainkar 2009) put the citizenship of Muslims at risk. Under the spotlights of surveillance and facing interrogation (both real and metaphorical, as they were challenged to prove their loyalty), Muslim communities were further marginalized. Even if they had full legal citizenship, they were seen as cultural aliens. At the height of the panic, as the disjuncture between the state and the nation started to grow, many Muslims who were citizens or residents considered changing their names, and some of them did, as a way of smuggling themselves back into the nation. They wanted to avoid becoming victims of the nation's wrath (e.g., discrimination in employment, bullying at school). Muslims—who were still protected by the state and its legal structures—no longer felt themselves protected by the nation and its public sentiment. The homeland was insecure; neither Muslims nor the American "nation" could feel at home. Both Muslims and America as a whole entered an era of heightened anxiety. This general climate is still felt most acutely at airports, the internal borders of the nation where entry to and exit from the homeland take place.

Muslim identity entered the American public imagination—forcibly—through airplanes and airports; ever since, these places have become an interface between Muslim lives and American law. Not only do all citizens feel the consequences of 9/11 most immediately at the airport, but more importantly, the airport has become the ultimate site of Muslim visibility (fig. I.1). I shall thus use the airport as a point of departure for my discussion of American Islam. With the takeoff, the journey begins—and so do the fear, anxiety, and risk.

Airport: The Interface of Alien-Nation

As a place of transition, the airport is a liminal space. It is an entry and exit point to and from the nation-state. With its strict rules and rites of passage, it has all the characteristics of a threshold place (Gottdiener 2001, 11). At this "edge" of the nation, some members of the nation take off while others land. Pieces of the whole split off and reunite. Outwardly it is a hub of diasporization, inwardly a port of homecoming. Solidarity is constantly tested at this ritualized border, where various forms of surveillance and control are exerted. The airport filters "flows, friends, and foes" (Lyon 2008). Especially since 9/11, widespread anxiety about aviation security, ever-more-intrusive screening procedures, and the creation of no-fly lists all have given rise to "societies of control," a condition Deleuze imagined to be the next stage of surveillance after Foucault's disciplinary society (1992). The airport thus provides a condensed version of the surveillance and control carried out by the "safety state" (Lyon 2003). It is at this site of passage that Muslim visibility and anxiety reach new heights. Muslim membership in the nation is tested here both literally and metaphorically. Passage requires *passports*, which, as proofs of membership, establish loyalty, transparency, and familiarity (Torpey 2000).

Muslims experience the split between the nation and themselves as aliens most directly at the airport. This silent fact comes through loud and clear when a person with a distinctly Muslim appearance walks into an airport. Someone who so far has been treated as more or less ordinary suddenly becomes suspect. The gulf that stretches between him and the nation is flooded with anxiety. At this border where "in" and "not in" meet, the sovereign power encounters an irregularity, a countercurrent. The seemingly resistant object must be arrested and "cleared" before it can be allowed to proceed. Entry into the airport takes the Muslim passenger out of his inconspicuousness with respect to the nation and subjects him to a dreadful visibility and externality. Even those Muslims who do not consider themselves particularly profiled or discriminated against in everyday life suddenly begin to feel uneasy at the airport. Citizens are asked to report suspicious behavior or persons. The state of alert now expected of all travelers is experienced most intensely by Muslim passengers, who are often exhausted by too much self-awareness. Here the Muslim self creates its double in the form of "consciousness" and carries the burden of "alienation." It feels and appears at war, as it were, with itself. Until they are seated on board, all travelers feel this exilic unease to some degree. Indeed, this sense of struggle with the self (awareness of self and others as demanded by the call for alertness) characterizes the overall airport experience.

At the airport human beings are stripped of their language along with their shoes. From the electromagnetic point of view, they become completely naked. The distinction between public and private is partly suspended as security personnel fumble with previously sacrosanct bodies. Strip searches and other security rites of passage show people the "hard edge of the nation" (Bosniak 2006, 4).

Close questioning by security agents who are trained to detect inappropriate emotional reactions (Salter 2007, 49) and scrutiny of travelers' faces for signs of ill intent are two particularly interesting aspects of the airport experience. Security policies increasingly focus on arresting and stabilizing what is loose and flexible. At the airport, both speech (logos) and expression (the face)—which philosopher Emmanuel Levinas famously interpreted as the source of unpredictability and transcendence—meet the pressures of objectification and control.

The face of the terrorist remains the most elusive part of this elusive enemy. If we fail to identify the terrorist through his actions or his speech, we look at his face and even into his eyes. The sovereign biopolitics, here, holds in its hand the tool of biometrics, a *Gestell* (enframing) that pursues and entraps (Heidegger 1977, 21). Still, indeterminacy pervades all human interactions. "The observation of human behavior is probably the hardest thing to defeat," says Waverly Cousin, a checkpoint screener and supervisor of the behavior detection unit at Dulles International Airport. "You just don't know what I am going to see."[2] This insuperable uncertainty is a serious matter: going through security, one must carefully guard one's tongue and facial expression.

Because at the airport the relationship between Muslim identity and American sovereignty comes into the open, it is not surprising that many reported Muslim civil rights violations and a significant portion of everyday Muslim conversation concern airport experiences. Muslims are surprised when they are not selected for random search on a given trip. People jokingly say that driving while black has been replaced by flying while Muslim.

A striking outcome of the securitization of society is the ban on jokes at the airport. Making jokes in the security check area is strictly prohibited. An interesting outgrowth of this is the attempt on the part of Muslim ethnic comedians to turn the stage into a symbolic airport (see chapter 6). Not only do they draw much of their material from their airport experiences, but some literally enter the stage with a simulated ritual of passing through metal detectors and being frisked by mock Transportation Security Administration staff. The turning of airports into no-joke zones and the turning of the Muslim comic zone into a symbolic airport are two symptoms of the same phenomenon. At one and the same time, 9/11, as a device of differentiation, has produced fear and laughter, Islamophobia and Muslim comedy, exclusion and visibility.

Here is an interesting phenomenon: Muslims are susceptible to exclusion only because, for the first time, they are being included. Awareness of Muslims, even as it remains discriminatory, makes them part of American society. Muslims are, as it were, incorporated into American life by virtue of their exclusion. The iconic illustration of this fact is the attempt by some states and groups to legislate a "ban on sharia law." Why do they bother? They negatively recognize Islam and include it in American law by trying to exclude it. Islam is inserted into state laws, and Muslim identity becomes a weapon in party politics at the highest level. One need only recall that 20 percent of the American people believe that President Barack Hussein Obama is Muslim. Being granted relevance in the form of exclusion is one step up from silence and invisibility, which neither excludes nor includes. Today Muslims are a *domestic* problem—a problem people try to solve in everyday conversations, in interfaith dialogue, in the courts, and in congressional hearings.

Part of this study deals with the ways in which Muslims undo exclusion by using their newfound visibility to extinguish the fear and anxiety that surround them. Feeling that their citizenship is at risk in the aftermath of 9/11, they try to bridge the gap that has opened between them and the rest of American society. There is a failure of communication, a crisis of community occasioned by the lack of connection between what feels like a severed limb and the rest of the body.

This book divides into two parts: the first half deals with Muslim anxieties about their Islamic identity in an American environment, the second with anxieties about the preservation of their American citizenship. There is a common theme throughout: the labor of appropriation and inhabitation. The chapters of the book explore the Muslim inhabitation of various American forms: space, land, language, citizenship, religion, and humor. How is the (terrifying) nearness of the perceived intruder transformed into the (tranquilizing) familiarity of a fellow inhabitant? This is the story of a part's cultivation of membership in the whole. It is a story of solidarity, or the development of an American *asabiyya*.[3]

Hermeneutics of the Immigrant as a Subject of Citizenship

The legal term for membership in the nation is "citizenship." It refers to participation in "the city," a naturalized *entanglement* in the communal life of a place. The community-city is today's nation-state. Those called citizen at home are known as nationals outside their neighborhood. Those who are inside the nation and yet not citizens are either aliens (whether legally visiting or illegally sneaking in) or immigrants (aliens who have embarked on the path to citizenship). The immigrant is an alien who needs to be included (made our *own*). He occupies a stretch between alien and citizen—the former speaks to his obscurity, while the latter represents familiarity and transparency.[4] The immigrant seeks release from this tension. As an alien, he is *no-longer,* but as a citizen, he is *not-yet.* He is a person in transit: *thrown* and not yet landed. This loose entity carries with him risk and danger, which needs to be filtered out at border spaces like Ellis Island and Angel Island and like those now found at every checkpoint inside the homeland.

Immigrant's Anxiety and Citizen's Security

Compared with the citizen, the immigrant is marked by struggle and anxiety. The immigrant stranger exerts his will to become a citizen (this is made explicit in the citizenship oath that every alien who has crossed the bridge of immigration must take). Therefore, the immigrant is a "becoming," while the citizen is a "being." Becoming is in flux (like a current), whereas being is stabilized (like an atmosphere). It is no wonder that the benign view of the immigrant (i.e., the view from liberal inclusiveness) perceives him as an incomplete citizen, while the malign view (exclusive nativism) sees him as an alien intruder. As a "becoming," the immigrant wants to find rest and become a "being," a citizen. The citizen, on the other hand, has no distance to travel, no oath to take, and no burden to carry. He does not need to make a covenant because he is always already attached. He is native to his destiny. He is not a party to a marriage but a child of a family. His belonging is fluent.

The immigrant is restless because he is not at home—yet. Being diasporic, he carries a burden (which is himself) and struggles to come to his own as a full citizen. The sight of his uncanny face is unsettling not only to the citizen but also to the immigrant himself, who sees himself in the mirror of the citizen. His own face appears either deficient or excessive, his behavior strange and out of sync. The immigrant needs to be extinguished so that citizens can relax.

If "man is the animal that has not yet been established" (Nietzsche 1999, 56), one can say that an immigrant is a citizen who has not yet been naturalized. Here nature is used in the sense of both natal place and resting place—a haven and a heaven. The native is natural and established; the immigrant is up in the air. The native is well rooted, solid; the stranger suffers from anomic looseness. He seeks settlement. Citizen and immigrant thus correspond to common sense and ideology respectively: only when "diasporized" does common sense shrink to ideology. This is exactly what happens to the native language and culture of the immigrant when he moves to another culture—they become an accent, something exotic.

As ideology, the immigrant is delivered over to himself. He has a "thesis" and carries the burden of proof. The subject of ideology is restless and has clear boundaries (he is "Muslim"). His speech sounds ideological, marred by an accent. Hard to understand, it generates obscurity. The immigrant is subject to objectification and is seen from a distance. He is "edgy" not only in accent but also in appearance, taste, and so on. In contrast to the immigrant, the citizen represents common sense. A citizen is not objectifiable and has no visible boundaries. Common sense, unlike ideology, has no "thesis" to prove but rather "facts" that are *obvious*. As understood by Aristotle, *doxa* is not a seeking but a "view already." It is light and transparent and taken for granted.

Every ideology—as soon as it recognizes itself as such—wants to annihilate itself as ideology and rise to the level of common sense (what Marxists call "hegemony"; Bourdieu, "*doxa*"; anthropologists, "culture"; and sociologists, "social structure"). That is, it desires its thesis to become fact, its accent to become the standard language. When an ideology achieves this in a given society, it simply vanishes from sight, becoming no longer an object with edges. Instead of carrying the burden of itself, it loses self-consciousness; its boundaries now correspond with the horizons of common sense. When Zarathustra decides to descend from his place high in the mountains and to associate with mankind, he comes across an old hermit, who asks him, "You lived in solitude as in the sea, and the sea bore you. Alas, do you want to go ashore? Alas, do you want again to drag your body yourself?" (Nietzsche 2006, 255). Here Zarathustra, who had been a citizen (residing in the peace of common sense, a perfect dweller with no edges), decides to become an immigrant (with the anxiety of ideology, an imperfect dweller with visible boundaries). By going ashore, Zarathustra clothes himself in boundaries and edges. He puts on anxiety and becomes accented. The cup that was full is now empty again.

We have boundaries, we exist within them, yet we need to transcend them (Simmel 2010, 1–2). We find ourselves within limits, but as soon as we think about what is beyond, we have already crossed the boundary. It is as though we have a *hunger* to cross boundaries and conquer what is beyond. We are consumers of borders. We make them or find them already established, and then we transcend them. They are like handholds for a mountain climber. Once crossed, they become indistinguishable in the mind's eye from the continuity that preceded them. Borders are horizons within which life assumes its forms, yet life is always overflowing these forms, pouring out toward new horizons. Simmel put his finger on the restlessness of this vital flow with his characterization of life as "more-life" and "more-than-life" (1971; 2010, 13).

The Expansion of Citizenship

As a formal membership in a polity, citizenship is an office the size of a cell in a corporate body. It is often expressed as a collection of rights and obligations into which the native is born and the immigrant tries to fit. Politically speaking, citizenship is a mass of cellular offices through which the incorporated entity rules and is ruled. Citizenship offers universality and equality to its insiders and closure and exclusion to its outsiders.[5] That is to say, it both unifies by sorting and leveling and denies by limiting and excluding. T. H. Marshall, in his famous treatise *Citizenship and Social Class* (1964; originally published in 1950), approaches citizenship as a mode of incorporating excluded groups. As a mechanism of inclusion and exclusion, citizenship is a product of struggles among various political, social, economic, and cultural groups. American citizenship in particular has always been a politically charged and contested status (R. Smith 1997, 14). Outsiders (e.g., slaves, women, the working classes, aliens) have struggled to gain citizenship so that they can attain formal equality. The leveling effect of citizenship gives them rights while it undercuts the privileges of the exclusive groups. Not only have waves of excluded groups demolished the walls of privilege in terms of rights, but domains of equality have expanded correspondingly. Today perhaps more people are citizens in a given society but more aspects of life are also brought into the fold of citizenship.

In this expansive movement, Marshall identifies three dimensions of citizenship: civil, political, and social. Civil citizenship refers to the legal rights developed in the seventeenth and eighteenth centuries in response to absolutism. It is institutionalized in the right of habeas corpus. Political citizenship, the second dimension, describes the right to participate in the exercise of power. Developed with the emergence of parliamentary democracy in the eighteenth and nineteenth centuries, political citizenship refers to the right to vote, the right to freedom of association, and so on. Marshall's third dimension of citizenship, social citizenship, emerged in the twentieth century and goes beyond the conventional notion that membership in a community is predominantly a political matter (Shafir 1998, 13). It transforms social hierarchies toward greater egalitarianism. Social citizenship thus takes aim at the problem of exclusion generated by the tension between citizenship's promise of universal equality and the social inequality produced by market forces (Somers 2008, 9).

"Citizenship requires a direct sense of community membership based on loyalty to a civilization which is a common possession" (Marshall 1964, 24). Citizenship always entails a common culture to which loyalty is asked (Hindess 1993, 26) but that common culture can be subject to change. In other words, one has to become American even though the definition of what "American" is may change over time in response to new entrants. The history of citizenship rights shows that social status and a sense of equality have played a key role in the development of citizenship (Marshall 1964, 18, 33; Shklar 1991, 2, 19). Citizenship as membership in a community and ownership of a status has been internally generous and externally selfish: it bestows enjoyment on insiders and deprivation on outsiders.

Today globalization and immigration have altered the character of liberal democratic societies. Legally or not, today many outsiders are in. And the newcomers arrive bearing new identities, religions, and cultural needs. This has given rise to a literature that focuses on citizenship from the point of view of identity (Isin and Turner 2002; Kymlicka 1998; Isin and Wood 1999). This dimension comes to the fore in different contexts, from the European unification process (Delgado-Moreira 1997) to Asian and Latino immigrant communities in the United States (Ong 1996;

Rosaldo 1997). Cultural citizenship, the fourth generation of citizenship, represents a symbolic and ideational turn in the conception of membership (Pakulski 1997, 83).

An important implication of cultural citizenship is that the demand for dignity, recognition, and equality is pursued with respect not only to the formal head of the nation (state) but also to its informal body. What cultural citizenship, commonly referred to under the umbrella term "multiculturalism," shows is the fact that citizenship is deepening its grip, becoming visceral and psychic. The demand for solidarity is now spreading its channels beyond the state, into the realm of national sentiment. Not only is citizenship deepening and expanding, but the very institution of sovereignty, to which citizenship was historically attached, is increasingly being subordinated to citizenship itself. The differentiation between the ruler and the ruled has been continuously—at least formally—eroded. This regicide by democratic revolution has produced *governmentality*—the logic of a sovereign body without organs (Foucault 1991, 103). Governmentality should not be interpreted simply as excessive penetration of the state. It is also the consummation of democratic citizenship in a given space. When the sovereign head (still autonomous in Hobbes) is cut off by the popular body (regicide in Foucault), the royal court is replaced by the national territory (Elias).

Today citizenship is still reaching out toward new horizons and is in the throes of globalization. The famous tension between "humanity" and "nation-state" (the powers of liberal universalism and democratic particularism) has now entered a new configuration because of the proliferation of nonstate and interstate populations and infra- and suprastate powers. This new situation has been called the *postnational constellation* (Habermas 2001). In an attempt to transcend the tension between human rights and citizenship rights (Arendt 1973, 267), philosophers call for a universal solidarity aiming "to incorporate citizenship claims into a universal human rights regime" (Benhabib 2004, 22). In short, the city's walls, at least in theory, are expanding to a point where they will have to disappear.

Overall, one sees a gradual penetration of citizenship into different domains for the sake of establishing solidarity, equality, and unity. While it may never achieve it entirely, citizenship is formally a leveler. By binding insiders to each other, it draws them closer together. It produces at once the private sphere and the public sphere, the home and the homeland. Since the purpose of citizenship is integrating pieces and domains that are loose and far from the body, it is important that the civic blood (Constitution or American culture) circulate well into all the cells and animate them. In this process, the immigrant must submit to and allow himself to be conquered by the city. Like a pious ascetic, the immigrant creates more and more surfaces of contact, an openness to the voice of the city, to the calling of his destination. He cultivates receptivity to the surrounding environment. By sensitizing his interior to his exterior, the immigrant submits and becomes conducive to the flow of *asabiyya*. He can now absorb and be absorbed by the body that surrounds him. The immigrant anxiously seeking security is in a struggle to fit into the "soul of the citizen" (Gordon 1987, 293).

Thus, the life of the Muslim immigrant must be reshaped into the form of a citizen. The immigrant has to prune away the excess and fill in the gaps. In this meticulous work of discipline and care of the self, the subject purifies itself and fulfills its vocation.

American Muslims: On the Way from Diaspora to Home

If they were not already aliens, 9/11 threw Muslims in America far out into left field. Not all Muslims are immigrants, but all Muslims are alienated or seen to be in need of and under the obligation of solidarity. Even native converts are seen as having departed from their own culture into alienage, if not betrayal. Therefore, they all share a common "vocation" opened up by the fateful event. Now as part of their destiny they have to arrive at their destination.

Let us first familiarize ourselves with the travelers before we focus on the path. Who are the American Muslims? What does American Islam look like? Perhaps I should start with a local answer to this global question. After all, most of the research that this study draws on was conducted in Detroit, a microcosm of Islam in America. It is also the birthplace of various Muslim movements and institutions. Detroit is home to the first mosque in America. It is the birthplace of the Nation of Islam. As in the rest of America, the majority of Muslims are immigrants to Detroit, but the story of Islam is not exclusively a story of immigration. Large African American convert communities—now second- and third-generation Muslim Americans—are an important part of the Muslim landscape. In Detroit one can easily find both first- and third-generation immigrants, converts, and mosques.

Islam in Detroit, as in all of America, is divided along the lines of race, ethnicity, time of immigration, language competence, and sect. Detroit's first mosque was established in Highland Park in 1921 by Lebanese Sunni immigrants. Mufti Muhammad Sadiq led the first prayer at the Highland

Park mosque and gave a historic speech that was reported by the *Detroit News* on June 9, 1921, under the headline "City's Mohammedans Open New Mosque, First in U.S." Missionaries from the heterodox Ahmadiyya movement of India arrived in Detroit around the same time. And in 1930 the Nation of Islam, started by Wallace D. Fard and led until 1975 by Elijah Muhammad, opened its first "temple" in Detroit.[6]

The Detroit metropolitan area, including the city of Dearborn, has seen several influxes of refugees. In the first quarter of the twentieth century they were mostly economic refugees from Syria, then an Ottoman province. Later, Palestinian and Lebanese refugees came to the region fleeing regional and civil wars. More recently, waves of Bosnian and Iraqi refugees and Yemeni, Indian, Pakistani, and Bangladeshi immigrants have all settled in the area. And the list goes on. Suffice it to say that one can find in Detroit both Albanians, one of the oldest communities, and Senegalese, among the newest. Some of these communities are Shia; others are Sunni.[7] There are both inner-city and suburban mosques. An extensive documentation of these mosques has been produced by the Building Islam in Detroit Project.[8]

Muslim communities are so diverse that only a few strands unite them: Islam as a religion and the American experience. The question of the incorporation of these different groups into the larger society as Americans is at the same time dependent on their articulation of a common "Muslim" identity among themselves. Common identity requires a variety of convergences. One of them is convergence in a common language, both linguistic and cultural.[9]

I was always fascinated by how these communities named their institutions. Let me give just one example to illustrate how factors such as time of immigration, class, and acquisition of English play out in the symbolic process of self-identification. Here are the names of three Detroit mosques: Masjid al Tawheed, Tawheed Center, and Unity Center.

Masjid al Tawheed is located on Warren Avenue in Detroit and has a congregation made up predominantly of recent Yemeni immigrants. The imam does not speak any English and relies on a translator. He is quite prejudiced against other Muslim groups (Shias in particular) and thinks the best way to live in America as Muslims is to minimize contact with non-Muslim Americans. His community is mostly poor: a number of them drive ice-cream trucks for a living, and you always see a small fleet of them parked behind the mosque at prayer time. The second mosque, Tawheed Center, is located in Farmington Hills, a somewhat more affluent suburb. Its congregation is mostly lower middle class. The mosque has an introverted but not entirely unwelcoming character. Compared with Masjid al Tawheed members, they are an older generation of immigrants. Tawheed Center has an ethnically mixed (mostly Arab and South Asian) congregation and does not involve itself much in interfaith activities. The third mosque, the Unity Center in Bloomfield Hills, is located in one of the richest suburbs of Detroit. The congregation is multiethnic and upper middle class. It includes relatively more established immigrants as well as converts. The orientation of the mosque is very ecumenical, both with respect to Islamic sects and to other faith groups. The leaders of the Unity Center are among the most active Muslims on the Detroit interfaith scene.

Now the interesting thing is that all these mosques actually have the same name. *Tawheed* means "unity" and refers simultaneously to the oneness of God and the unity of the Muslim community. The evolution of a single name—from pure transliterated Arabic (*masjid al tawheed*), to a mix of Arabic and English (Tawheed Center), to an entirely anglicized form (Unity Center)—perfectly encapsulates the three mosques' degrees of internal diversity, time of immigration, involvement in interfaith activities, and overall level of engagement with their American environment.

The density of the Muslim community and the diversity of mosque cultures in Detroit make this area a perfect destination for discovering patterns of community development. Andrew Shryock observes one such pattern in the "developmental arc of mosque creation" in Detroit, which begins with "the acquisition of a prayer space, then a move to a house or apartment, then the purchase and refurbishment of an existing structure (a church, a warehouse, an old workshop, a restaurant, a bank), the construction of a mosque 'from the ground up,' and finally the establishment of the mosque-school-cultural center, which is now the aspiration of nearly every active mosque community" (2007, 7).

The three largest Muslim ethnic groups in the United States (and in Detroit) are Arabs, South Asians, and African Americans.[10] About two-thirds of Muslims are foreign born. Estimates of the number of Muslims in the United States vary widely. The most commonly cited number is six million, but it is not a reliable figure.[11] What is agreed upon, however, is that American Muslims are on average better educated and financially better off than their fellow citizens. According to the Pew Research Center's 2007 report, American Muslims are mostly middle class, have moderate political views, and share mainstream values. The same report also found that a majority of Muslims "believe that it has become more difficult to be a Muslim in the U.S. since 9/11. Most also believe that the government 'singles out' Muslims for increased surveillance and monitoring" (2007, 6).

On the shelves of bookstores one can observe the growing interest in Islam and Muslims. The literature on Islam has been growing steadily since 9/11. Some of it can be called alarmist or Islamophobic literature, some of it consists of editions of standard religious texts, and other works are "Islam for Dummies"–type introductions. Muslims themselves are also producing work in response to the demand for knowledge about Islam.

The classic works on Islam in America are for the most part the work of Islamicists, that is, scholars of Islamic studies (Haddad 2002; J. Smith 1999; Haddad and Esposito 2000; Haddad and Smith 2002). Most of this early generation of scholarship provides snapshots of the experience of being Muslim in America. Works on Muslim slaves (Austin 1997; Diouf 1998), convert Muslims (Abdallah 2006), and the African American experience (Jackson 2005) are drawing increasing attention. Popular works representing journalistic interest in American Muslims (Abdo 2006; Barrett 2007) share the shelves with a literature of Muslim self-justification and apology. For example, in 2005 when I walked into a Borders bookstore to check out the new releases, there were two Islam-related books in the storefront display of popular mainstream titles. The first was Khaled Abou El Fadl's *The Great Theft: Wrestling Islam from the Extremists* (2005). The second book was by Corporal James Yee, the former Muslim chaplain at Guantánamo Bay who was accused of espionage by the US government. After a highly publicized case, all the charges against him were dropped. His book's title reflects the tension that gave him both recognition and victimhood: *For God and Country: Faith and Patriotism under Fire* (2005). My first thought was that this is how Islam enters the mainstream, through apologetics and victimhood. Finally, rounding out the picture is a fast-growing literature by Muslim public intellectuals who propose future directions for the community (M. Khan 2002; Safi 2003; Shakir 2005). The landscape is changing rapidly as the demand for Muslim voices and the need for self-explanation lead to an outpouring of new genres. We have arrived at a moment when the second-generation experience is being articulated in new ways. Muslims are no longer simply victims or objects of Hollywood misrepresentation; they are creators of new superhero comics (Naif al-Mutawwa's phenomenal series *The 99*) and performers on Comedy Central (Aasif Mandvi, the Muslim correspondent on Jon Stewart's *The Daily Show*). Publishers now see more aspects of Muslim experience as relevant: hence the proliferation of books like *The American Muslim Teenager's Handbook*, a self-help guide marketed to both Muslim teens and their curious non-Muslim classmates. Efforts toward depicting Muslims as mainstream citizens include a recent reality-television series, *All American Muslim*, which chronicles the everyday lives of Muslim families in Dearborn. Broadcast on TLC, the show follows in the footsteps of a show about a polygamous Mormon family (*Sister Wives*). Young Muslim artists and writers are reaching out to new genres (like the urban Islamic fiction of Umm Juwayriyah's *The Size of a Mustard Seed*, 2009) and new media (such as the highly rated blog *My Halal Kitchen* by Yvonne Maffei).

Academically, the field of American Muslim studies is still new and fragmentary (Leonard 2003b). In the past, most works focused exclusively on immigrant Muslim experiences. The few that dealt with the African American experience tended to treat it separately. Comprehensive, in-depth studies that are grounded in fieldwork are still relatively rare (Ahmed 2010; Baker and Shryock 2009; Bakalian and Bozorgmehr 2009; Schmidt 2004; Shryock 2004a; Moore 1995; Cesari 2004). Today, we have works on the history of American Islam (GhaneaBassiri 2010; Curtis 2009) and studies of the aesthetic aspects of mosques (Kahera 2002) and the proliferation of Muslim expressions in fiction, film, and the like (Cooke and Lawrence 2005). Needless to say, the themes of politics and Islam and Islam and gender remain well-published areas. But this expanding literature, perhaps unsurprisingly, lags behind the flourishing of new Muslim practices ranging from Muslim comedy to Abrahamic discourse. In this book I have deliberately chosen themes that have either escaped attention (are already taken for granted) or have not yet fully appeared above the horizon (are postdiasporic).

I approach American Muslims as a religious/cultural minority, paying particular attention to the process of cultural settlement and to citizenship practices that allow Muslims to inhabit various forms of American culture. I also trace the transformations that take place among the second and third generations of people and institutions that are no longer either immigrant or convert. Muslims are engaged in a range of boundary work. The "symbolic boundaries" that separate "us" from "not us" (Bail 2008; Zubrzycki 2006, 210; Lamont 1992, 9) seem at times to appear and then swiftly vanish, while at other times they remain stubborn. Muslim identity in the United States is an outcome of processes of *boundary crossing* and *boundary shifting* (Zolberg and Woon 1999, 8–9). The concept of boundary crossing entails an investigation of the symbolic violence and disorientation experienced by newcomers. The concept of boundary shifting, on the other hand, makes us attentive to the transformative influence that newcomers aspire to have on their host environment. Rather than the making of boundaries, I am interested in how Muslims consume and transform the boundaries between them and America. Especially after the exclusion generated by 9/11, how do American Muslims unmake boundaries so as to include themselves in the nation?

Theoretical Orientation: The Agonistic Approach in Cultural Sociology

This book is about Muslims and Islam in America. While it has elements of both sociology of religion and immigration studies, its subject matter is not covered by either alone. Those who look for a straightforward engagement with either of those literatures may be surprised not to find them immediately. This book is more precisely a study in cultural sociology and social theory. As a cultural sociologist, I take an agonistic approach to the experience of an emergent community and explore how such a community engages in the constitution of new realities and the dissolution of old ones. In many ways my sociology overlaps with both philosophy and anthropology. It easily blends in with the "sciences" of human experience. I draw on Simmel in sociology and Heidegger in philosophy (the affinities between the two are a subject for future research). My work constitutes at once a Heideggerian sociology and a Simmelian philosophy. It pays homage to Bourdieu but remains critical of his monomothetic reductionism with respect to power. In other words, while I do not feel at home in the shrunken world of most of the symbolic interactionist approaches to sociology, neither am I satisfied with Bourdieu's abrogation of phenomenology through his ultimate translation of everything into power relations, regardless of how "fine" the varieties of power he may identify. I believe that cultural sociology, when informed phenomenologically, should pay particular attention to questions of historicity, the fragility of the subjective and intersubjective worlds and their temporal and spatial processes. Such a phenomenology reflects true human experience, which is always grounded in time and place. This tradition has its origins in the philosophy of Husserl and Heidegger and its (Husserlian) sociological articulation in the work of Schutz, Berger, and Luckmann.[12] A less restrictive list would include philosophers like Nietzsche and Foucault and sociologists like Simmel and Weber.

Agonistic sociology has several sensibilities: these are (*a*) historicization of rationality and attention to the genesis and degeneration of rule, (*b*) primacy of the agonistic elements of charisma, anomie, and life, and

(c) sensitivity to temporality. This type of sociology pays attention to the margins more than to the mainstream, to lived experience more than to floating abstractions, and to the residues of chaos as yet untouched by formatting. I take to heart the observations of Norbert Elias—another Simmelian—that, for example, anomie is not the opposite of social structure but a part of it (Elias 1994b, 177). Contrary to Bryan Wilson's claim, charisma is similarly not a residue of the past in today's world of rationality but something lurking beneath and at the beginning of every rationality. "Not following a rule" (found as a principle in the philosophies of both Heidegger and the later Wittgenstein) is simultaneously a quality of this approach with respect to disciplinary bureaucracy and a point of departure for understanding the dynamics of social action.

We should remain cognizant of the primacy of experience vis-à-vis the ideal types and the rules. Ideal types in Weber are the winners of the tug-of-war between Neo-Kantian and Nietzschean currents at the foundations of sociology. These half-abstracted, formalized reports of experiences "elsewhere" and "in the past" are at best smart averages, a form of reluctant generalization. There is no way to avoid them, since the very ethnographic account one produces based on experience turns into an inventory of ideal types for another interpreter/reader. Following disciplinary convention, I continue to use the language of subject and object, although I consider it problematic. We need to remember that not only the subjects (often treated as "objects") of our research but also we ourselves are beings in-the-world. That is to say, we are in "an irreducible ontological relationship with the world" (Moran 2000, 3). The location of our involvement in the world shapes and "decides what an observer can and cannot see. You can observe only that which can be observed from there. No observer can disclose 'the' world as such" (Fuchs 2001, 4).

Generalization and abstraction are always problematic ventures and can sever the connection between ideal types and their origins in the lifeworld. Instead of seeking applications or instances of laws, we need to first see instances of unique practices and how they generate what we perceive to be rules or laws. The contrast between ideal types and experience is similar to the relationship between rationality and charisma. We often forget that rationality is nothing but a routinized charisma. What makes a rationality rational is not that it is not arbitrary, which it is, but that it is agreed upon and thus routinized. Instead of setting charisma and rationality in opposition to one another, we need to chart their relation on a continuum of nascence and congealment. We need to reestablish the singular and the creative as part of social ontology rather than relegate them to the status of pathology and exception. Bourdieu's antitheoretical theory of practice is an attempt to restore charismatic edge to particular experience (action) against the once-and-for-all abstract universalism of structuralism.

It is remarkable that despite classic theory's anxiety about standardization and bureaucratization, modern-day sociology has succumbed to the desire for abstract generalizations and methodological bureaucracy. This crust of rational abstractness is fractured by ethnographic experience in life. The confrontation between these two traditions has a long history in the opposition between life and reason, between Pascal and Descartes.

My agonistic approach recognizes a certain degree of opacity in the social world. It is humble but not resigned. It strives for elucidation and edification. It also does not waste its energy on wrong assumptions about complete laws and fixity in the world of things that are always becoming. Nor is it interested in piling up empirical data. Unlike a camera (or naïve versions of thick description), it does not report everything and does not presume to see everything. It is always *perspectival* (Nietzsche 1967, 119) and respectfully *selective*. Our understanding of reality is "only a constant approximation" (Dilthey 1962, 109). The hard truth is that social science is "one genre of literature" (Rorty 1982, xliii). As I study that which is historical (not in the sense of what has become past but in the sense of what makes the future), my inquiry itself is historical and takes its place humbly in the journey of a human person: me. Agonistic sociology combines the openness that the notion of "event" (Foucault 2005, 326; Badiou 2006) demands, the recognition of the due rights/truth of the empirical world we inhabit, and the "creativity of action" (Joas 1997) that we possess as moral agents.[13]

Critics like Adorno remind us that methical thinking is always a variant of the metaphysics of presence (i.e., foundationalism) (Shapiro and Sica 1984, 8). In other words, the Cartesian character of modern sciences, in seeking certainty for humanity, has led them to arrest the world as a picture (Heidegger 1977, 115). By trying to stabilize the fleeting world, the modern sciences turn becomings into beings.

Agonistic sociology rescues and resuscitates "the ownness," "the unique," and "the creative" from the blind universalism of Kantian sociology and its tendency toward nomothetic closures to reality. We should not close our eyes to the arrival of new "forms of life" beyond law, language, and theory—a vigilance called for by theories of practice, emergence, or performativity.[14] This openness to history-making respects the "reasons" of the established but safeguards the entry of newness into the world. The agonistic approach pays heed to the "silence" of later Wittgenstein rather than the brilliant and prolific formulas of early

Wittgenstein. It normatively sees the Habermasian *system* as only a massive tool in the hands of *lifeworld*. Without the hand, the tool is lifeless—but without the tool, the hand is still free. The tool is welcome as long as it stays light and submits to the hand. Therefore, what should be prized is not the sea of data but the wisdom of elucidation.

In agonistic sociology, the researcher starts from the self, crosses an ocean of objects, gives them their due place (*aufheben*), and arrives at the *realization* of truth. The agonistic approach keeps the horizon of *uncertainty* open, requires the elucidation of whatever is present-at-hand, and humbly and receptively arrives at the threshold. There, it patiently awaits the bestowal of the *event*. Most important of all, in the agonistic approach the "person" (long lost in most social sciences and only recently sought [C. Smith 2010]) is always present. As a matter of fact, no object of research goes untouched by the person, the seeker of the knowledge. As the questioning being par excellence, the person is what gives unity, meaning, and lucidity to knowledge. For the knowledge is *to* him and *for* him. The knowledge sought after in the agonistic approach is thus not encyclopedic knowledge (information) but wisdom (in the sense of practical wisdom that remains embedded in and at the service of the life of the human person). It is not "objective culture" but "subjective culture" (Simmel 1997).

Because it has lost the person, modern knowledge never arrives at the certainty it seeks. It is seeking the impossible and chasing a mirage—which accounts for the incessant accumulation of knowledge and perpetual dissatisfaction with it in much of science. When it discovers the person as both the origin and the destination, it will acquire a certainty—not the certainty of law, but that of the virtues of calm wisdom and discerning judgment. We should thus be more receptive to critiques of the Kantian legacy in sociology, a good example of which is Georg Simmel's "The Law of the Individual" (2010, 100–154). Post-Bourdieu sociology will benefit immensely from turning its attention toward the key insights of Continental philosophy and much-neglected American pragmatism. The right method for me for knowing another person is "understanding." I know and can explain *things*, but other people, having a dignity not found in things, demand understanding.

My Understanding: *A Personal Interpretation*

Understanding as a basis of interpretive sociology is an alternative not only to positivist explanation but also to simple description. Phenomenological sociology in particular is often accused of being merely descriptive. True phenomenology acquires hermeneutical qualities, and true hermeneutics should lead to new openings in the world of its participants. The methodological line adopted here is hermeneutical, but it is a forward-looking hermeneutics—more humble and more receptive to that which lies ahead. It moves forward not for prediction and control but for edification and inhabitation.

Things that exist under the law are "beings"; those that make the law are "becomings." The human body as an object is a being—it can be explained, and the laws that govern its functioning can be discovered. Even its form of becoming (its development) is predictable because it is subject to law. However, the human spirit (or whatever it is that makes persons more than a body) follows a law only because it chooses to do so—and thus it can only be understood. Explanation is possible only because there is first understanding. In the language of Habermas, the lifeworld has priority over the system and should not be colonized by it. The explanation of experience (*practice*) cannot be rational in a narrow sense. *Practice* precedes all rationality, for it makes history.

I adopt the language of *verstehen* (understanding) as it was appropriated by figures ranging from Dilthey to Weber and Gadamer (2004). Dilthey expressed the essence of hermeneutical procedure in those terms when he said, "understanding is the rediscovery of the I in the Thou" (1962, 67). Through "understanding" the human subject finds relief from opacity and comes to himself. "To Dasein's being, an understanding of being belongs" (Heidegger 1962, 118). As the ground for interpretation, understanding should not be conceived as merely cognitive and textual. This insight is a contribution made philosophically by Heidegger and articulated sociologically by Bourdieu, who encapsulated it in his notion of *habitus*.

All cognitive forms of knowing are founded upon a more primordial form of knowing. This more primordial form of knowing is understanding. As a kind of knowledge it is nonrational (prereflexive, habitual, bodily) and nontheoretical. It is the knowledge that emerges in the domain of "givenness." It is the "naïve" knowledge of "nativity." This nativity, the unmediated engagement with the world—that is, the native experience of the world—refers to *familiarity*.

Based on this insight we can see why both *habitus* and *practice* in Bourdieu remain beyond the complete grasp of rationality. One is prerational and the other, postrational. A deeper articulation of understanding is found in Heidegger's later "thinking," which goes beyond the hermeneutic phenomenology of *Being and Time* (Dreyfus 1984, 66).

The connection between agonistic sociology and this particular form of understanding can be highlighted by the importance of the domain of *facticity*. In other words, there are moments when things are *true* without being *correct*, *ethical* without being *moral*. One can have a lifeworld without a system and encounter "forms of life" without concepts. Equally hard to see for our rationalist eyes is the fact that there can be *aletheia* without *veritas*: we should be prepared to *understand* charisma before it becomes rationality, and we should dare to appreciate madness before it is tamed into civilization. Here lies one of the reasons why art, sport, humor, violence, terrorism, revolution, and so on still remain largely outside the theoretical grasp of sociology.

We cannot ascribe originality only to the totality of society. In trying to stake out a scientific ground of its own, mainstream sociology has either reduced the individual to divisions of the whole (which is the dominant meaning of the individual in sociology) or seen as individual only the whole (which is the treatment of society as an individual). Yes, only society is moral in sociology because it is the only individuality in sociology (Simmel 1991, 144). *Humanity* in Kant became *society* in sociology. In this universalistic conversion, we lost all "persons" except for one: society (Simmel 1950, 58; 2010, 150). Of course (and thank God), most sociologists honor their discipline more in the breach of these principles. A sociology true to its claims of social facts, autonomy, and objectivity, an impoverished yet specific perspective on human life, would look more like Donald Black's pure sociology—which sociologists seem to find shocking (C. Smith 2010, 265).

What has been lost in the constitutive violence that gave rise to sociology is also what makes elusive the notions of action and practice. With structures and laws we stand comfortably within sociology, but when it comes to human agency *within* society, we find ourselves at the periphery of sociology, closer to the humanities. Why is that? I consider sociology to be the anthropology of the Western self; and anthropology, the sociology of the other. In sociology the human ground of scientific activity gets lost in the language of science and objectivity, but in the study of other people, it intrudes and becomes impossible not to reckon with. That is why the sociology of other people always becomes an anthropological endeavor even when it does not have this name, whereas the sociology of one's own society is a forgotten anthropology. Once we truly understand the nature of practice or the creativity of action, we can loosen our claim to scientism and choose a better approach to our objects of study. All this is germane not only to the mistaken boundary between the humanities and social science but also to a question that is frequently asked and hardly ever answered satisfactorily: what is a "case"?

In the process of understanding and interpreting practices we tend to generate metaphysics and rules. As Bourdieu and others have observed, in theoretical theory, rule colonizes action. It chains practices and makes them line up as evidence of its jurisdiction. Here the rule is a standard in search of verification. It achieves its continuity by seeking, arresting, and torturing practices and turning them into cases that confess its validity (Nietzsche 2006, 117; Simmel 2010, 110). The disinterested objectivity of rules and laws might appear neat and abstract but it does violence to the reality and the truth. No wonder a certain philosophical beast smells "cruelty" even in Kant's "categorical imperative" (Nietzsche 1967, 64). A case, thus, is a practice imprisoned by a concept. Although theory's law arrests reality with its concepts, reality always escapes into the future as *practice*. It is for this reason that the study of human beings and their culture restlessly refuses the language of natural sciences. "The rigor of mathematical physical science is exactitude. . . . The humanistic sciences, in contrast, indeed all the sciences concerned with life, must necessarily be inexact just in order to remain rigorous" (Heidegger 1977, 120).

Tahqiq: *Evincing the Real*

I name the methodological aspect of my agonistic sociology *tahqiq*, an Arabic word that means "realization," in the sense of letting the Real be— "to give each that has a right its due right" (Chittick 2007, 71). *Tahqiq*, a classical procedure of truth-seeking, is revived here in response to the need to recover the person from the objectifying laws of positivistic science and the Cartesian split between subject and object. *Tahqiq* is derived from the word *haqq*, which means all the following at once: real, true, proper, appropriate, right, and just (Chittick 2007, 78). *Tahqiq*, grammatically, means to let *haqq* happen or to make it manifest. Here I use the word *tahqiq* in the sense of *appropriation* of truth through *realization* of the true. It demands a labor, a personal devotion. As a practice of research it searches for practices and lets them stand in their meanings by not incarcerating them in the prison of law after arresting and torturing them. *Tahqiq* is not mere investigative sociologism. It does not put the sociologist in the sterile position of an "abstract" researcher seeking perfect knowledge or the perfection of objective knowledge. Here the subject is not engaged in "disinterested" (Bourdieu 1998, 75; Nietzsche 1967, 119) research for discovering the truth. Rather, the truth the researcher discovers has "rebound effects" on him (Foucault 2005, 16).

In *tahqiqi* method, the subject is exposed to and contaminated by the truth he or she lets be (realizes). In this method, the truth is not only unconcealed but also made the researcher's *own*. For only that which can become one's own is true.

Why Ethnography?

In this section I attempt a brief theorization of methods to justify my preference for ethnographic method. Occasionally one comes across the naïve insistence on a certain methodological approach. Such demands are no different from missionary activities wherein a believer demands that another person believe in *his* God. In the secular world of social science, however, the prevailing culture is and must be polytheism. Weber, who managed to suppress gods and demons in his sociology, had to bring them back when it came to matters of values and value neutrality.

Methodological choice is simply a matter of taste, of one's understanding of the research activity. Here is my taste in matters of methods. As an ethnographer, I would like to show—ironically, with numbers (albeit in their most qualitative incarnation)—what each method does to reality and what it means to *me*. In doing this, I borrow three (and no more) terms from Charles S. Peirce, the American pragmatist philosopher. When he first came up with this idea, he confessed that he knew it sounded crazy but that things could most usefully be understood in terms of three categories: *firstness*, *secondness*, and *thirdness* (1935, 52). He described these categories as pure relations. Here I am applying them to three methodological approaches. Since Simmel also harbored a comparable list of relations, my juxtaposition of methods in these terms should not sound too strange.

Peirce described firstness as a *quality* or a *feeling*. Here one experiences or observes as a participant. The researcher is *in* the world and *in* the "case," which reveals itself to him. He does not suppress it or arrest it. He is overwhelmed by it. He gracefully (with *charis*) lets it be. The truth he shares is the truth he witnesses as his "own." It has an *event* character. The subject is not objective. He should not be. He appears native and naïve. He simply says, "Here is my understanding." For understanding is always "mine." In this method (also known as ethnography), research activity is a human endeavor. Our involvement in the world is part of our understanding of it. We can understand it only because we are involved in it. An interpretation that shares such an understanding, therefore, is "never a presuppositionless apprehending of something presented to us" (Heidegger 1962, 191).[15] Rather, presuppositions (as implicit understanding) are the past (retentions) that make the future ("protentions") possible. That is why, despite all efforts toward its bureaucratization, ethnography remains an art and a craft. It is no mere cognitive operation but requires a practical sense: a feeling for the field. It does not predict but can make judgments. It is subjective and personal.

Comparative method corresponds to the Peircean category of secondness, which is a *reaction*. Here we have a comparison, a measurement against each other and mutual verification between two (or more) cases. By pitting two cases against one another, the researcher implicitly acknowledges that one case by itself merely "is." It cannot be subject to right or wrong. It is simply true in itself. To judge it rationally, the researcher brings in another case and uses both cases as mirrors and prisons for each other. Each is arrested by the other by means of *rectitude* and *assimilatio*: each appears as either deficient or excessive, as either weak or strong, with respect to the other. Their comparative fate, set by a rate, depletes their individuality. They appear in dependence on each other, and the originality of each is routinized along the lines of the other. In comparative method, perspectivalism has not yet been lost. This method is a mediated interpretation that goes under the guise of explanation. It departs from the *event* but is not yet a *law*. It represents a flirtation with scientism and its naïve notions of objectivity. Unlike the ethnographer, the comparative researcher can hide behind the correspondence and may claim scientism. With this half interpretation and half explanation, the researcher is still half personal. A rudimentary "measure" shields the researcher from accusations of subjectivity. But the researcher's conscience remains torn between loyalty to the uniqueness of each case and the tendency toward reducing them to one another or to a third ideal.

Thirdness, according to Peirce, is *mediation* and *representation*. This is the survey method. In this method, the researcher is simply lost. In survey, the categorical imperative has chained multiple "cases" together and assimilates them to their average (which does not correspond to any of them, unless by coincidence). Survey speaks a universal language: perspective (location) is extinguished. The researcher is invisible. You cannot see him, because he is nowhere. In the words of Bourdieu, "logic can be everywhere only because it is truly present nowhere" (1990, 87). The researcher is often happy to appear as an extension of his computer—to be precise and objective and to count as a scientist. He has become, as

Thoreau would have it, the tool of his tools, an employee of a research project. The view is not his but the computer's, which is from above—a synoptic, God's-eye view. The correspondence is now not between two cases but among many. "In the midst of all that is correct, the true will withdraw" (Heidegger 1977, 26). In the prison of categories, cases are calculated and pulled by each other so that they remain in custody of each other. The cases are simple embodiments and victims of laws. Survey explains "things" that are present-at-hand as data, and it comes closest to the objective ideal of science. Its voice is that of "one" ("the They" in Heidegger, *das Man*).

In the language of Weber, ethnography corresponds to charisma, comparative method to routinization, and survey to bureaucracy. In order of appearance they are life, arrest/detention, and the iron cage. The ethnographer is an artist or a criminal; the comparativist, a policeman; and the survey researcher, a prison guard. Thus, I ask you to either enjoy my artwork or excuse my crime of passion!

Sites of Exposure and Ways of Familiarization

In some sense, this book is my own story, an autoethnography as an American Muslim. But I am not speaking about myself as such. Rather, I share in what I see sociologically. Put otherwise, this book is more properly a work in *philosophical anthropology* done by a sociologist. As such it may strike my fellow sociologists as a strange book. Yet in this I am a student of the now forgotten philosophical sociology of Simmel.

I gathered my ethnographic data through casual conversations, taped informal interviews, and documentary-archival materials such as community magazines, weekly newspaper, flyers, and audiovisual media. I also observed and listened to what is not spoken, what is taken for granted. Indeed, the first half of this book is precisely about matters that are increasingly being taken for granted, things that will soon sink forever beneath the waves of common sense.

My preliminary fieldwork began in the summer of 2003, when I spent two months as an intern at the national office of the Council on American-Islamic Relations (CAIR) in Washington, DC. Working as an intern, I had the opportunity to gain firsthand insight into the functioning of one of the main Muslim organizations in the United States. After this initial exposure, I continued to keep an eye on the field. I conducted most of my active fieldwork in the Detroit metropolitan area between 2005 and 2007. Part of my data and insight comes from the Building Islam in Detroit Project, where I was a member of a research team exploring various aspects of the collective spaces Muslims have built in Detroit. The Detroit metropolitan area is home to more than fifty mosques and provides an ideal setting for observing the naturalization of Islam and the institutionalization of Muslim identity. The density and diversity of Muslims in the Detroit area allowed me to think comparatively across time and space.

In addition to my research in Detroit and Washington, DC, I have attended community events at both the regional and the national levels, from fundraising dinners and community lectures to gatherings sponsored by national organizations. In particular, I attended several annual conventions of the Islamic Society of North America (ISNA), an organization that has been historically very influential in the shaping of American Islam. I also attended locally organized conventions, campus study circles, and other activities. The multiple sites of my ethnographic fieldwork enabled me to link the national and local levels of community experience.

Stations of the Journey

The book is divided into two parts: "Cultural Settlement" and "Citizenship Practices." The individual chapters form a coherent stream but are broken into two parts for analytical purposes. The first part deals with the orientations, translations, and cultural fine-tuning that take place at the interface of Muslim life and American forms. It examines how Muslims overcome the symbolic violence they initially feel upon coming into a non-Muslim environment. The second part examines Muslim strategies once inside the city, where the breakage caused by 9/11 is knit with civic attention, familial care, and healing humor. The first part reflects the spirit of Muslims as diasporic—oriented *toward* America but still coming at it from outside. The second part understands Muslims as already on the inside, showing them as Americans practicing citizenship.

For early Muslim immigrants, America was an unformatted territory, which generated anxieties about preservation of their Islamic identity. They had to engage in a series of codifications: determining the direction toward Mecca, thinking about the ways of making English a Muslim language, and deciding whether America could qualify as a religiously legitimate homeland. America as a space, culture, and domicile needed to be naturalized.

Chapter 1 explores how Muslims arriving on the American continent faced the question of establishing the direction toward Mecca (qibla). As

America was outside the Muslim sacred canopy, it became a frontier that needed to be incorporated in the Muslim spatial imagination. Determination of the direction toward Mecca is an important way in which Islamic nomos was introduced into an otherwise-profane space. Such codification efforts required the canonization of one "correct direction" at the expense of multiple directions. It emerged gradually over the course of Muslim settlement in America. Unification of qibla among American Muslims is a symbolic unification of the disparate Muslim communities as well. The practical and theoretical debates around the question of qibla in North America provide a metaphorical starting point for my discussion of Muslim membership in American society.

Chapter 2 examines another transition or translation that Muslims in the United States had to make. Muslims historically met with English primarily in two contexts: as the language of Christian missionaries and of European colonizers. Skepticism toward the English language persisted among religious Muslims for some time. With economic globalization and the emergence of English-speaking Muslim minorities, Muslim attitudes underwent a change. In this chapter I trace the genealogy of the encounter between English and Islam and discuss Muslim efforts to make English a Muslim language.

Chapter 3 deals with the difficulty some Muslims have had in seeing America as a homeland. Historically, Muslim exposure to non-Muslim environments was discouraged. Residence outside the lands of Islam (*dar al Islam*) was either temporary or out of necessity. With the rise of permanent Muslim minorities in the West, Muslims had to juridically justify their presence in a non-Muslim environment. This chapter contextualizes the origins of Muslim values and discourses about America—which stand in stark contrast to the anti-Americanism one finds in some parts of the Muslim world. I trace here how America gradually evolved in the minds of its Muslim inhabitants from a land of chaos (*dar al harb*) to a land of Islam (*dar al Islam*).

The formative experiences captured in these three phenomena (direction, language, and home) are increasingly taken for granted by second-generation Muslims. As such they are the vanishing sites of negotiations that formed the backbone of American Muslim identity. During my fieldwork, I witnessed transitions whose traces are being lost over time. These three chapters provide a perspective on the constitution of Muslim common sense and primary domains of inhabitation in the United States.

The second half of the book focuses on the citizenship practices of American Muslims in relation to the larger American public. Unlike earlier chapters, these sections deal with Muslim practices that are relatively recent or still emergent. American Muslims facing the risk of losing their civil liberties and human rights engage in various practices of undoing exclusion. They assert three interrelated messages: "We are citizens" (civil rights), "we are kin" (Abrahamic discourse), and "we are human" (comedy). These are the themes of the final three chapters, dealing with avenues for cultivating and protecting Muslim membership in American society after the traumatic appearance of a gap between the nation and its aliens.

In chapter 4, I explore how Muslims as novice Americans suddenly found themselves on the front lines of the struggle for civil rights. As noted earlier, the impact of 9/11 on Muslims created both exclusion and visibility. It has also forced Muslims to seek recourse in the legal institutions of citizenship, which has led to increased sensitization to Muslim identity on the part of American law. The story of the largest Muslim civil rights group, CAIR, provides an illustration of the dual outcomes of crises like 9/11. Through a discourse of victimhood, Muslims (but only those Muslims who are protected by the law) have been able to fight discrimination. While 9/11 produced discrimination and stigma for Muslims, it also forced American law and Muslim citizens to speak to one another. Muslims train themselves under the pressure of and toward the possibilities of American law. In this work of cultivating fitness with respect to the law, the Muslim immigrant or dormant citizen is awakened as an active American bearer of rights.

Chapter 5 argues that Muslims have recognized the fact that the appeal to civil rights and formal membership alone is not sufficient to secure Muslim belonging in America. Not unlike the need that arose for political, social, and cultural layers of citizenship rights, legal and rational membership alone is not enough for complete solidarity. The mutual possession needs to be deepened. They must also reach out to other faith groups through involvement in interfaith work. Exploring the landscape of interfaith work in the Detroit metropolitan area, I discuss the causes of the discovery of "Abrahamic language" and its significance for the establishment of Muslim membership in Judeo-Christian civilization. Responding in part to the "visceral" language of nativism confronting them (and the welcoming arms of support extended by some religious communities), Muslims gravitate toward a genealogical language of faith. Through Abraham, Islam becomes familiar as it becomes familial. But even Abraham is merely a stop on the way to the universalism of American civil religion. In claiming their membership in American society, Muslims increasingly appropriate the language of American religion.

Chapter 6 ventures onto "funny" ground: the emergence of Muslim comedy after the tragedy of 9/11. By examining the rise of comedy troupes such as Allah Made Me Funny and Axis of Evil, I link Muslim comedy to Islamophobia and the emergence of the "negative charisma" of Muslims in the post-9/11 era. I interpret Muslim ethnic comedy as a plea to humanity by stand-up comedians, a way of undoing otherness on a more personal level. A second-generation phenomenon, Muslim comedy is also a symptom of Muslims' Americanization. I conclude my discussion by offering a new theoretical framework for understanding ethnic comedy in general. Here we reach the frontier of our subject. The Muslim subject and his American object—separated by alienation and a countering desire to overcome it—meet here in the most personal way. At this stage, on the stage, the Muslim subject *enjoys* himself as an American. Having left the weight of the world behind, he finally reaches his destination. Laughing, he comes into his own.

The conclusion looks back at the journey, offering a theory of inhabitation. It clarifies the meanings of being diasporic and being at home. It offers a series of concepts that facilitate the understanding of "nativity" as a general human condition. How do the alienated regain solidarity with the world? How does the opaque object that a subject struggles "with" become a transparent equipment the subject is fluent "in"? This concluding section delineates the acquisition of "learned ignorance" (Bourdieu) or "inconspicuous familiarity" (Heidegger) that is at the heart of inhabitation. It lays out the ethical elements of the intricate process through which the diasporic stranger becomes a native citizen, a virtuoso of dwelling. As such it is an invitation to further thinking on the often-neglected notions of appropriation and inhabitation.

PART ONE

Cultural Settlement

Finding Mecca in America: Muslim Directionality and the Codification of American Space

Muzaphar Shukor has a problem. As Malaysia's first astronaut, he's scheduled to lift off October 10 in a Russian Soyuz spacecraft for a nine-day visit during the holy month of Ramadan to the International Space Station. He's a devout Muslim and when he says his daily prayers he wants to face Mecca, specifically the Ka'aba, the holiest place in Islam. That's where the trouble comes in. From ISS, orbiting 220 miles above the surface of the Earth, the qibla (an Arabic word meaning the direction a Muslim should pray toward Mecca) changes from second to second. What's a devout Muslim to do? Malaysia's space agency, Angkasa, convened a conference last year to wrestle with these and other questions.

PATRICK DIJUSTO, "A MUSLIM ASTRONAUT'S DILEMMA: HOW TO FACE MECCA FROM SPACE," *WIRED*, SEPTEMBER 26, 2007

If a tower were to be built in Mecca such that it could be seen from North America, in which direction would that tower appear? The question seems a simple one. Yet the answer has far-ranging consequences for Muslims in the United States. Far from hypothetical, it has a direct impact on the everyday lives of practicing Muslims. The most immediate consequence is that such a direction would determine where Muslims turn during their five daily prayers. It would also affect the architecture of their mosques and the way they bury their dead. In other words, to carry out their everyday lives as Muslims, they must identify the direction toward Mecca.

The immigration of Muslims to the United States triggers this question, one no longer asked in their countries of origin. At the same time, Americans who convert to Islam—thereby crossing another kind of boundary—are faced with the same issue, one that surely never occurred to them in their non-Muslim past. An obvious implication of this question is that Muslims engage in a process of reorientation wherever they move so that they can locate themselves with respect to Mecca. Muslim directionality—taken for granted and routinized in historically Muslim countries—becomes a problem when Muslims move to an unfamiliar place.

Historical accounts show that Muslim slaves who were brought to America turned in prayer toward the east. Immigrant Muslims, the bulk of whom arrived after the change in immigration policies in 1965, turned for many years to the southeast. African Americans who converted to Islam under the Nation of Islam and were known as Black Muslims turned, at least for a time, toward the west.

When I ask this question of young Muslims in the Detroit metropolitan area, the answer I get most often is "none of the above." They respond very quickly and easily: "Of course, the tower will appear in the northeast." Today, for the overwhelming majority of Muslims, it is common sense and established fact that the direction of Mecca in America is northeast.

Muslims' encounter with American space required them to mentally digest their new environment, which meant inscribing Islamic nomos on American geography. The direction toward Mecca had to be extended in such a way that America, a previously external geography, could be included in the Muslim spatial imagination. Multiple directions emerged in the anomic space of North America because it was literally a New World for Muslims; it came to them as terra incognita.[1] The shift from old directions to new has left architectural scars, much like an accent in language, in some Detroit-area mosques. In this chapter, I explore a symbolic aspect of the Muslim encounter with America and ask how Muslims appropriate and codify American space.

America as Ocean and Storm

In the month of Ramadan, Muslims fast and pay greater attention to their spiritual lives; they read the Qur'an more frequently than at other times of the year. On October 7, 2005, a Friday during Ramadan, I was at the Muslim Unity Center in Bloomfield Hills, Michigan, for *jumah*, congregational prayer. The mosque is always well attended on Fridays; today, because of Ramadan, it was fuller than usual. The Unity Center is a relatively affluent community whose membership is multiethnic and professional. Many of them are physicians, engineers, or business people. Imam Musa, the spiritual leader of the mosque, is an immigrant from Egypt who speaks English with an accent. All of his sermons and speeches that I heard were very ecumenical, moderate, and spiritual. I also learned from others that he used to have a more conservative outlook and that he changed significantly as he moved from one community to another. At the end of his sermon on October 7, 2005, which was about the Prophet's practices during the month of Ramadan, he encouraged the congregation to make donations to the mosque. He reminded them of the Prophet's generosity during Ramadan, then turned to the story of Noah to emphasize the need to support community infrastructure in an environment where Muslims live as a minority. Mosques, Imam Musa told his audience, were like Noah's ark, buffeted by the challenges of ocean and storm. "We should donate," he said, "for the safety of our children; so that we *don't get lost.*"

Imam Musa's remarks about the danger of assimilation into a Christian society were not unusual. Most Muslim community leaders and clerics seek to promote two often contradictory imperatives. They want new generations to interact with the majority culture and be fluent in it, but they also want them to maintain their Muslim identity. In the absence of necessary community institutions and crystallized normative guidelines, there is a perception that Muslims are very chaotic in their practices. Converts surf the Internet for the most congenial style of their newfound religion and "shop around" for suitable mosques in their areas. The second generation often finds their immigrant parents and community leaders inept at dealing with the American context and with other faiths. Imams themselves usually oscillate in their sermons between catering to the mores of the older generation and soothing the exasperation of the young.

Imams face constant challenges over their roles in the American mosque, which can be dramatically different from mosques overseas. Here they are expected to assume the role of counselor as well as prayer leader. Even mosques that started their lives as simple prayer spaces have gradually become community centers with basketball courts, schools, libraries, and soup kitchens—and as such they create new roles and expectations for their imams. Practices vary significantly, however, depending on their particular constituencies' class and ethnic backgrounds.

Community leaders like Imam Musa present mosques as ships that will allow Muslims to navigate the anomic environment of American society. Enduring storms in the ocean of America, they imply, is possible only if Muslims take refuge in the mosques. Avoiding assimilation and constructing an American Muslim identity require symbolic unity among Muslims. That unity finds its metaphorical expression in what Muslims believe unites them all around the world: qibla, the direction toward Mecca. At mosques like the Unity Center, Muslims collectively turn toward Mecca.

The idea of coming together as a congregation and facing one common direction has a powerful place in the imagination of Muslims as a global community. It is not only a matter of symbolic unity but also a practical requirement of their religion, which is probably why Muslims were pioneers in the invention of such direction-finding instruments as astrolabes. Pursuing the larger implications of Imam Musa's metaphor of Noah's ark, we can say that Muslim life in American society is a matter of survival in a spiritually threatening environment. Muslims can survive as a community only to the extent that they see their mosques as ships and find their way (qibla) through the storm and chaos created by displacement. America does not so much pose a threat to Muslims as it induces a sense of agoraphobia: it represents a disorienting open space. This perception is most visible in the experience of early mosques, which, as the first ships floating in the ocean of America, had to change their direction and sail uncharted waters.[2]

Mosques Seeking Their Qiblas: Ships and Astrolabes

The Detroit metropolitan area is a unique place for the study of Muslim experience in America. It has one of the largest concentrations of Arabs and Muslims in the United States. It is a historical destination of Muslim immigration and the birthplace of African American Islam. It is home to the earliest mosques in America. In no other place is Islam as naturalized and institutionalized as in the cities of Detroit and Dearborn, where there are more than fifty mosques. If anywhere, the Detroit area must be the best place to look for the itinerary of Muslim life in its passage to America.

My visits to the dozens of mosques in the Detroit area taught me the most basic fact about the Muslim community: its bewildering diversity. From Bangladeshis to Bosnians, Lebanese to Yemenis, Iraqis to Albanians,

Senegalese to African Americans, a whole range of ethnicities, languages, and sects are represented. A middle way between treating them all as one and getting lost in the wilderness of their diversity is to classify them based on size and cultural proximity. The three major Muslim groups that constitute the bulk of Muslims in the Detroit area and represent the majority of the overall American Muslim population are South Asians, Arabs, and African Americans. They all have mosques and community centers in the Detroit area. Some are inner-city mosques; others are located in rich suburbs. The overwhelming majority of these institutions are very new. Most of them opened within the last two decades. Many of the mosques are converted buildings that used to be churches, houses, workshops, night clubs, banks, and even bowling alleys. To mention just a few, the American Muslim Center used to be a church, the Muslim Center of Detroit was a bank, and the Islamic Institute of Knowledge was once a bowling alley.

The first mosque in the United States was established in Highland Park, now a city within the boundaries of Detroit. The Building Islam in Detroit Project research team unearthed documentary evidence that this first mosque was opened in 1921. There are mosques with competing claims to being the oldest in the country (Khalidi 2000, 317). The first imam of the Highland Park mosque was Imam Hussien Karoub. When I talked to his grandson, Carl Karoub, the first thing he said was, "At the time of my grandfather, Islam was not bad; it was unknown." Imam Karoub was originally from Syria. He came to Michigan in 1914 to work at the Ford plant.

Built on Victor Avenue in Highland Park, this first mosque was initially known as the "Muhammadan Prayer Hall," as it was called on a fundraising flier from the 1920s that Carl Karoub showed me (fig. 1.1). Unfortunately, his grandfather's mosque did not survive long. After his Highland Park experiment, Imam Hussien Karoub led another mosque. This new mosque was built in 1937 at the end of the Great Depression near Ford's new Rouge Plant in Dearborn's Southend. Imam Hussien Karoub himself continued to serve the community as imam until he died in 1973.[3]

Imam Karoub's second mosque still exists on Dix Road and is officially called the American Moslem Society, but people simply call it the Dix Mosque. Built by Lebanese immigrants, Dix Mosque is now a predominantly Yemeni mosque in a poor industrial neighborhood. It was established in 1937 and is the oldest surviving mosque in the Detroit area. It has undergone several renovations and expansions and its ethnic/racial

1.1 Fundraising flyer for the first mosque in Detroit, ca.1921 (courtesy of Carl Karoub), and the gravestone of its first imam, Hussien Karoub.

composition has also shifted significantly. Among the mosque's historical oddities is the fact that early immigrant communities used to congregate there on Sundays rather than Fridays, the Muslim sabbath. Used as a social hall, the space was often appropriated for weddings and dancing, something that would never happen in a mosque in the Middle East. When believers prayed, they prayed toward the east or southeast. Then "one Friday in 1976 a group of Muslims gathered on the doorstep of the Dix Mosque in the Southend of Dearborn. Finding the door locked, they forced their way in and proceeded to do what Muslims all over the world do every Friday at midday: perform *Jumaa* communal prayers. For this group [mostly Yemeni and Palestinian] their dramatic entrance into the mosque symbolized its reclamation by 'authentic' Muslims" (Abraham 2000, 279).

The story of Dix Mosque is interesting in many ways. One interpretation of this particular episode in its history is that the newcomer immigrant Muslims were troubled by what they saw to be the alienation of their fellow Muslims. They saw the earlier immigrants as simply "lost" in the ocean of America. They had lost their spatial and temporal bearings. In the eyes of newly arrived and conservative immigrants, the assimilated Lebanese immigrants had come unmoored from Muslim time and calendar.

"That the Dix Mosque was not open on Fridays was abnormal, even scandalous, in the eyes of the immigrant Muslim community." As Nabeel Abraham describes, the newcomers—who eventually came to outnumber the old immigrants—declared that "henceforth, there will be no singing or dancing in this house of worship" (2000, 280). The Islam that reached the shores of America came in waves; its history is therefore one of constant adjustments and reorientations. The case of the Dix Mosque is just one among many where new immigrants brought in more traditional religious expertise and introduced changes that led to more orthodox practices.

Long before the arrival of Yemenis and Palestinians, new mosques were being opened in various parts of Detroit. If Imam Hussien Karoub was the first Sunni imam in the area, Imam Muhammad Jawad Chirri was his Shia counterpart. Imam Chirri led the Shia community and established one of the most effective and affluent religious organizations in the area. The Shia community once led by Imam Chirri now owns a major mosque complex that is increasingly becoming an icon of American Islam: the Islamic Center of America. It is located on Ford Road, very near the birthplace of Henry Ford.

Today, of several dozen mosques in Detroit, only a few are almost half a century old and still in use. Around the time the Lebanese Shia community was building the first Islamic Center of America in Dearborn, Albanian Muslims had already opened their Albanian Islamic Center in Harper Woods. Established in 1963 and 1962, respectively, these two mosques are of the same generation and can be distinguished from other mosques in several ways. First of all, they were built as mosques and not converted from another use (building conversion is still the most common way of starting mosques). Second, they had larger immigrant bases, which helped the communities reach critical mass. Third and most important, these two mosques each have two mihrabs (see fig. 1.2). The mihrab is a niche in the wall in the direction of Mecca, both giving the prayer area its orientation and designating the place where the imam stands to lead the prayer.

In both of the mosques, the imams no longer use the original mihrabs that were built into the walls then thought to be facing Mecca. Instead, they face a different direction, which is not inscribed in the wall as a niche but is highlighted by the placement of a prayer rug and the organization of carpets. Accordingly, each congregation also forms lines behind the imam and faces a direction different from the original orientation of the mosque. In terms of use of space, there is a cartographic incongruence between the worshipers' positioning and the shape of the hall where they pray.

Albanian Islamic Center
(two qiblas)

NORTHEAST   SOUTHEAST

1.2 The old and the new directions toward Mecca at the Albanian Islamic Center in Harper
Woods, Michigan. The old direction is indicated by the tiled mihrab; the new one, by prayer
rugs.

I wondered about the background story of the two mihrabs. When
I asked Imam Shuajb Gerguri of the Albanian Islamic Center about the
reason for the change, he gave me a clear answer: "Back then they did not
know; they used the flat map." He told me the direction was corrected
in the early 1980s when it became clear that the qibla was northeast and
not southeast. At the time of construction of these mosques, the direction to Mecca and thus the placement of the mihrab were determined
on the basis of a Mercator map rather than a spherical projection. And
when the qibla was changed, it left a permanent scar on the architecture
of these two mosques.

Though most visible in these mosques, the consequences of qibla
change were not limited to them. Muslim graves also had to be reori-
ented. The arrangement reached with Roseland Park Cemetery, where
Imam Hussien Karoub and many other Muslims are buried, was that because of the "improper positioning of the plots," Muslim remains were
to be reinterred "in another section of the cemetery in accordance with
Islamic requirement" (Abraham 2000, 300).

From the repositioning of cemetery plots to the abandoned mihrabs
in old-generation mosques, the changing answers to the question of the

direction in which the imaginary tower in Mecca would be seen in America have had important consequences. To prepare the ground for a detailed discussion of what is known as "the qibla debate in America," we need first to explore the symbolic meaning of the two ends of qibla: Mecca and America.

I begin the next section by discussing the significance of Mecca, as both the focus of pilgrimage and the source of qibla. I will go about this in a counterintuitive way: explaining an empirical yet unfamiliar social object by means of a theoretical and philosophical discussion. I am well aware of the relative unfamiliarity of the two parties I am putting in dialogue here. Nevertheless, I find that the best way to give a degree of conceptual legibility to the phenomenon of Muslim directionality is by resorting to theoretical tools familiar to my audience in the social sciences.

Muslim Directionality: Linking Mecca and America

Muslims have a rule. Wherever they are they should turn toward Mecca for their religious rituals. Therefore, they live with a spatial orientation comparable to the concept of intentionality in phenomenology. To understand the dynamics of this directionality as part of Muslim religious life, we need to explain the importance and centrality of Mecca for Muslims.

Mecca is the holiest city in Islam. The birthplace of Prophet Muhammad, Mecca is also home to the most sacred structure for Muslims: the Kaaba. It is believed that the Kaaba was first built by Abraham. "Kaaba" literally means "cube," in reference to the building's shape. Hajj, one of the five pillars of Islam, requires Muslims who have the material resources and health to visit Mecca at least once in their lifetime.[4]

Every year, Mecca hosts millions of Muslims from all over the world; the pilgrimage is the largest continuously held transnational convocation of people. As part of the ritual, pilgrims circumambulate the Kaaba. In this rite of passage, pilgrims strip themselves of all status symbols and dress identically. They shed their ethnic and gender differences and form *communitas* as they enter Mecca's liminal space of exception and the spatial aura of the Kaaba (V. Turner 1973). They also follow a specific code of conduct. After completing hajj the pilgrims assume a new status and gain the title of *hajji* or *al hajj*.[5]

Although hajj is a major religious requirement in Islam, it is only one aspect of the Muslim relationship to Mecca. Muslims also engage with

Mecca on a daily basis. Another pillar of Islam requires them to pray five times a day, and in those five daily prayers, Muslims face Mecca, more specifically the Kaaba. The Kaaba is the source of qibla. It should be noted, however, that the first qibla in the formative years of Islam was not Kaaba but Jerusalem (Bashear 1991, 267). Early Islam shared the direction with Judaism, and the first Muslims also prayed in Christian churches in locations where they did not have a prayer space of their own. It was only later that Prophet Muhammad changed qibla permanently to the Kaaba. Although some scholars of early Islam argue that "one cannot speak of 'one original *qibla* of Islam,' but rather of several currents in the search for one" (Bashear 1991, 282), what is important in this symbolic unfolding of Islam is that the change of qibla allowed Islam to gradually distinguish itself from both Christianity and Judaism. As Zerubavel shows in his discussion of Easter and Passover, a unique symbolic system, be it temporal (calendar) or spatial (qibla), "accentuates the similitude among group members while, at the same time, establish[ing] intergroup boundaries" (1982, 284).[6]

The revelation on the basis of which Prophet Muhammad changed the qibla came to him while he was praying in a mosque in Medina. This mosque—now among the city's pilgrimage sites—is called Masjid al Qiblatain, "the mosque with two qiblas." The fact that qibla changed in the early history of Islam is inscribed in the structure of this mosque. All the other mosques in Muslim-inhabited geographies have one single qibla. That is, they have one mihrab. They are all oriented toward the Kaaba in Mecca. The mosque with two directions is thus a unique mosque: it is the site where the decision about the qibla was made. It is the site of the decision that precedes the norm. Its similarity with the two mosques in Detroit therefore says a great deal about the nature of rules and rationality. At the bottom of a rule one finds an arbitrary decision. As Foucault notes in his essay "Nietzsche, Genealogy, History," "what is found at the historical beginnings of things is not the inviolable identity of their origin; it is the dissension from other things. It is disparity" (2003, 353). When a decision is repeated so that it becomes congealed into a norm, we lose sight of the original decision. The parallelism between the spatial origin of Islam and its frontiers in North America is an interesting issue to which I will return toward the end of this chapter.

The Kaaba is the center of global Muslim spatial structure. It appropriates, disciplines, and owns. Also called "the house of God," the Kaaba is the embodiment of divine sovereignty, toward which all sacred practices and rituals are oriented. In congregational prayers worshipers form lines that, if connected, would constitute concentric circles around the Kaaba and across the earth. When Muslims slaughter animals, they turn toward the Kaaba, and they bury their dead in such a way that the graves are oriented toward Kaaba. The work of the Kaaba is similar to that of Heidegger's Greek temple: "It is the temple-work that first fits together and at the same time gathers around itself the unity of those paths and relations in which birth and death, disaster and blessing, victory and disgrace, endurance and decline acquire the shape of destiny for human being" (Heidegger 1971, 41). In the words of Henri Lefebvre, the author of *The Production of Space*, "man does not live by words alone: all 'subjects' are situated in a space in which they must either recognize themselves or lose themselves, a space which they may both enjoy and modify" (1991, 35).

In other words, the Kaaba makes the *worlding* of the world possible by standing there; it "first brings to light the light of the day, the breadth of sky, the darkness of the night. The temple's firm towering makes visible the invisible space of air" (Heidegger 1971, 41). As a temple, the Kaaba translates nature into culture, bare geography into directionality. It punctuates space, producing order out of chaos. It creates nearness and distance; it "holds" the world as an oriented space—not unlike the poet Wallace Stevens's "jar in Tennessee."[7]

The focal point of Muslim imagination, the Kaaba is also a symbol, one that Hegel would call the ultimate symbol of Islamic monotheism. In *The Philosophy of History*, he writes:

The object of Mahometan worship is purely intellectual; no image, no representation of Allah is tolerated. Mahomet is a prophet but still man—not elevated above human weaknesses. The leading features of Mahometanism involve this—that in actual existence nothing can become fixed, but that everything is destined to expand itself in activity and life in the boundless amplitude of the world, so that the worship of the One remains the only bond by which the whole is capable of uniting. In this expansion, this active energy, all limits, all national and caste distinctions vanish; no particular race, political claim of birth or possession is regarded—only *man* as a *believer*. (1956, 357)

The idea of Islam as a monotheistic religion that strictly polices the transcendence and unity of God and works as a racial equalizer finds its best symbolic expression in the act of hajj (pilgrimage). The impact of hajj as an experience is particularly visible in convert narratives. Most famously, in his autobiography Malcolm X writes, "I have met, talked to, and even eaten with people who in America would have been considered 'white'—but the 'white' attitude was removed from their minds by the religion of Islam. I have never before seen *sincere* and *true* brotherhood practiced by all colors together, irrespective of their color" (1964, 391).

In an article on pilgrimage and ritual process, "The Center Out There: Pilgrim's Goal," Victor Turner quotes this paragraph to illustrate the concept of *communitas* (1973, 193), which he further develops in *The Ritual Process* (1969).

From anywhere in the world one must turn toward the Kaaba, and from any place there is only *one* correct direction to the Kaaba; yet from within the Kaaba *all* directions are correct. Someone who prays inside the Kaaba can turn toward any direction. This is an extremely important matter because it designates the Kaaba as an exception to the rule of directionality. The Kaaba as an exception is sacred. In spaces of exception the rule is suspended, or to put it differently, there is no rule. The Kaaba therefore is characterized by an *originary indistinction* (Agamben 2005, 6). The Kaaba as a center gives rise to the world around it, and while structuring that world, itself escapes structurality (Derrida 1980, 278).

Before being structured, the center and the structure are identical. Once difference is introduced, they become constitutive "others," with the center occupying the privileged place. The concept of "center" as it is employed here draws on its use not only by Jacques Derrida (1980) but also by Edward Shils (1972) and Victor Turner (1973). That the Kaaba escapes structurality (i.e., directionality) indicates its status as exception (Agamben 2005; Schmitt 1988). That the Kaaba structures the world around itself points to its charismatic character as a space (Weber 1968). Charisma[8] is that which rule (or rationality) cannot explain, where explanation means subjection to a comparison and regularity. Since later readings of the Weberian concept of charisma have unfortunately focused on religious and political authority and leadership, the understanding of charisma has been limited and its obverse needs to be brought to light. Here, I would like to make two interventions based on my treatment of the Kaaba as a charismatic space. First, as Bourdieu (1991, 250) and Agamben (2005, 85) have aptly noted, charisma should be treated as a quality not of a person but of a position. Second, I would argue that there are two types of charisma: *positive charisma* and *negative charisma*. I will explain these two points below.

Weber's charismatic leader, for example, has *exceptional* qualities; people follow him or her without question. But this is only one way that charisma makes its appearance. What does it mean that charisma is a quality of location or position and not person? It means something counterintuitive: it is not that great leaders emerge in times of crisis, but that in times of crisis (states of exception) the leaders that emerge appear great (charismatic). This understanding of charisma goes beyond "charisma of the office." Once we dissociate charisma from the psychologized person and return it to its rightful owner, person-in-location, we can begin to look for other locations where charisma makes its appearance.

In my conceptualization, charisma is the structural equivalent of exception and anomie[9] in that it refers to locations where structure or nomos is absent (i.e., Turner's "anti-structure"). Such locations cannot be subjected to the rule—as in the case of the Kaaba. Or they may not yet have been claimed, appropriated, or subjected to the rule—as in the case of early Muslims' perception of America. The rule can be a rationality, a legal code, or a language of communication. In our case, the rule is directionality. Irregularities, violations of the rule, are indeed charismatic, but in a different way. In the case of positive charisma, such irregularities are approached with fascination and special treatment (they are seen as above the law). Thus, suspension of the rule of directionality inside the Kaaba marks it as divine. The empty space inside the Kaaba thus becomes the location of an omnipresent God. As the house of God, the Kaaba therefore has positive charisma. It is omnidirectional.

The same absence of rule is present in the case of negative charisma, too, but such irregularities are treated as pathologies and considered repulsive (below the law, substandard, incorrect). The contrast can be seen in the ways irregular language use is interpreted. While elites might seek distinction by deviating from the most widespread usage of language, immigrants seek to eliminate the differences that make them accented and incomplete (Bourdieu 1991, 46). Here again we see the two ends of charisma: positive charisma, which one seeks to maintain, and negative charisma, which one seeks to eliminate. Again, the translation of this to our case would be that Muslims strive to get close to the Kaaba (through pilgrimage) while showing anxiety toward full immersion in America. The former represents the source of nomos; the latter, the lack of nomos (anomie).

In short, if positive charisma is associated with creativity and leadership, negative charisma should be associated with chaos/anomie and lack of status. Negative charisma, I would argue, is also the location of what Victor Turner calls *communitas*. Both positive and negative charisma "emerge where social structure is not" (Turner 1969, 126). In that liminal or anomic space where symbolic violence has not yet produced structure, there is neither hierarchy nor distinction. In a sense, negative charisma is naked, bare life (Agamben 1998). It is the unformatted surface, a geography without a qibla. It needs to be arrested, tamed, and formatted. Negative charisma is anomic and must be subjected to discipline. It is forced to acquire docility, legibility, submissiveness to the rule. With the following statement about *communitas*, Turner summarizes the

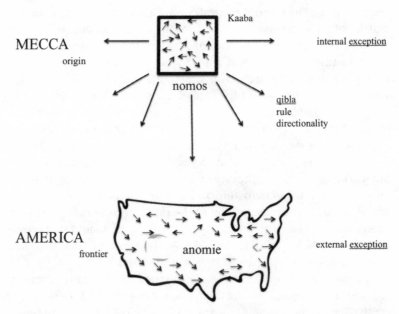

1.3 Center and margin: the exceptional space of Kaaba gives structure to the not-yet-formatted space of America through the imposition of nomos (directionality).

ways in which charisma makes its appearance at various locations of the structure: "*Communitas* breaks in through the interstices of structure, in liminality; at the edges of structure, in marginality; and from beneath the structure, in inferiority" (1969, 128).

Between the positive and negative locations of charisma lies the territory of the rule. Yet the rule has a direction. It starts from positive charisma (the center, Kaaba) and flows toward the rest of the space with the ultimate objective of subjecting that space to its rule (by routinization and rationalization). As it flows, the rule clears and cleans, since that which is *unclear* is often seen as *unclean* (Douglas 1966; Zerubavel 1991, 37). Mecca and America are two spaces linked together by a rule. The rule originates in Mecca as directionality and reaches America as a new surface (fig. 1.3).

The sense of universalism generated by the Kaaba is an effect of the monotheistic exclusion of anything and anyone from the locus of divinity. The Kaaba is the house of a transcendent God, and no other entity can claim that location. All the social and geographic space around and outside the Kaaba is subjected to a set of rules. This subjection produces believers and their orientation. Kaaba is a powerful example of what Foucault calls a *dispositif* (an apparatus) (1980, 196). Agamben usefully elucidates the term, describing it as "anything that has in some way the capacity to capture, orient, determine, intercept, model, control, or secure the gestures, opinions, or discourses of living beings" (2009, 14). In ways both physical and conceptual, the Kaaba resembles the panopticon that Jeremy Bentham developed and Michel Foucault analyzed. The architectural structure of the panopticon was simple: "at the periphery,

1.4 Structural homology of Bentham's panopticon and the Kaaba, focal point of Islamic sacred space.

an annular building; at the center, a tower" (Foucault 1977, 200). The Kaaba is a cubical tower at the center; at its periphery is a square building with rounded corners. The building around the Kaaba is called Masjidul Haram (the Sacred Mosque). If the panopticon has a periphery of partitioned space with isolated cells, the Kaaba's periphery includes both open and covered spaces for prayer. The spaces are punctuated by pillars, but they are not isolated. While the panopticon is a closed disciplinary machine, the Kaaba is an open device for spiritual discipline or for the disciplining of souls. Although Foucault considers panopticism the ultimate modality of disciplinary power in modern times and a technique of control that transcends the architecture of the panopticon, the Kaaba cannot be considered equally embedded in power or a product of modern times. Yet it exercises a similar function as a device that symbolically formats an open surface and produces space (fig. 1.4).

As a modality of partitioning space and providing orientation, the similarities between the panopticon and the Kaaba are striking. Both the tower and the Kaaba see everything but cannot be seen. In its ideal use, the panopticon needs no guardian in its tower, since it is supposed to wield an impersonal and unverifiable power over its subjects. Inmates in the cells cannot see the guardian in the tower, while the guardian in the tower sees them all. Whether they are physically in Mecca or not, Muslims all turn toward an empty building.[10] An empty building with opaque walls, the Kaaba makes visible that which is invisible. It brings forth a world by allowing for the partitioning of space into directions. The Kaaba is a mental pole and the constitutive lack that allows the Muslim layer of direction (a metaphysical construct) to emerge as presence. Annemarie Schimmel notes that for Muslims the Kaaba is "the navel of the earth" (1994, 57). The Kaaba is a "temple" that, "in its standing there, first gives to things their look and to men their outlook on themselves" (Heidegger 1971, 42).[11]

America as Margin: Extension of Qibla and Erasure of Negative Charisma

Upon leaving the Arabian Peninsula, wherever Muslims went they codified place and time according to their religious calendar and sense of direction. Determination of qibla therefore is an archaic issue for the people of the lands where Islam has a long history. The issue of direction to Mecca resurfaces in geographies where Muslim presence is more recent.

The Muslim encounter with America as a geography and culture (i.e., through immigration) is marked by the reemergence of the question of the direction to Mecca. The same is true for the American, especially the African American, encounter with Islam (i.e., through conversion). Both immigrant and convert Muslims engaged in a search for qibla. This search was both literal and metaphorical: it required a cultural digestion of the American environment or orthodox Islam, or both.

Muslim immigrants initially perceived America as a Christian country. They employed medieval juridical distinctions that divided the world into *dar al Islam* (the abode of Islam/peace) and *dar al harb* (the abode of war/chaos) (Haddad 2004, 32; Leonard 2003a, 154). The initial application of Islamic nomos to American space, that is, the first appropriation of America by Muslims, conceived of America in its externality to Islam as a space of exception; Muslim presence in it was construed under the rubric of necessity (*darura*). Immigrants who came to the United States in the 1960s and 1970s wanted only to avoid the negative influence of American society (Schumann 2007, 5). This perception, however, changed over time (Haddad and Lummis 1987).

I leave an extended discussion of this change to the chapter on the transformation of Muslim discourses on America (chapter 3). However, suffice it to say that in the beginning Muslims perceived America as an undifferentiated entity and a space of impurity. In particular, the students who constituted the institutional core of the immigrant Muslim population had a diasporic orientation; they saw America as a temporary way station.

America was foreign to Muslims and Muslims were foreign to America. The initial conceptions of America in externality to Islam defined it as an anomic periphery. Legislating this anomic periphery meant, for example, extension of qibla, the Muslim directional order. The attempt to find the direction to Mecca in America is one way Muslims engaged with American space. Put differently, to appropriate America and turn it into a navigable territory, Muslims had to connect Mecca and America through the Islamic rule of direction (qibla).

In theoretical terms, America and the Kaaba in Mecca occupy the two ends of the rule of qibla, since they both stand outside it. In other words, they are places of exception. Both characterized by their absence of structure, America is an external exception and the Kaaba is an internal exception.

As America has been temporarily and for practical reasons left outside the legislation, it forms an external exception in that it lies beyond the reach of the rule and remains in a juridical void. And because the rule has not yet conquered it, it is an anomic site where *multiple directions arise*. It remains bare geography, a nature yet to be converted into a culture. As a space over which the protective shield of the rule, the "sacred canopy" (Berger 1969), needs to be extended, America remains profane and risky. It emanates anomic terror. It causes confusion and disorientation. Practices in such a place fall under the rule of necessity and state of emergency where normal rules are unavailable. In this anomic space the differentiation of right direction from wrong direction has not yet been achieved: boundaries have not yet been definitively drawn. Therefore, religiously speaking, being in America generates anxiety, confusion, and agoraphobia (Zerubavel 1991, 49) for immigrant Muslims because America appears as an unbounded and unnavigable environment.

The Storm and the Port: The Qibla Debate

Throughout the history of Islam, Muslim astronomers devoted part of their work to establishing the principles for determining qibla and making instruments such as the astrolabe, which were indispensable for navigation and exploration. Qibla was thus always bound up with cultural and geographical frontiers. The question of qibla hardly ever occurs to people in Muslim-inhabited geographies today, as it was resolved centuries ago. It is the mobility and dispersal of populations brought about by colonialism, globalization, and immigration that have given rise to Muslim minorities outside the traditional lands of Islam. These movements create the need to determine qibla in formerly unimaginable locations like America, Australia, and New Zealand.

As we have said, most of the early immigrant mosques, including the first mosque in Detroit, faced east or southeast. In the seventies, as the number of mosques began to increase significantly in tandem with the rise in the number of Muslim immigrants, the question of qibla became an issue. In 1978 S. Kamal Abdali, an expert on Islam and a National Science Foundation scientist, published his *Prayer Schedules for North America*. Based on his expertise and research, Abdali argued that the qibla for North America was northeast. His conclusion was supported by major Islamic organizations in the United States and soon became the norm. Mosques made the required change to fix their directions. Muslims who used to face southeast henceforth faced northeast. The mosques that had mihrabs in the wall in the old direction left them untouched and simply reorganized the layout of prayer rugs to redirect their congregations. But newly built mosques and mosques undergoing expansion or renovation adopted the new direction and carved their mihrabs accordingly. It is only in the oldest mosques that one can see the architectural scar of this reorientation.

As for the two mosques in the Detroit area that still display evidence of the old qibla, the Albanian Islamic Center is planning to rebuild or move to a new location, and the Islamic Center of America has already done so. It has moved from its old place on Joy Road to a new mosque complex on Ford Road. The new mosque was completed in 2005. In one of my visits to the new mosque, I spoke about the old qibla with Eide Alawan, an interfaith activist and community spokesperson for the Islamic Center. He usually complains about what he calls "immigrant" ways of doing things. A proud American-born Muslim, he always emphasizes values that Weber would call Protestant, like "punctuality." In response to my question he said, "Tell you what, actually there is one guy who still thinks that qibla should be southeast. He's an old guy. People don't give up their habits that easily."

In the early 1990s two scholars from the Arab world visited the United States and reignited what can be called the "qibla debate" with a pamphlet entitled *The Substantiation of the People of Truth That the Direction of al-Qibla in the United States and Canada Is to the Southeast*. The authors, Nachef and Kadi (1990), argued that for both jurisprudential and technical reasons, the direction of Mecca in North America was southeast. The authors also declared the prayers of people who had used the northeast direction invalid and asked for a return to the southeastern qibla. Imam Haroon of Masjid un Nur in Highland Park also remembered this controversy when he said, "Back in the late 1980s two brothers from overseas wanted to change but we did not pay attention to them."

Their disagreements mostly revolved around definitions in the religious texts and the technicalities of using maps. For example, what does it mean to be "facing Mecca?" Such Qur'anic verses as "wherever you are, turn your faces toward Kaaba" (Qur'an 1:150) could be interpreted in different ways. Apart from such jurisprudential disagreements, the technical dispute was between Mercator projection maps and gnomonic (spherical) projection maps. The puzzle was whether one should use the "rhumb line" or the "great circle" to determine the shortest distance between Mecca and America.

In response to their arguments and criticism, S. Kamal Abdali published an online article in 1997 titled "The Correct Qibla." The discussion mushroomed on the websites of major Muslim organizations like the Islamic Society of North America. Some Muslim scholarly institutions outside the United States (e.g., Al Azhar University in Cairo) also became involved in the debate, issuing their own fatwas (legal rulings).

Participants in the debate tended to charge their opponents both with being scientifically incorrect and with trying to divide the community. For example, Waheed Younis, the author of the article "*Qibla* in North America," wrote:

This article is written to clarify the issue of correct direction of prayers (*qibla*) for Muslims in North America. Unfortunately, it has become a big issue and Muslims are being divided on it. It is also unfortunate that in this age of Mathematics, Geography and Computer when the Science of Navigation, Calculation and Cartography are reaching their pinnacle, and with the help of those tools, others did not have any problem finding the direction, navigating through and traveling to the Moon, we still do not have consensus on this small issue. (Younis 2006)

The most recent contribution—which (like its predecessors) aspires to be the last word on the subject—comes from Nuh Ha Mim Keller, an American convert and religious scholar. Keller's book, *Port in a Storm: A Fiqh Solution to the* Qibla *of North America* (2001), includes scientific illustrations and cites religious sources in Arabic. On the cover is an image of an ancient astrolabe. Keller brings together both religious arguments and specialized technical knowledge. His book is probably the most comprehensive work on the subject available in English. Apart from jurisprudential reasons, Keller's objection to those who push for a qibla change back to the southeast is based on two grounds: the authority of science and the need for American Muslims to develop their own religious knowledge instead of relying on speculations from overseas.

Islam is spreading to the far corners of the earth, and if the only way we can establish the *qibla* of the new mosque in Tierra del Fuego, for example, is by the visit of an impressive scholar from Algeria and hearing his opinion, the *qibla* will only last until an even more impressive scholar from Iraq arrives and gives the contrary opinion. People in our times are unable to accept such a process. The real world and not subjective personal preference must be our home port, and we can only put into it with religion and intelligence. (Keller 2001, 175)

If America was a stormy sea where Muslims risked losing their bearings, according to Keller, the fault lay with neither the religion nor America but with the irrationality of those who failed to make the move from a personal understanding to a scientific one. Muslims would find their home port through rationality and through autonomy from overseas "experts." Like Imam Shuajb and Eide Alawan, Keller treats the northeast direction as an objective fact. Northeast qibla inscribes itself both in the physical architecture of new mosques and in the minds of communities who increasingly think of the northeast qibla as the standard, correct qibla. Once the northeast qibla is established as objective orthodoxy, it becomes common sense, and the southeast qibla is reduced to the level of subjective ideology. It gradually vanishes.

In the immigrant Muslim experience, finding the direction to Mecca is a matter of mentally penetrating into America and linking it to Mecca. A similar process took place in the African American Muslim experience as well. In their case, the challenge was to link their American experience to the center of Islam in Mecca. Various discursive and symbolic moves within the African American convert community—including a qibla change—brought them closer to their immigrant coreligionists.

Black Mecca and the Bilalians

The earliest Muslims in America were slaves. Of the enslaved Africans from West Africa, approximately 12 percent were Muslims from the region of Senegambia (Diouf 1998, 49). Among the many slave narratives that have come down to us today are stories of Muslim slaves who struggled to maintain their religion against all odds. One example is Salih Bilali (Old Tom) of the Sea Islands off the coast of Georgia, who was a respected leader and elder of slaves on a plantation. The grandson of Thomas Spalding, Bilali's master, reports that his grandfather's slaves were "devout Mussulmans, who prayed to Allah . . . morning, noon and evening." He also adds that Bilali "*faced east* to call upon Allah" (Diouf 1998, 62; my italics).

The stories of Muslim slaves that are available to us suggest that, in the absence of community and technical knowledge, Bilali and other Muslims turned toward the east when they prayed. One can identify several reasons for that. Most of the Muslim slaves brought to America were from West Africa, so Mecca in their consciousness was in the east. The slaves also came increasingly under the influence of Christian culture, so that east, the Holy Land, Jerusalem, and the sunrise tended to melt into one sacred direction. Muslim slaves' search for the direction toward Mecca overlapped with this imagination, and it reinforced the perception of east as qibla.

Not only the direction but also the religious terminology was gradually subsumed under a new culture and language. When the descendants of Bilali were interviewed for a project that attempted to retrieve the oral history of Georgia's Sea Islands, they vaguely remembered some of the words their grandmothers uttered during prayers; these words were heard as indistinguishable exotic sounds such as "hakabara" (which researchers familiar with Islam later identified as "Allahu Akbar").

Islam not only gradually disappeared but in some instances merged with Christianity. In 1860 a Muslim slave woman known as "Old Lizzy Gray" died in Edgefield County. Her obituary appeared on the front page of the *Edgefield Advertiser* on September 12, 1860. Her owner, Dr. E. J. Mims, wrote that she always said that "Christ built the first church in Mecca" (Muhammad 1998, 44).

The stories of Muslim slaves remained unknown for a very long time, as few paid attention to the Muslim component of their identities. Kunta Kinte in Alex Haley's *Roots* (1976) was a Muslim, although Haley's account downplays Muslim elements. Recent studies, such as Allan Austin's *African Muslims in Antebellum America*, have been recovering the stories of Muslim individuals and their spiritual struggles. As Umar Ibn Said, a slave from Fayetteville, North Carolina, wrote (in Arabic) in his 1831 autobiography: "When I came to the Christian country, my religion was the religion of Mohammed, the Apostle of God. . . . And now I pray 'Our Father, etc.,' in the words of Jesus the Messiah" (Austin 1997, 16). A recent PBS documentary, *Prince among Slaves* (2007), similarly tells the story of a Muslim prince enslaved in America.

Unlike in some Muslim communities in the Caribbean and South America, the Islam that came with African slaves to North America was not fated to survive.[12] But it left its traces in the memory and consciousness of African Americans. One example of this is to be found in the Gullah dialect of Georgia's Sea Islands, where transculturation of African languages and English produced a creole that combined elements from both (L. Turner 1949), including the survival of some Islamic terminology. Julie Dash's movie *Daughters of the Dust* (1992) recovers the oral history of Gullah-speaking slave communities, some prominent members of which were Muslim. Nonetheless, the contemporary African American experience of Islam must be considered more recent: it dates back to the first quarter of the twentieth century.[13]

The story of immigrants and their ways of finding their qibla is in some ways paralleled by the story of those who were already Americans but yet were looking for a qibla. African Americans who chose to become Muslim saw themselves as reclaiming the Muslim identity of their ancestors. This is best expressed in the extended name of the Nation of Islam: the Lost-Found Nation of Islam in the Wilderness of North America. The Black Muslim movement was simultaneously a restoration of racial dignity and a reclamation of Islam.

These early Black Muslim communities were hybrid in many ways. They included elements from both Islam and Christianity. Even when the content was Islamic, oftentimes the form was Christian. Like their immigrant coreligionists, these Black Muslim communities also experienced gradual reorientation and cultural fine-tuning. Two prominent Detroit mosques reflect the history of this transition: Masjid Wali Muhammad and the Muslim Center of Detroit.

The Muslim Center of Detroit was opened in 1985 and has much more in common with immigrant mosques than the older Masjid Wali Muhammad. What is now Masjid Wali Muhammad used to be called Muhammad Temple Number One under the Nation of Islam and its leader, Elijah Muhammad. The members of the Nation of Islam at the temple used to pray toward Chicago, where the headquarters of the Nation of Islam were located. Many practices of the Nation of Islam were incompatible with the orthodox practices of Muslims in the rest of the world. How did Muhammad Temple Number One become Masjid Wali Muhammad and the Nation of Islam become the Muslim American Society?

On February 18, 2005, in a group interview with Imam Saleem Rahman of Masjid Wali Muhammad and his assistant Imam Gary Al Kassab, Imam Saleem described this transition:

Our temples were not mosques proper. . . . We saw others as weird and they saw us as weird. We felt like Allah came to us with Master Farad [Fard]. Allah came in the person of Farad and chose Honorable Elijah Muhammad as His messenger.

The transition [after Warith Deen Mohammed assumed the leadership] was difficult for many of us. I thought, "This is 'our' religion." Mine was very small, what I was thinking. This man was talking about the universal. Many of us thought we were Muslims proper [but] we were not. The imam said, "Most of y'all are Christians masquerading as Muslims." We were being taught the Bible. . . . The Qur'an was always held up as "the book to come." Many of us had it. We had it on our shelves. And Elijah Muhammad said, "In time we will get to the Qur'an. Right now I am teaching from the Bible."

At this point, the assistant imam intervened and said that "when Muhammad was mentioned in the Qur'an, we thought that it refers to the Honorable Elijah Muhammad. When my brother became Muslim through immigrants, we had discussions about that."

Imam Saleem continued with what happened after Warith Deen Mohammed assumed the leadership of the Nation of Islam in 1975 after the death of his father: "This place used to be Muhammad Temple Number One. In 1975 Imam Warith Deen Mohammed changed it into Masjid Wali Muhammad. All we did, we took out chairs and brought in carpets and *changed the direction from west to qibla* [my italics]."

I asked Imam Abdullah El-Amin of the Muslim Center of Detroit, another mosque that follows the teachings of W. D. Mohammed, about the transition to orthodox Islam. El-Amin also emphasized the suddenness of the transformation:

You know, it's almost like when the Prophet changed the direction of prayer from Jerusalem to Mecca. So, on Linwood over there [i.e., at Masjid Wali Muhammad], they used to pray to the west, and they were praying to the west all those years, but Imam Muhammed said no, the direction is to Mecca. So instantly the whole community turned to face Mecca. It was almost the same as the Prophet receiving the revelation to change, and instantly all the Muslims without question turned their qibla toward Mecca. So it was a very powerful event, I think.

When W. D. Mohammed assumed the leadership of the Nation of Islam he introduced several dramatic changes. Islam would no longer be "the black man's religion" but a universal religion. It would be open to whites too. This move away from Nation of Islam doctrine toward mainstream Islam was symbolically crowned with the introduction of the word "Bilalian" as an alternative to "Negro," "black," or "Afro-American" (Mamiya 1982). The Nation's newspaper, *Muhammad Speaks*, underwent a similar change under W. D. Mohammed's leadership and became the *Bilalian News*.

African Americans, in their search for Mecca in America, thus found their qibla in a historical figure who was simultaneously African and Meccan: Bilal ibn Rabah, who later became known as Bilal al Habashi (Bilal the Ethiopian). Bilal ibn Rabah was the first black Muslim in history. A contemporary of Prophet Muhammad, he became Muslim when he was a slave. After his conversion and later emancipation, he assumed an honorable status as a companion of the Prophet[14] and the first muezzin (caller to prayer). The figure of Bilal forged a perfect link between African Americans and Islam.[15] His story resonated with the black experience in America.[16] The theme of Ethiopianism is also in harmony with Christian biblical culture. Ethiopia is an ancient African kingdom with a long tradition of Christianity. Through the figure of Bilal, African American Muslims were simultaneously creating a channel of engagement with Islamic orthodoxy and remaining within the religious and racial discourse of the larger African American community.[17]

The very name of the organization, the Nation of Islam, was also changed—not once but several times. In each renaming one sees the elements of convergence with the universalism of mainstream Islam and more importantly a closer embrace of mainstream America. This becomes clear through the evolving names of the Nation of Islam: Nation of Islam (1930); World Community of al Islam in the West (1976); American Muslim Mission (1980); The Ministry of W. D. Mohammed (1985); Muslim American Society (1997). Warith Deen Mohammed's name and honorifics have also evolved in a similar direction. Soon after he became the leader of the organization, his title was changed from supreme minister (1975) to chief imam (1976).

Qibla changes in both African American and immigrant Muslim histories, and various acts of naming and renaming, all bring the two lineages of American Islam closer together. In addition to the unification of qibla, there has been a growing compatibility between the two groups' theological discourses. Initially ethnic or racial, they have both increasingly become religious. More importantly, their convergence also encourages further embrace of Americanness as an identification compatible with Islam.

Both immigrant scholars like Taha Jabir al-Alwani and indigenous leaders like W. D. Mohammed encourage the possibility of interpreting Islam in the context of its minority status in America (al-Alwani 2003). The search for an Islamic legal thinking that takes the minority status of Muslims seriously into account is an attempt at carving out autonomy for Muslims in the United States. The road to such a possibility is full of obstacles, though, and the discussions cannot always be reduced to immigrant versus native differences.

In the case of the qibla debate, for example, it is important to note that what appears to be a simple technical problem is rather a complex one. The debate between opposing views is a conflict between an "organic" (subjective) conception of space and a technical (objective) conception. Both sides can draw on sacred texts and prophetic traditions that confirm their approach. While it might be possible for the qibla debate to reach a technical resolution, we should remember that the debate is never purely rational or technical, for it is taking place under structural constraints such as the requirements of organized modern life in America and the imperative of unifying Muslims as a minority so that collective interests can be pursued. One such collective interest is the recognition of Muslim holidays in public calendars and institutional arrangements.[18]

One can see the gradual emergence of structure, order, and orthodoxy in the evolution of names that both immigrant and convert Muslims gave to their religious institutions. They called their meeting places temples or halls: the earliest mosques in Detroit under the Nation of Islam were called temples, and the early immigrant mosques, such as the one in Highland Park and the precursor of the Islamic Center of America, were called Muhammadan Hall and Hashemite Hall, respectively. Both communities initially congregated and prayed on Sundays instead of Fridays. They faced various directions during prayers, ranging from west to southeast. Their qiblas also eventually converged, a process of transformation whose traces are increasingly vanishing.

Conclusion

Translation of Islam into the American context requires both spatial and temporal boundary work, where immigrants and converts alike engage in cultural fine-tuning and seek convergence between their practices. In the formative, contested moment prior to the emergence of orthodoxy, there is no rule, only multiple practices. After one of those practices gains canonical status through codification and others are marginalized—as in the case of the northeast qibla—one observes the emergence of a rule and the subtle disappearance of symbolic violence into taken-for-granted (commonsense) reality. Muslims initially lived with a cacophony of directions: southeast, west, northeast, and east. When the standard is produced through constitution of one claim as the commonsense or scientific fact, the symbolic violence that once left scars in the interiors of mosques and created an accent in the Muslim sense of direction assumes normality and naturalness. Now it has become constitutive and productive. It is taken for granted that qibla is northeast. The transition from anomie to nomos is accomplished, and the elimination of negative charisma achieved. What was once felt as symbolic violence, like speaking a new language, has now become "nature," like a native language. This is the contrast between Imam Shuajb or Eide Alawan, who take the northeast qibla for granted, and the old man who still thinks that the southeast qibla is right. It is the contrast between the two old mosques with two mihrabs and the many new ones with only one. And it is the contrast between first-generation immigrants and the American-born generations.

The direction of symbolic change for both immigrant Muslims of various kinds and W. D. Mohammed's Muslim American Society has been a convergence toward orthodoxy in Islam. Yet this orthodoxy is not necessarily an orthodox Islam in general but one mediated by the American experience. In this convergence no party represents a preordained orthodoxy. Rather, orthodoxy is constituted through interaction and negotiation. This interaction and convergence make possible the cultural settlement of Islam and lead to the crystallization of an American Islam. The contours of the development of American Islam can be traced through various sectors of American life that are being codified by Muslims. Those sectors include qibla, moon sighting, gender-based partitioning of space in the mosques, development of halal food standards, sporadic neighborhood debates (e.g., call-to-prayer controversies), and mosque soundscapes. All represent moments and sites of a negotiation between Islam and its new American environment.

Qibla unification represents the symbolic unification of a community that is racially, ethnically, culturally, and even linguistically divided. In this sense, the American context for Muslims of various backgrounds looks very much like the situation of pilgrims in Mecca. Like American Muslims, pilgrims in Mecca come from various cultures, ethnicities, and language backgrounds, but they are symbolically unified through the centrality of the Kaaba. Finding Mecca in America, therefore, is a story of the cultural settlement of Islam as an American religion in the eyes of Muslims. Whether Islam has become or will become an American religion in the eyes of non-Muslim Americans is another question entirely. The naturalization of Islam in America is contingent on the completion of the naturalization of America in Islam. Such a naturalization is made possible through the introduction of Islamic nomos in the form of Muslim directionality and the development of localized Muslim religious standards.

TWO

The English Language and Islam: Genealogy of an Encounter

Etymologically both the words *kalam* ("speech") and *kalima* ("word") derive from *kalm*, which the Arabic dictionaries define as *jarh*, which means to cut or wound. *Jarh* in turn is explained more generally to mean *ta'thir*, to leave traces and marks. CHITTICK 2007, 59

Unlike Arabic, Farsi, Turkish, Urdu, or Malay, English is not among the historically Muslim languages. It is basically a language that has no history of hosting Islam as either religion or culture. Only recently has English become a "Muslim language" in the sense that a significant number of people in the United States and across the globe speak it as their native language while practicing Islam as their religion/culture. The connection between language and culture is important because languages are embedded in the cultures of their speakers; linguistic and cultural categories inform and nurture one another. The challenge of translation from one language to another becomes more acute when the cultures in question are dramatically different. In such situations, linguistic translation becomes a cultural reinterpretation. A number of questions naturally arise: What happens when a set of practices and its attendant vocabulary adopt a new, culturally alien language as their habitat? Does the language put limitations on the culture? How does the culture or religion carve its own space in the language?

Today the English language is the lingua franca of Muslims in the diaspora. Diasporic Islam is not only communicated but, more importantly, increasingly *produced* in English. For instance, Hamza Yusuf, a prominent American Muslim scholar, is popular among Scandinavian Muslim youth (Schmidt 2005). The Islamic Center of America in Dearborn hosts speakers from Australia. One of the most popular convert public intellectuals among American Muslim youth is Abdal Hakim Murad (Tim Winter), who lives in England and teaches at Cambridge. The link among all these people spatially removed from one another is Islam and English. Unfortunately, both the English language, which is new to Islam, and the mutual influence between English and Islam are taken for granted. The traces of their encounter increasingly vanish as Muslims become naturalized. The encounter between Muslims and the English language is a neglected issue in the scholarship on Islam in America.[1] Yet it is crucial for delineating the contemporary nature of American or globalized Islam because of the tensions and privileges it engenders.

In this chapter, I discuss the cultural implications of the encounter between the English language and Islam. Examining both its historical and contemporary moments, I explore the impact of English on the understanding of Islam and the transformative appropriation of English by American Muslims. In other words, I investigate the ways in which Muslims perceived the English language in the past and how they now make it a Muslim language in the English-speaking American society where they are a minority. The framework in which I work is not linguistic but rather a cultural sociology based on ethnographic research into the English language in relation to its Muslim speakers. As such, it investigates an important dimension of citizenship, namely the process of linguistic membership in a society and how Muslims overcome the symbolic violence incurred in their gradual immersion in the English language.

Linguistic Nomos and Symbolic Violence

Key to the discussion that follows is the idea of language acquisition as a form of symbolic violence. Symbolic violence refers to the operation of naming or renaming.[2] It is the imposition of a nomos, the formative and collective form of which is language. Before further expanding the idea of symbolic violence, let me first explain what "nomos" means. Nomos is a crucial concept for understanding the relationship between order and orientation. Carl Schmitt describes nomos as "the Greek word for the first measure of all subsequent measures, for the first land-appropriation understood as the first partition and classification of space, for the primeval division and distribution" (2003, 67). Bourdieu similarly defines nomos as "a word that is narrowly translated as 'law' and would be better rendered as 'constitution,' a term which better recalls the arbitrary act of institution, or as 'principle of vision and division'" (2000, 96).

As an imposition of nomos, symbolic violence can be of two types.[3] First, it may be constitutive. Such symbolic violence is productive in the sense that it establishes boundaries and generates entities by naming them. This kind of symbolic violence is the work of the limits into which one is born. Pure, constitutive symbolic violence is the primary form of classification; it is what Bourdieu (1984, 466) calls the "habitus." One example of constitutive symbolic violence would be a person's relationship to his or her culture and native language. The learning of a first language is pure symbolic violence in the sense that it is not the imposition of boundaries on an already-formatted surface, but the first formatting of that surface. This symbolic inscription of culture or language is constitutive and productive. It produces subjects.

The second type of symbolic violence is the imposition of boundaries on entities whose existence and shape precede the newly imposed limits. It has a restrictive, if not always repressive, character. Unlike the first type of symbolic violence, it is felt and can leave scars on its subjects. These scars include accent in speech (an immigrant's broken English), incompatibility of body language (Bourdieu's Béarnais peasants who cannot dance), discrepancy between thought and expression (Muslim clerics' inability to explain certain elements of Islam in English), and a general sense of disorientation (popularly known as culture shock). Speakers of second languages and practitioners of new religions—where a new culture is superimposed upon an existing one—are subject to such symbolic violence. Most immigrants and converts subject themselves to this kind of violence voluntarily.

The difference between the two types of symbolic violence stems from whether symbolic violence is exercised for the first time (constitutive) or not (restrictive). It is often a matter of time for the imposition of boundaries to lose its impositional character and be regarded as natural. It usually does not happen in one generation, but does so over two or three generations as the effects of symbolic violence come to be perceived as natural and objective. Cultural settlement in a new language therefore can be defined as the eventual resolution of the tension between the old linguistic/cultural grid (habitus) and the new one (habitat).

A native language is home. The native speaker feels at home in the world because the world is *in* him, in the form of habitus (Bourdieu 2000, 143). There is a perfect correspondence between our habitus and our habitat, our perception of the world and the world itself. Everything seems natural, harmonious. We become what we are and the world appears to us as it is through our native language. Anything native has the quality of being "ready-to-hand." But when we speak another ("foreign") language, we are in a foreign land. Things do not seem natural and harmonious. They are merely "present-at-hand." We have now moved from the moment of enjoyment (immediacy) to that of reflection, the exile of subject from object. A gap between our internal world and this external world emerges. Our effort to bridge this gap causes a lapse in time and the ordeal of internal translation. We do not feel at home; we stay on mental guard. Our turning of the new environment into a home takes time and may face obstacles from the ontological filter and restrictions of the new language. Once the new habitat—through appropriation—sediments in our bodies, it becomes the new habitus for us; only then do we feel at home again and can speak of inhabitation.

If, as Saussure argues (1959, 68), the essence of language is "convention," then language cannot exist outside the culture of its speakers. That is, until sedimentation is achieved through time and across community, any new acculturation will feel unnatural, nonstandard, and strange. The mental fields and ontological categories carved by each language may not correspond neatly with those of another. In situations of immigration or displacement, a discordance may emerge between habitus and habitat. The impact of finding oneself in "another" language is that the symbolic violence that is invisibly exercised in the production of our "native" language (in a way that precedes our history and awareness) all of a sudden surfaces in our consciousness and becomes visible. In transition from one language to another one may experience linguistic anomie,[4] where the original nomos is no longer valid and the new nomos is not yet fully internalized or naturalized. Over time and through attunement and appropriation the new language is given transparency. This transition is almost never perfect, as the old home survives in the new one in the form of accent and delay. The naturalization process is an erasure of the disjuncture and an articulation of a new harmony between habitus and habitat. When fully inhabited, a language becomes a true instrument (like a glove) instead of a necessary but uncomfortable one (like an ill-fitting shoe).

This chapter captures a vanishing aspect of the cultural settlement of Muslims in American society and culture. Like the problem of the codification of space (i.e., finding qibla), the encounter with English belongs to the set of challenges Muslims faced in the initial stages of their entry into American culture: it is part of the genesis of American Islam. Oftentimes, these problems and challenges are forgotten by the later generations, for whom all things historical[5] now appear quite natural and unremarkable. But scholarship on Islam in America needs to avoid taking them for granted.

The process of globalization has led to the spread of English as a global language and the spread of Islam as a global religion. The latter is also responsible for the emergence of Muslim minorities in English-speaking, historically non-Muslim countries such as the United States, Britain, Australia, and New Zealand. The framework with which Muslims have perceived and interpreted the English language has also shifted over time. Two moments can be distinguished in the encounter between English and Islam. These are the historical encounter, marked by colonialism and Christian missionaries, and the contemporary encounter, marked by globalization and Muslim minorities.

Historical Encounter: Colonialism and Christianity

English: Colonial and Christian

The early encounters between Muslims and the English language took place in colonial contexts. Muslims who were colonized by Europeans identified European languages with Christianity, domination, and cultural conversion. Not only Muslims but all colonized peoples harbored a strong suspicion toward the language of the colonizer. The colonizer's language was part of a larger colonial discourse where cultures and languages were placed in a hierarchy. It is not surprising that the first chapter of Frantz Fanon's classic book *Black Skin, White Masks*, is on language. Early on he notes not only how "mastery of the colonizer's language affords remarkable power" but also how it represents a tragic loss of authenticity. He observes, "Every colonized people—in other words, every people in whose soul an inferiority complex has been created by the death and burial of its local cultural originality—finds itself face to face with the language of the civilizing nation" (1967, 18).

That anticolonial movements have an ambivalent relationship with the language of the colonizer has a great deal to do with the colonial context, where the identity and authenticity of the colonized are balanced against the seductive power of the colonizer's language. In the case of Muslims, where the difference in language is paired with a difference in religion, suspicion toward the language of the colonizer becomes inevitable. In other words, the colonizer's language never comes to the colonized independently and simply as a language. It is never a means of communication alone. Rather, it comes initially in a tightly knit bundle with colonial domination and its cultural apparatus—including Christianity and missionary education.

When Islam and the English language came into contact in colonial environments, English was accordingly seen as the language of "the colonizer" and "the Christians." As Ali Mazrui, a prominent scholar of Africa, notes, "The equation of the English language with [Christian] missionary education was a major factor in conditioning Islamic attitudes towards it. Muslims became suspicious of the English language on the basis of a presumed guilt by association. This was aggravated by the sense of cultural defensiveness which developed among Muslim communities" (1971, 180).

Thus, learning English historically meant learning the language of Christian missionaries or that of the colonizers. "Being associated with conquest and colonialism, English was seen as inherently inhospitable to Islam and as syntactically and discursively different from any of the major Islamic languages," another scholar writes (Malak 2005, 2). In other words, due to the historical baggage of colonialism and Christianity, English has been perceived by many Muslims as a *kafir* (infidel) language (Pennycook 1994, 314). This perception—which has dramatically changed over time—did not make the distinction between learning a language and adopting its culture.

If the Christian convictions of English speakers led Muslims to approach the language with suspicion, how did colonialism affect Muslims' appropriation and use of the English language? If English entered the Muslim imagination and experience through colonization, how did this shape the ways in which Muslims entered the discursive world of English? These questions lead us to a striking dimension of the encounter between Islam and the English language.

Diasporic Islam: An Identity-centric Islam

The first Islamic texts written in English or translated into English and made available to English-speaking audiences were produced by Muslims living in colonized lands, notably India and Egypt. The most famous example is Abul Ala Mawdudi,[6] who, together with Sayyid Qutb, is considered among the founding figures of modern political Islamism. Their colonial background informed the ways people constructed themselves,

69

and more importantly it affected their articulation of religion. Even the mere use of English in the communication of religion and social issues inadvertently put authors and the users of that language in dialogue with the colonizing culture, thereby inviting a hidden transcript of *anti-colonialism*. Hence, not only was English a means of communication for people who were colonized, but this fact shaped the content and deployment of texts written in English. If so, what can be said about the nature of Islam as it was constructed in texts written in English?

Early Islam in English was marked by postcolonial nationalism and a sense of displacement. The audiences of such texts were either displaced Muslims speaking English or Muslims subjected to colonial rule. The Islam produced in English can thus be defined as a "diasporic Islam." Consequently, one characteristic of Islam in the English language is that it approaches itself not as a religion—or not only as a religion—but as an *identity*. This distinction becomes harder to detect in our age of identity politics, not to mention in the context of the scholarly tendency to reduce religion to identity.

The encounter between the English language and Islam was mediated by the colonial experience and produced an identity-centric Islam, which at times would culminate in Muslim nativism. It is this diasporic foundation that arguably finds an echo in contemporary Muslim radicalism in the Western world. The impact finds expression in the anticolonial baggage of early writings. Intellectuals or scholarly figures who wrote in English or whose writings were translated early on into English were anticolonial thinkers. They often placed Islam in opposition to Western culture and civilization. And, not surprisingly, they produced a totalistic understanding of Islam that later became the ground for political Islamism. One might ask why this anticolonial sentiment and reaction had a lasting impact. I contend that this moment was, to use Bourdieu's terms, an "inaugural moment" (Bourdieu 2000, 95) in the institution of Islam in the English language. For practical reasons of path dependency, those writings and their diasporic Islam had a lasting influence on how Muslims entering into the sphere of English through immigration (and those English speakers entering the sphere of Islam through conversion) made sense of themselves and their new environment.

If one walks into the libraries of most of the mosques in North America—as I have done often of late[7]—in pursuit of the textual sources of American Islam, one is likely to notice the presence of English-language works by Mawdudi, Qutb, and many others (fig. 2.1). Yet only a decade or two ago, the libraries of Islamic centers were largely empty of English-language books. The few such books available would most likely have

2.1 A typical mosque library shelf. This one, at the Tawheed Center in Farmington Hills, Michigan, includes Sayyid Qutb's *Milestones*, Abul Ala Mawdudi's *Towards Understanding Islam*, and Muhammad Asad's *The Road to Makkah*.

been those of Mawdudi and Qutb. The reason for this is not necessarily ideological. As a matter of fact, the wide presence of such books and the absence of others were due to the unavailability of Islamic works in English. Those that were available, therefore, became common and later classic.[8] And they exercised a certain influence on American mosque culture and global Islam in general. Although there is today a proliferation of new Islamic works produced by indigenous American Muslims, the works of Mawdudi and Qutb continue to enjoy the status of classics of Islam in English.

A good illustration of the place of such works in the imagination of American Muslims can be traced in a recent statement by Dawud Walid. Walid is an African American Muslim who is a vice imam at a mosque affiliated with Warith Deen Mohammed (Elijah Muhammad's son); he is also the director of the local chapter of the Council on American-Islamic Relations (CAIR), a Muslim advocacy group.[9] When asked which authors he most likes to read, Walid said that he reads "Sayyid Qutb, Imam Khomeini, Maulana Mawdudi, Ismail Faruqi, and Imam Warith Deen Mohammed."[10] Although Imam Khomeini and Imam Warith Deen Mohammed are not technically diasporic, the remaining names are diasporic Muslims who produced Islamic works either in English or for English-speaking Muslims. What connects an African American Muslim from Detroit to Muslim scholar-activists from India and Egypt of decades ago? The English language. I shall further develop the relationship between the English language and postcolonial Muslim intellectuals when I discuss the case of Ismail al-Faruqi and his approach to English.

In short, the impact of colonialism and the English language on Muslims resulted in an anticolonial culture and identity-centric, diasporic understanding of Islam. Although the early Muslim intellectuals who wrote in or were translated into English successfully overcame their suspicion toward the English language, this was achieved at the price of turning Islam into an "identity" deployed in opposition to Western culture. This fact can also be restated from the other direction, as Mazrui does: "Although learning English will certainly lead to a certain degree of Westernization, it was the English educated, those who could speak the colonizers' language, who came to articulate anticolonial sentiments" (1975 statement quoted in Mohd-Asraf 1996, 367).

Contemporary Encounter: Globalization and Muslim Minorities

As noted earlier, the story of the relationship between Islam and the English language is marked by two large-scale phenomena: colonialism and globalization. While the former characterizes the historical encounter of Muslims with the English language, the latter describes an ongoing process. Similarly, while the Muslim attitude toward the English language during the colonial encounter was one of rejection, in the contemporary world, it is increasingly becoming one of acceptance. Unlike the colonial situation, where English was the language of the colonizer and of Christianity, today Muslims are in the process of making English a Muslim language and detaching it from its colonial past. It has also become the lingua franca for a significant number of Muslims.

Globalization has brought English and Islam into closer contact. Once total strangers, globalization has turned them into friend and foe at the same time. While English allows for the articulation of a global Islam, becoming a vessel for its dissemination, the same English is often presented as an antidote to the international terrorism associated with Islam.[11] Globalization of English and globalization of Islam have dramatically changed the interaction of both. English is no longer seen by many outsiders as tied to any culture or nation: it has now become the property of the entire world.[12] The same can be said for Islam. Both English and Islam are now at large.

Today one can speak of two ways in which Muslims think about the English language in relation to Islam. These are the issues of "English in Islam" and "Islam in English," respectively. The first issue has to do with carving a space for English in Islam and among Muslims. This problem arises at the periphery of the language, in Muslim majority contexts where English is a foreign language. The second one has to do with carving a space for Islam within the English language and Western culture. This issue appears at the periphery of Islam, in Muslim minority contexts.[13] These two approaches also mark the gradual immersion of Muslims in the English language. In the beginning, English was external to Islam and was treated as something that had to be accommodated or legitimized. Later, when Muslims became fully embedded in the English language through immigration and naturalization, it was Islam that seemed external to their setting (habitat) and in need of accommodation.

English in Islam: Language as a Tool

The pragmatic approach to English is a direct outcome of economic globalization and focuses on the instrumentality of English as the language of globalization and technology. It emerges out of Muslim majority contexts and is best illustrated by the case of Malaysia. It comes as no surprise that Malaysia, a Muslim nation that has embraced economic globalization, is at the same time the first and perhaps the only nation to host a conference specifically dealing with the relationship between Islam and English. Held in 1996 at the International Islamic University in Malaysia, this conference was presented as a response to the needs of Muslims in a globalizing world where the English language plays an increasingly crucial role. The interaction between Islam and English, the two globalizers, was deployed in terms of a parallelism. Jalal Uddin Khan, the coeditor of the published proceedings of the conference, noted that the conference was "perhaps the first of its kind in the world," and he then juxtaposed Islam and English as follows:

Neither of them remained confined to the place of its origin, having reached far and wide across the languages and cultures of the world. Both are equally global and pluralistic, with the result that Islam today does not mean whatever is Arab only and English whatever is Western or Christian. There are Arab Christians as there are English-speaking Muslims or Muslims who are native English speakers. English has been the most widely used means of expression and communication as Islam has been the fastest growing or most resurgent religion in today's world. (J. Khan and Hare 1996, x)

The timing, location, and themes of the conference reflected the nature of the transition that Muslim nations like Malaysia were undergoing. From a framework of colonialism, Malaysia had moved to one of globalization, where English is being embraced as an imperative of development and progress. One could even surmise here a certain concurrence, if not complicity, between Islam and the globalization of English (Karmani 2003a). Many Malay Muslims believed that "when we learn English, we will be rewarded by Allah" because "when one seeks knowledge or learns another language, one earns God's pleasure" (Mohd-Asraf 2005, 111). Thus, learning English was not only Islamically legitimate but also desirable. In the words of African Muslim Dahiru M. Argungu, "Muslims definitely need English today, in particular, in education. Apart from education, English is a strategic bridge linking Muslims with a vast English-speaking non-Muslim world with great potentials for outreach *da'awah*[14] activities, business and international relations" (1996, 336).

The following quotation from another participant of the conference brings out how the suspicion toward English was overcome and highlights the role postcolonial Muslim thinkers played in appropriating the language:

It is possible to be highly proficient in English and still maintain one's identity as Muslims. In fact, there are many Muslims from among our contemporaries as well as those in our past, such as Allama Muhammad Iqbal, Fazlur Rahman, Sayyid Muhammad Naquib al-Attas, Seyyed Hossein Nasr, and Ismail Faruqi, to name but among the most prominent ones, who are highly proficient in English and who have used their ability in the language for the purpose of Islam. (Mohd-Asraf 1996, 363)

In the approach championed by the Malaysian conference, the English language was appropriated for Muslim purposes of global economic competitiveness, propagation of Islam, and the fulfillment of a religious requirement about gaining knowledge.[15] English was thus detached from its Christian-colonial baggage and embraced as a tool for economic development and religious service. This treatment of English as an instrument of development in the age of globalization neutralized the negative history of the language. Yet English still remained external to the Muslim context, something to be incorporated and used. This was significantly different from the next approach, which emerged at the "center" of the English-speaking world, where Muslims lived as minorities.

Islam in English: Accommodating Islam

The second way in which Muslims thought about the English language was related to postcolonial immigration and the rise of English-speaking Muslim minorities in Anglophone societies. In this case, the use of English was no longer optional. When suspicions toward English lingered, they derived from a concern about its capacity to accommodate Islam. The question here was how to make English a Muslim language. The following section discusses two articulations of "Islam in English" and notes two moments in the cultural settlement of Islam in the linguistic habitat of America.

Al-Faruqi's Project of "Islamic English"

A Biography of Diasporic Islam in America

Founded in 1982, the Islamic Society of North America (ISNA) is currently the largest Muslim national organization in the United States. ISNA was born of the fact that many Muslim students who came to America to study ended up not going back to their home countries. As their plans to return home gradually faded away, they decided to build institutions that would support their diasporic life. The first major Muslim organization and nucleus of immigrant Muslim institution building in the United States was, after all, the Muslim Student Association (MSA). Despite the commonsense impression, MSA is not a branch of ISNA; rather, ISNA came out of MSA.

Ismail Raji al-Faruqi's (1921–86) biography is, in a sense, also the history of immigrant Muslim experience in America. Not only did he articulate a vision for the Muslim community in his writings, but he also played a key role in its institutionalization. Most of the institutions with which he was involved as either founder or promoter are now major national organizations: MSA, ISNA, and the International Institute of Islamic Thought (IIIT). Al-Faruqi was also the first president and founder of the Association of Muslim Social Scientists (AMSS).

Al-Faruqi was a Palestinian refugee who came to the United States to pursue his academic studies. He received a doctorate in philosophy in

1952 from the University of Indiana. He wrote extensively on Judaism, Christianity, and Islam. Although initially an Arab nationalist (al-Faruqi 1962), he gradually abandoned his Arabism in favor of Islamism. Al-Faruqi's ideological orientation and intellectual identity, in both its Arabist and Islamist phases, were in many ways postcolonial. After failed attempts to intellectually articulate a culturally essentialist idea of Arabism, he found in Islam what he had been looking for: a non-Western universalism and authenticity. The guiding theme of his intellectual career was an urge to create an authentic ground for himself (and other Muslims) outside Western discourse. The diversity of the Muslim student community with which he interacted contributed to his gradual transition to Islamic universalism. He saw in the presence of Muslim students in America the possibility of a pure *ummah* (community of Muslims).

As a visionary intellectual and community leader, al-Faruqi articulated a diasporic conception of Muslimness in which ethnic and geographical origins were to be transcended in favor of an Islamic universalism. His distinctly diasporic orientation treated America as a precious meeting point for Muslims from all over the world. Although they were in America (as students), they were nevertheless oriented toward the Muslim lands. Most of the institutions initiated by al-Faruqi and his colleagues had transnational and diasporic names—their community and institutions were "in" America, but they were not necessarily "American."

His colleagues, some of whom I had the opportunity to meet during my visit to the IIIT in Herndon, Virginia, and at the annual conferences of AMSS, have specialized in such varied disciplines as Islamic studies, finance, and political science. Even though all are American educated, they are more inclined to see things in a transnational framework. (Not surprisingly, one of the senior members of IIIT told me during a conversation that he had visited more than a hundred countries—which struck me as quite diasporic and not quite American.) The legacy of al-Faruqi looms large over IIIT, AMSS, and ISNA. His contribution to Islamic thought is so significant as to constitute an exception: American Muslims are more likely to "import" Islamic knowledge from overseas, and al-Faruqi is one of the few Muslim thinkers in America whose work has had a decisive impact on Muslims in other parts of the world.[16] What was al-Faruqi's contribution that could be exported from America to overseas Muslim contexts?

Al-Faruqi's main project, which informed much of his institution-building work, was the idea of "Islamization of knowledge" (al-Faruqi 1982). This project was based on the assumption that modern science and knowledge need to be rehabilitated so as to be compatible with the Islamic conception of the world. Despite (or perhaps because of) its instant popularity among Muslims at the time, the Islamization of knowledge project was a very ambitious one. As an epistemological critique of Western science and its metaphysical presuppositions, Islamization of knowledge was a reluctant engagement with Western modernity (Zaidi 2011).

IIIT was established to serve this agenda. The Muslim students attracted to this project were to obtain Western knowledge but "Islamize" it upon taking it back to their home countries. In this way, they would become agents of an epistemological rectification (Ghamari-Tabrizi 2004, 72). When it became clear that many of these students were not actually going back to their countries of origin, their presence in America inspired individuals like al-Faruqi to dream of a Muslim *ummah* here. This microcosm of the greater Muslim *ummah* was to be based in America, yet still oriented toward the Muslim world.

Al-Faruqi recognized early on that the common language for all these Muslims coming from different ethnic and linguistic backgrounds was not Arabic but English. In other words, this emergent community was tied together by their Muslim identity and shared American experience. Al-Faruqi published a small book in 1986 in his Islamization of Knowledge Series that dealt with the question of English. This programmatic essay bore the title *Toward Islamic English*.

Toward Islamic English

Al-Faruqi's *Toward Islamic English* does not even ask whether Muslims can or should use the English language; this is already treated as given. The question, rather, is how to make the English language sensitive to the culture and worldview of Muslims. What is needed, al-Faruqi argues, is an "Islamic English." Al-Faruqi defines Islamic English as "the English language modified to enable it to carry Islamic proper nouns and meanings without distortion, and, thus to serve the linguistic needs of Muslim users of the English language" (1986, 7). But who are the Muslim users of English? Al-Faruqi answers:

Muslim users of the English language are, first, the Muslim citizens and permanent residents of the English-speaking countries, namely, the UK, the USA, Canada, Australia, and New Zealand. To these, the non-citizen Muslim students should be added. The term also includes the Muslim citizens and permanent residents of those countries around the world where English is the official language, such as Pakistan, India, Ceylon, Malaysia, the Philippines in Asia, and Nigeria, Ghana, Uganda, Kenya, Ethiopia, Tanzania and others in Africa and around the globe. (1986, 7)

Al-Faruqi sees a serious problem in the relationship between Islam and English that urgently requires intervention: "The present situation of the English language—when it expresses matters pertaining to Islam, its culture, history and civilization, to the Muslim World or the Muslims, whether used by Muslims or non-Muslims—is chaotic. It constitutes an intellectual and spiritual disaster of the highest magnitude. And it carries a universal injustice against the human spirit" (1986, 8).

Giving examples of how Muslim names are "mutilated" in transliteration, al-Faruqi calls for a creative appropriation of the language on the part of Muslims. According to him, Muslim speakers need to transform the English language at two levels: transliteration and translation. The problem with transliteration lies in the lack of standardization. There are multiple systems and no central power to choose which is legitimate. Different spellings exist for Arabic terms that are increasingly used in English. For example, should the Arabic term for Muslim pilgrimage to Mecca be spelled *hajj* or *hadj*? Is it Muhammad or Mohamed? Even the name of the religion itself still begs standardization; is it Islam or Islaam?

The problems faced are not limited to transliteration. Through standardization and codification, al-Faruqi argues, transliteration problems can be eliminated. It should be noted that al-Faruqi insists on a scholarly transliteration and direct use of Arabic words in English. In other words, not only should their transliteration be fixed, but they should also not be translated. Many Arabic words, he says, are not translatable into English, and many others are rendered into English only with difficulty. Furthermore, Muslims cannot rely on the orientalists' translations of Islamic terms. "The orientalists may have used such translations with impunity because for them it is a foregone conclusion that all Islamic meanings must fit themselves under Western categories" (al-Faruqi 1986, 11). There are certain concepts in Islam that cannot be translated. "To give an English translation of them is to reduce; and often to ruin, those meanings" (al-Faruqi 1986, 12).

Al-Faruqi—and other Muslim intellectuals, such as Naquib al Attas, who were influenced by his ideas—argue that language reflects ontology, that is, the nature of truth and reality as understood by a religion or culture (Mohd-Asraf 2005, 114). They also emphasize that the languages of all Muslim peoples have been infused with basic Islamic vocabulary, which projects a distinctly Islamic worldview. Therefore, the Islamic ontology and conception of the world cannot be properly expressed through the English language unless it is adjusted. The adjustment that al-Faruqi suggests in his Islamic English, in the words of Argungu, "is a remedial measure which aims at *bending* the English language to accommodate" Islam (1996, 332; my italics).

The lack of exact correspondence between the ontology of the English language and the ontology of Islam can be illustrated in several registers. Al-Faruqi himself provides some of them. For example, the word "prayer" does not distinguish between *dua* (spontaneous supplication) and *salat* (the five daily fixed-time prayers). It collapses the two categories into one and erases the ontological distinction between the two. The same can be said about "almsgiving," which fails to distinguish between *zakat* (the annual obligatory public welfare tax) and *sadaqah* (altruistic, voluntary charity) (al-Faruqi 1986, 11–12).

There can also be conceptual misfits. For instance, some Muslims may find the expression "good luck" to be un-Islamic because it implies that things happen by luck. Similarly, some Muslims might find themselves uncomfortable with the use of the future tense in English because "when native speakers of English make reference to the future, they do not feel a need to 'soften the arrogant assumption' that the future will occur, and appeal to the benevolence of God on such an occasion by adding 'God willing' (*insha'allah*)" (Mohd-Asraf 1996, 355).[17] This point is exemplified in the following paragraph from al-Faruqi's *Toward Islamic English*, where he frames the purpose of Islamic English as a spiritual rehabilitation of the English language for Muslim users and performs what is suggested here by inserting *insha'allah* in the future-tense sentence:

In modern times, the English language stands in need of the precepts and values of Islam which only the Qur'anic language can provide. Constant use of their Arabic form will help to shield the English-speaking Muslims from the onslaught of materialism, utilitarianism, skepticism, relativism, secularism and hedonism that the last two hundred years have established firmly in English consciousness. And it will—insha'Allah—inject a reforming and salutary influence into the consciousness of all English speaking Muslims, pulling them out of their tragic predicament in modern times. (1986, 14–15)

There are also religious words that are secularized and universalized in the language and that Muslims may find alienating. Such Christian words used in a nonreligious sense include "bible, biblical, christen, christian, Christian name" (Brown 1996, 310). Also, some Islamic terms are given Western interpretations that may not correspond to the Muslim conceptions of them (e.g., jihad, mecca).[18]

To all of the above problems one can add the culturally produced errors of English. If the Muslim appropriation of English is relatively recent and marked by a past colonial encounter, the English language's encounter with Islam is old and marked by a history of orientalism and cultural prejudice. A good example of such cultural prejudice invested in language would be the notion of "Mohammedanism,"[19] which implies that Muslims worship Muhammad, a false prophet claiming to be a god. al-Faruqi rightly points to the "Maumet" entry in *Webster's International Dictionary* (al-Faruqi 1986, 10).

Part of the prescriptive project of al-Faruqi's Islamic English assigns Muslims the task of decolonizing English. Decolonization of the English vocabulary about Islam and codification of the Islamic vocabulary that is increasingly used in English are two avenues for the articulation of an Islamic English.[20]

Islamic English or Muslim English?

How Much Islamization Is Too Much?

On February 3, 2003, a young Australian Muslim, Irfan Yusuf, published a short essay criticizing Ismail al-Faruqi's idea of Islamic English. Published on a popular American Muslim website, MuslimWakeUp!, the essay was entitled "The Islaam of Double Vowels." MuslimWakeUp! is a website that caters to young professional Muslims who are second or third generation and also very critical of mainstream Muslim conservatism. The website provides a forum for discussion in addition to a cornucopia of content, ranging from critical essays to satire and poetry. Revealing a gap between al-Faruqi's vision and the perception of new generations of Muslims in English-speaking countries, the essay starts with a teasing question:

Do we all remember that really cool Palestinian American academic, the late Dr. Ismail Faruqi? And what about his cool wife, Lamya? One wrote on Islamic thought, the other on Islamic art. A whole generation of young Muslims in North America was apparently brought up on that stuff. Well, that's what we in Australia think. You see, we are really not quite sure. The Faruqis lived in an era before the Internet became popular and before we could chat with bruzzerrz and sistarrz across the globe. So in presuming the extent of Dr. Faruqi's influence, we relied on the inside jackets and back covers of his books.

Anyway, Dr. Faruqi and his "Islamisation of Knowledge" project was quite grand although it did at times enter the realms of the absurd. Take, for instance, his book, *Towards Islamic English*. What on earth is Islamic English? Is it just saying "masha-Allah" and "insh'Allah" every second word? Do we draw a little star after every capital "C" so that it looks like part of the Pakistani or Turkish flag? Then of course there is the Islam (or is it "Islaam") of double vowels.

The essay is a partly satirical rejection of al-Faruqi's insistence on infusing Islamic concepts and forms into the English language. "The Islaam of Double Vowels" is symptomatic of the growing gap between Muslims born into English-language environments and al-Faruqi's (and his generation's) call for an Islamic English. Unlike their immigrant parents or grandparents, the new Australian- or American-born generations of Muslims do not treat the English language as something alien to Islam or incapable of fully expressing it.

The same tension can be traced in another instance, where Islamic English is reconceptualized as Muslim English. In 2006 a popular Muslim online multimedia store and website, SoundVision.com, published an article that asked the same question that Ismail al-Faruqi asked two decades ago: "Can there be Muslim English?" (Mujahid 2006).[21] Intended as a guide to common Arabic usage in the English language, the article starts with the assumption that "in the absence of simple basic common rules, Muslim English is becoming difficult to read for *new Muslims, young Muslims* and *non Muslims*" (my italics).

Unlike al-Faruqi's programmatic and relatively purist "Islamic English," Abdul Malik Mujahid's article seeks to contribute to the standardization of "Muslim English." And while al-Faruqi asks for more Arabic in English, Mujahid asks for less. "If it is meant for a general audience, we suggest a minimum use of the basic Islamic terms in English. Loading a writing or a speech with Arabic terms may impress a reader or listener, but is certain to fail to communicate with a vast majority of Muslims (90%) who are not Arabs, are young Muslims, new Muslims, or non Muslims. If communication is the purpose, don't create problems for your audience."

SoundVision's guide to Muslim English makes a series of suggestions for both transliteration and translation of Islamic (Arabic) words and concepts. But it is minimalistic, asking that English not be burdened with unnecessary Arabic words.

A general rule of thumb is that if it is not in the English dictionary, don't use it. If it is not an Islamic term, just an Arabic word, don't use it. It is good that we import Islamic terms from Arabic into English instead of through other languages. Therefore, Muslim is better than Musalman or Musselman. . . . *Salat* is far better than *namaz*. If an Arabic term or its equivalent English word has become dominant in usage, let's keep using it for a while although it may not be a very accurate representation of Arabic sounds or terms. You cannot transform English into Arabgish or Engbic, can you?

Inviting his audience to a "pronunciation jihad" in English, Mujahid provides the formula "Simpler is better."

Quran is simpler than Qur'an, al-Qur'an, or al-Qur'aan while we are still struggling to stop the usage of Koran which does not seem to be ill motivated either. Usage of Islam is more dominant than Islaam or al-Islam or allslaam, or al Islam. So let's be happy with it. Dawa is simpler and better than Da'wa, Da'wah, or Dakwah.

Writing Allah or God has been a difficult issue for many. Some translations of the Quran use God others use Allah. Instead of taking a position on this issue we suggest [using] it interchangeably so that language becomes used to it instead of differentiating between the two names.

As a guide for the use of Islamic words for media purposes, the "Muslim English" approach differs strikingly from al-Faruqi's Islamic English. The rules suggested by SoundVision "are based more on common sense than any deductive logic or structure imposed by English or Arabic language. This is an effort to develop standards in usage of Arabic words in journalistic English for the layperson" (Mujahid 2006).

Although the SoundVision piece was not written in response to al-Faruqi's project, the contrast between the two approaches allows us to make a useful distinction between Islamic English and Muslim English. Islamic English treats the linguistic nomos of the English language as a hindrance to the proper presentation of Islam. The idea that English cannot fully express the Islamic conception of the world is certainly open to debate. Nevertheless, it leads to a defensive position. If the format of English is oppressive and restrictive toward Islamic ontology, then a structural adjustment is needed. Islamic English is an attempt to "bend" English so as to "protect" Islamic ontology. Muslim English, however, approaches English as having a format conducive to the expression of Islam. Not driven by the fear of losing Islam in translation, Muslim English does not demand any surgical intervention into the language. Instead, it seeks to make Islamic ontological categories communicable without placing an additional burden on the structure of the language.

In that sense, there are two alternative views or rather two stages of linguistic sedimentation.

From Diasporic "Islamic English" to Doxic "Muslim English"

A closer look at the intellectual approach of Ismail al-Faruqi and the practical approach of Abdul Malik Mujahid reveals several important differences between the two. First of all, al-Faruqi's articulation of Islamic English is philosophical, whereas SoundVision's is commercial. Therefore, while al-Faruqi asks for a structural negotiation with the English language, the SoundVision author tends to accept the structure and seeks ways, to use al-Faruqi's word, to "fit" in. al-Faruqi's emphasis on and search for authenticity are indicative of the postcolonial character of his project. SoundVision's orientation, on the other hand, is both postdiasporic and American. It replaces authenticity with efficiency as its primary concern. Finally, the greatest difference between the two articulations of a Muslim-friendly English language lies in the nature of their audiences; while al-Faruqi's primary audience consisted of Muslim students whose experience was characterized by displacement and immigration, the primary audience of SoundVision is second- and third-generation Muslims whose experience is characterized by cultural settlement and integration with the larger society. While al-Faruqi's audience had an overseas (i.e., immigrant) habitus in an American habitat, SoundVision's audience has an American habitus in an American habitat.

An English-Speaking *Ummah*

Most American Muslim communities are still somewhere on the path between al-Faruqi and SoundVision, that is, between Islamic and Muslim English. The English language of Islam is in the process of crystallization, and this process is paralleled by the formation of a community imagined through English. The fact that Arabic is the sacred language in Islam often prevents us from seeing the crucial role played by English in the formation of American Muslimness.

Today, Islam in America has two universal languages: Arabic and English. Arabic is the language of ritual and symbolizes ritualistic unity, whereas English is the language of communication and symbolizes communal unity. In an interesting twist, in America the Muslim idea of *ummah* (community) is possible only through one language—and that language is not Arabic but English. Muslims coming from different ethnic and linguistic backgrounds connect with each other through English. English serves many functions for Muslims in American society. It is an instrument of legitimation, a means of connection with other Muslims (both locally and globally), a path to integration with the larger (American) society, and a vehicle for reaching out to non-Muslims (in *dawah*).

Language Dynamics of Mosques

As mosque communities lose their original immigrant insularity and become more and more ethnically diverse, they face the challenge of finding clerics who can function in two languages: Arabic and English. The early imams could survive with Arabic and the ethnic language of their congregation. (In the case of Arab immigrants that would be Arabic, but it could be Urdu or Albanian for other communities.) The need for competence in English emerged only with the coming of the second generation—and has intensified with the third. It comes as no surprise that early imams, like Imam Mohammad Chirri of the Islamic Center of America and Imam Vehbi Ismail of the Albanian Islamic Center, found it necessary to write basic catechism pamphlets and books in English for their growing American congregations. As communities settled and grew in numbers, they lost their homogeneity through contact with other Muslims and through the influence of mainstream culture on the younger generation. The pressure toward more use of English was further intensified with the conversion of people whose first and often only language was English.

Most of the mosques try to strike a balance between their two—and, in many cases, three or more—languages. Even though Arabic remains a constant as the language of ritual, out of convenience most immigrants use their ethnic languages (Urdu, Albanian, Arabic, Bosnian, etc.) in daily communication. However, the lingua franca among Muslims of various backgrounds is English. Exclusive reliance on English alienates the first-generation immigrants, while its absence alienates both new generations whose primary language is English and Muslims of other ethnic backgrounds. The extreme diversity of the Muslim community in the United States therefore encourages two phenomena: greater emphasis on the concept of *ummah* (Muslim community) as a unifying identity and the rise of English as the language of communication for that *ummah*.

Today almost all mosques deliver most of their Friday sermons in English, though the proportion of English-language use varies from imam to mam and congregation to congregation. English-language competence is becoming more central to recruiting and hiring imams. As 9/11 and other factors created the need for outreach and interfaith activism, the language imperative for imams and community leaders has intensified. Lectures and extracurricular activities outside regular prayers have also contributed to the growing need for English-language competence.

English and the Postcolonial Network

The disproportionate representation of, for example, South African imams and intellectuals in the United States illustrates the crucial role that English plays in gaining access to global markets of Islamic clerical and intellectual knowledge production. As American congregations began to seek imams who would combine strong Islamic credentials with proficiency in English, they naturally turned to the once-colonized hinterlands of Islam. In the Detroit metropolitan area alone, three of the most prominent local scholars are examples of this trend: Imam Achmat Salie of Oakland County, who is the former imam of the Islamic Association of Greater Detroit, and Muneer Fareed, who is the current secretary general of ISNA, are both from South Africa; and Imam Ali Suleyman Ali of the Canton mosque is originally from Ghana. Prominent Muslim academics in the United States like Farid Esack and Ebrahim Moosa are also from South Africa. What makes possible the disproportionate representation in America of South African Muslims—who are a tiny minority in their own country—is the English language.

The same dynamics also explain the origins of key figures involved in the polemics with Christianity. A case in point is the popularity of Ahmed Deedat's books and videos. Deedat, who died recently, was a Muslim scholar from South Africa who was well known for his knowledge of Christian scripture and his debates with Christian clerics. Most American Muslim bookstores still carry Deedat's books.

Avenues of Authenticity: English and Islamic Knowledge

One can even discuss the presence of a politics of English in the American Muslim community, in the sense that mastery of English can empower one group or one leader over another. Religious competence being equal, an imam who speaks English is often preferred. Communities may even sacrifice a degree of religious competence in exchange for language skills (i.e., employing an American-born imam rather than someone from overseas who has greater knowledge of Islam). Therefore, imams attempt to acquire competence in English and American culture. A young Muslim student recently told me that Shaikh Yaqoubi of the Zaytuna Institute is memorizing Shakespeare in order to better communicate Islam.

The rise of the Zaytuna Institute demonstrates how those with simultaneous access to local American culture and overseas Islamic knowledge enjoy the highest popularity and prestige, especially among young Muslims. Hamza Yusuf and Zaid Shakir, both American converts and Islamic scholars associated with the Zaytuna Institute in California, are increasingly becoming popular among a new generation of American Muslims. In a *New York Times* story about the institute, a nineteen-year-old student from New York states that "Sheik Hamza Yusuf and Imam Zaid Shakir have grown up here after having studied abroad, you can really connect with them. The scholars who come from abroad," he adds, "they can't connect with the people. They are ignorant of the life here."[22] The search for a Muslim English has also given rise to what Marcia Hermansen calls "Islam-speak": "peppering one's conversation or presentation with pious formulae is a common feature of Muslim performance. It is a demarcator of Muslim discourse and a means of Islamizing English" (2004, 393).

The African American Muslim Voice

In the short run, the desire for native-born scholars has tended to privilege African American imams (e.g., the popularity of Imam Siraj Wahhaj on the MSA speaking circuit), suggesting an ever-closer convergence between black and immigrant language practices. At the same time, however, the different dynamics of the black Muslim community lead them to choose a distinct path through the pragmatics of Islamic and Muslim English.

Unlike immigrant Muslims, African American Muslims have a fairly comfortable relationship with Christianity.[23] When I attended Friday services at the Muslim Center of Detroit or at Masjid Wali Muhammad, which was Temple Number One of the former Nation of Islam, I observed that the style and frame of reference of sermons were very different from those of the immigrant mosques. The speakers assumed their listeners to be intimately familiar with both the phrasing and stories of the King James Bible. They often supplemented Muslim ethical exhortations with biblical aphorisms and illustrated their points with reference to stories not present in the Qur'an. The speakers differed little in cadence and manner from the typical African Methodist Episcopal or

Baptist preacher. And their audiences received them in a fitting manner, with loud exclamations of "Amen" and "You tell it, Brother!" resounding from all parts of the mosque (including the women's section).

Translations of the Qur'an

Although it is most actively felt in African American mosques today, it is worth remembering that biblical language is—if only indirectly—a part of the inheritance of all English-speaking Muslims. The English translations of the Qur'an most popular with Muslims in America today were all produced by either colonial Muslims in diaspora (e.g., Abdullah Yusuf Ali, a British Indian Muslim) or Western converts to Islam (e.g., Muhammad Asad, an Austrian Jew).[24] These translators shaped their diction in imitation of (or, rarely, in reaction against) the King James Bible, the gold standard of elevated, "sacred" style in English. Because of the unavailability of *tafsir* (interpretation) of the Qur'an in English, the translations included somewhat-detailed footnotes and translator's notes, where verses were sometimes explained through the invocation of biblical passages. For example, Muhammad Marmaduke Pickthall's introductory note regarding the first chapter in the Qur'an starts in the following manner: "*Al-Fatihah*, 'The Opening,' or *Fatihatu'l-Kitab*, 'The Opening of the Scripture' or *Ummu'l-Qur'an*, 'The Essence of the Qur'an,' as it is variously named, has been called the Lord's Prayer of the Muslims" (Pickthall 1938, 1). The analogy made between the Fatihah and the Lord's Prayer shows how translation is always a cultural reinterpretation. Similarly, in the notes to Yusuf Ali's translation of the Qur'an, there are references to Shakespeare and Milton. The style of translation that emerged in colonial and early minority Muslim contexts is arguably still a part of the texture of the language of Islam in English. This awareness of and constant dialogue with biblical culture is a result of being a minority in a Christian majority society and demonstrates that Muslims have chosen a Christian interlocutor. Pickthall's introduction illustrates this point:

The aim of this work is to present to English readers what Muslims the world over hold to be the meaning of the words of the Qur'an and the nature of that Book, in not unworthy language and concisely, with a view to the requirements of English Muslims. It may be reasonably claimed that no Holy Scripture can be fairly presented by one who disbelieves its inspiration and its message; and this is the first English translation of the Qur'an by an Englishman who is a Muslim. (1938, iii)

If English translations of the Qur'an are inextricably linked both to Christianity and to the mind of the colonizer, immigrant and African American Muslims deal with this troublesome history in very different ways. For immigrant Muslims, the Christian interlocutor is an *other*, even a rival. For African Americans and converts, the Christian interlocutor is more often a family member or even their own past selves.

Another Mode of Authenticity

Perhaps because their personal histories are often bound up with Christianity, English speakers who adopt Islam have rather different attitudes toward the use of Arabic than do Muslims who adopt English. In other words, African American Muslim English is often different from immigrant Muslim English. While African Americans prefer Arabic words such as *al-Islam* (instead of "Islam") and *deen* (instead of "religion") as a way of authenticating themselves as Muslims, immigrants prefer English words such as "God" in order to authenticate their Americanness.

Conclusion

This chapter has traced a circle from the authenticity anxieties of Muslims in general as they tried to protect themselves from corruption via language to the (dueling) new authenticities of English-seeking immigrant scholars and English-fleeing American converts. The Muslim perception of the English language has changed over time from a defensive suspicion to an appropriative embrace. As Muslims found themselves deeper in and closer to the English-language sphere, they developed visions and strategies to detach the language from its Christian or colonial baggage and to articulate English as a Muslim language. The perceived tension between the authentic Islamic conception of the world and the linguistic nomos of English is also a reflection of the location of Muslims like al-Faruqi who developed the idea of Islamic English. In other words, Muslim theories about the English language are a function of their locations vis-à-vis the language. The misfit between the ontology of Islam as it was understood by al-Faruqi and the structure of English illustrated the temporal nature of the language-culture nexus. Displacement of Muslims through immigration put their Islamic habitus at odds with their new linguistic habitat. The symbolic violence that the new habitat exercised on the old habitus found its expression in linguistic anomie—or appeared, as it did to al-Faruqi, as chaos and injustice. It was this assumption that led al-Faruqi to employ words redolent of symbolic violence when he described the experience of Islam's translation into English. He countered its "mutilation," "reduction," and "ruin" with the suggestion of "bending" the English language to accommodate Islam.

The cultural settlement of Islam in the linguistic habitat of American society is an ongoing process. It produces a tension between Muslim life and American forms. The process requires Muslim arbiters of style to transform the multiplicity of linguistic practices that now characterize Islamic English into a commonly agreed set of rules. Once Muslim English becomes standardized, the anxieties and histories associated with its development will sink beneath the waves of common sense. The triumph of a new linguistic nomos will establish the order and orientation currently lacking in the relationship between Muslims and English in America.

THREE

Homeland Insecurity:
How Immigrant Muslims
Naturalize America in Islam

There has always been some kind of *nomos* of the earth. In all ages of mankind, the earth has been appropriated, divided, and cultivated. But before the age of the great discoveries, before the 16th century of our system of dating, men had no global concept of the planet on which they lived. . . . Every powerful people considered themselves to be the center of the earth and their domin- ion to be the domicile of freedom, beyond which war, barbarism, and chaos ruled. SCHMITT 2003, 351

Muslims who become immigrants in the United States face a challenge unusual in the Muslim world: living as a minority in a non-Muslim society. This experience, which we in con- temporary multicultural society take for granted, is a new situation for the majority of Muslim immigrants. It is not that Muslims never had minorities among themselves. On the contrary, there have always been non-Muslim minori- ties living in lands dominated by Muslims. But the reverse has not always been true, especially in the case of Muslims residing in Western societies. Muslim reluctance to settle permanently, and a lack of tolerance toward Islam in the Western world, have both contributed to this historical outcome. Muslim presence in and exposure to non-Muslim environments were historically "temporary" and justified within the legal framework of "necessity" (i.e., due to ex- ception and emergency). The rise of Muslim minorities in contemporary European and American societies is in many ways a new situation for both the Muslims and the West and therefore poses a challenge to Islamic law and Muslim imagination as well as to the West. The emergence of "permanent" Muslim minorities has significant religious implications. Is it religiously permissible to live in a non-Muslim society? What should be the nature of one's relationship to such a social environment? These are questions that Muslims who are interested in religiously justifying their new environment frequently ask themselves. The answers they find, to employ the much-debated Muslim juridical terms, range from America as an abode of war/disbelief (*dar al harb*) to America as an abode of Islam/peace (*dar al Islam*). The evolution of the Muslim perception of "America as homeland" is an important cultural dimension of citizenship and constitutes an understudied aspect of Muslim cultural settlement in the United States. How do immigrant Muslims overcome their initial sense of "homeland insecurity" and begin to feel at home as Muslims in America?

This chapter is a phenomenological account of Muslim constructions of America as homeland. It starts by articulating the concept of home and what it means to feel at home. It continues with a brief inventory of the cultural idioms or topoi with which early Muslim immigrants and Muslims in the early stages of their immigration made sense of their presence in America. This diasporic moment and vocabulary changed over time as exposure and interaction led to a more nuanced understanding. In addition to these cultural idioms, there are crucial juridical tools by which Muslims religiously interpret America and produce an articulation of America as "home." Therefore, the fundamental question that this chapter answers is how Muslims naturalize the United States in Islam. I aim to capture the dynamics of the transition from being "in" America to being "of" America. In philosophical terms, this is the story of transition from being "present-at-hand" to being "ready-to-hand."

Reality and Its Anomies

One difference between an immigrant and a citizen is that for the citizen home and homeland are the same, while for the immigrant they are not. The correspondence between home and homeland is achieved through the extension of home into homeland: continuity between home and homeland, which is a condition of feeling at home, requires the projection of what is private and subjective (i.e., home, Muslim, communal) into what is public and intersubjective (i.e., city, American, national). Before engaging in a discussion of the transformation of Muslim

discourses on America, we need to establish some theoretical connections between feeling-at-home and homeland and between displacement
and the sense of anomie.

A defining characteristic of home is that it is a place where the relationship between the subject and space takes the form of a feeling:
feeling-at-home or being-in-the-world. A place is home only when inhabited.[1] It is inhabitation that turns *any* place into home. Hence, there is
nothing essentialist about home. When inhabitation generates the feeling of "feeling-at-home," we can say that a place has become home. What
is crucial for the sense of home is the experience of dwelling (Heidegger
1971, 143). This subjective recognition of a place as home is a temporal
process. The subject appropriates a given space as home only after she
projects into that space her subjective being, that is, when she dwells.
This projection is also a construction of the subjective world, which becomes the ground for the production of the intersubjective world (Berger
and Luckmann 1966, 20). (It must be noted here that this order is correct only for heuristic purposes. Ontologically, the intersubjective world
always precedes the subjective world.) In short, "with the dwelling the
latent birth of the world is produced" (Levinas 1969, 157).

Simmel provided an early sociological account of the tension or lack
of equilibrium between subjective and objective cultures (Simmel 1971;
Frisby and Featherstone 1997, 55–75). His discussion of the crisis in culture is in many ways a pioneering study on the topic of homelessness in
the general sense of the "homeless mind" of modernity (Berger, Berger,
and Kellner 1974). Simmel argued that the increasing division of labor
and proliferation of cultural products (objective culture) placed a disproportionate strain on the subject, who could no longer have a true com-
prehension of her cultural environment. This process of alienation from
the environment, or, in Simmel's own terms, the loss of equilibrium between subjective culture and objective culture, was a tragic consequence
of modernity.

Arendt also treated the idea of home as a staging ground for entry into
the intersubjective realm (Arendt 1998, 207) where different subjects meet
and where the encounter of different subjects produces objects (natural
or social). Thus, we feel at home where everything is subjective. That is,
all objects are subjectivized (e.g., the IKEA desk that is now my late-night
refuge); and subjective elements, objectivized (e.g., the arrangement of
things on my desk). The Simmelian idea of cultural crisis refers to the collapse of the flow between the subjective and the objective cultures.

In their treatise on the sociology of knowledge, Berger and Luckmann
(1966) provide a fascinating discussion of the way common sense (i.e.,

reality, the world as we know it) is produced and maintained. Any given society is an arena of reality construction where individual members participate in the production of objective reality. This reality is sustained as long as the intersubjective realm of lifeworld that underpins it remains available. Thus, any common sense or reality is precarious because "all societies are constructions in the face of chaos. The constant possibility of anomic terror is actualized whenever the legitimations that obscure the precariousness are threatened or collapse" (Berger and Luckmann 1966, 103).

Here, there are several themes that need to be made explicit. First, the reality that each society produces is constructed against a background of chaos. That is, it is produced through the introduction of nomos into a realm that is otherwise chaotic. Nomos (rule, law, regularity, sense) translates chaos into order and nature into culture. The idea of homeland is one such cultural construction produced on the surface of bare geography. Second, the reality to which nomos gives rise is historical, contingent, and fragile. Therefore, anomie, which is the loss of nomos, has a terrorizing effect, causing anxiety and insecurity. This includes the anxiety one feels when one is a long way from home and the insecurity of an unfamiliar abode. That is also why unfamiliar or mentally inaccessible things and places are associated with the uncanny. Referring to the fear of the unfamiliar, Freud (2003) links the uncanny to the unhomely and homeless.

Third, the anxiety and insecurity, normally repressed and swept under the carpet by intersubjective dwelling and everyday language, burst in when either the protective shield is removed (internal collapse) or those protected within it move outside it. Hence, anomic terror can happen either temporally (crisis) or spatially (finding oneself outside the coverage area of the shield). In other words, anomie, chaos, and bare nature all manifest themselves in marginal or *liminal* situations (V. Turner 1969, 95). That is to say, they manifest themselves either under the shield or beyond its limits. Outside the shield—or, to use Berger's (1969) own term, outside the "canopy"—all the distinctions dissolve. In the words of a political philosopher, "man erects around himself an artificial netting which conceals from him the abyss" (Strauss 1989, 36). The structure expires and antistructure (V. Turner 1969) begins. The margins reveal the historicity of the structure. At the edges and on the frontiers, the nomothetic format (i.e., constructed reality) ends, and the unformatted surface (chaos) appears, or to put it more precisely, what is beyond appears as chaotic. The relationship between nomos and chaos/anomie is crucial for a proper understanding of the experience of people who are displaced. The Durkheimian discussion of anomic suicide (1951, 241) is directly linked to such displacement. Displacement in this sense might entail encounter with a radically different culture, language, or both.

Immigration is one such displacement.[2] For immigrants, the most obvious challenge to their sense of reality is the requirement to speak another language, since language is the depository of common sense par excellence. But there are other challenges, especially if their religion is different or has a history of conflict with the religion of the host culture. In the next section, I trace the experience of Muslim immigrants who either find themselves at the frontiers or outside the juridical concept of Muslim homeland (*dar al Islam*).

Muslims Outside the Islamic Canopy?

Medieval Muslim jurists developed a binary opposition to distinguish the legal status of Muslim-controlled lands from the rest of the world. They designated as *dar al Islam* (abode of Islam, abode of peace) the lands where Islam was dominant or had been naturalized as mainstream culture. By that classification, all other places fell under the category of *dar al harb* (abode of war, abode of chaos) or *dar al kufr* (abode of disbelief). In this conception, *dar al Islam* becomes a spatial or geographic projection of the Islamic sacred canopy. Scholars have different opinions as to whether the canopy is held up by an Islamic political rule or by an Islamic mainstream culture even when the ruler is not necessarily Islamic (al-Alwani 2003, 28; Ramadan 2002, 166). What is decisive in either case is whether a certain land has been subject to Islamic nomos and has thus become conducive to an unrestricted, free practice of Islam. In short, *dar al Islam* describes a legal order (and not necessarily a political one[3]) where geography is codified through the imaginary inscription of Islamic law. The remainder of that geography is mentally "nihilated" (Berger and Luckmann 1966, 114) in order to create the sharp contrast that preserves "mental hygiene" (Zerubavel 1991, 37; Berger and Luckmann 1966, 156). This spiritual appropriation of land finds still another abstract expression in the juridical order of things. Identification of qibla, the direction of Mecca, is yet another form of religious appropriation of land, that is, introduction of nomos.[4]

As a juridical sphere, *dar al Islam* refers to the pacified, codified space enclosed within the canopy. Muslims living within *dar al Islam* are inhabitants of a familiar abode and members of a bounded community. This sphere that is under public law and familiar for jurisprudential purposes is surrounded by its constitutive other, *dar al harb*. What remains outside, therefore, becomes an extrajuridical, agonistic sphere. In that sense, *dar al harb* is similar to the Greek conception of "barbarian lands." Muslims venture into this unfamiliar abode, the uncanny, only at their spiritual peril.

Concerned with the protection of Islamic identity, the classical Muslim jurists saw no reason why Muslims should move to *dar al harb* permanently. They strongly discouraged people from leaving the abode of Islam unless their departure was due to *darura* (necessity).[5] This extrajuridical sphere was thus incorporated into the legal canopy through the state of emergency; sojourn in that sphere fell under the paradigm of *exception*.

The Significance of Darura

Darura, or necessity, occupies a special place in all legal traditions because it is the foundation of exception (Agamben 2005, 24). As a limit concept it is the borderline between juridical order and bare life, between facticity and norms (Habermas 1996). Where public law (in this case, Islam) ends, political fact (the agonistic sphere) begins. Therefore, law melts under the conditions of necessity, as implied by the ancient maxim *necessitas legem non habet* (necessity has no law) (Agamben 2005, 1), for necessity has the power to render the illicit (*haram*) licit (*halal*).[6] But this is not generalizable: necessity justifies only specific, individual cases of transgression through exception.[7]

The movement of Muslims from *dar al Islam* to *dar al harb* is a movement from inside legal order to outside it, from law to exception. According to Carl Schmitt (1976, 10), law has two fundamental elements: norm and decision. In the state of exception—that is, in *dar al harb*—the decision remains while the norm recedes. Put differently, the law loses its objective normalizing power and taken-for-granted character. More specifically, it loses its power of "convention," which is what makes a law law. The new environment does not lend itself to the applicability of the norm developed inside the canopy and demands (a new) decision, an act of construction. At that very moment the agency attributed to the law through reification falls back into the hands of the lawmaker.

The movement from rule (norm) to exception (decision) shifts our attention from the law itself to the lawmaker(s). What had been given now becomes an explicit object of human construction. It is a shift from an already-naturalized, habitualized reality to a reality that is witnessed at the moment of its construction by human subjects. This de-routiniza-tion also corresponds to what Agamben calls "force-of-law without law" (2005, 39).

Therefore, as will become evident later in this chapter, the analogies made by present-day Muslims to the time of Prophet Muhammad are not invalid: there are very real similarities between the contemporary fron-tiers (margins) of Islam and its center, its beginning. The similarities are both temporal (*hijra*, the early migration of Muslims and the first estab-lishment of Islam)[8] and spatial (choosing qibla and living in a land that is not yet *dar al Islam*).[9] Therefore, stepping outside the canopy is a return to the prehistory of the canopy. At the frontiers, where nomos is absent, there is an originary indistinction (chaos, anomie). After all, necessity is the first and original source of all law. It is this character of necessity and exception that explains the law and rule (Agamben 2005, 27; Schmitt 1976, 15). In that sense, it reveals the historicity and contingency of the law. At the spatial margins of Islam, Muslims have to reenact what those who codified Islam in the Muslim lands did many centuries ago. As Michel de Certeau has observed, "other lands restore to us what our own culture has seen fit to exclude from its own discourse" (1984, 14).

There are two possibilities for those who find themselves outside the canopy: they can either extend the canopy to cover their spot or engage in the construction of a new one. It will become clear in the case of Muslims that choosing the first seems to lead to the second, as far as the distinction between *dar al Islam* and *dar al harb* is concerned.

Extending the canopy under the paradigm of exception (*darura*) may be done for individual necessities, but if a large number of people reside not temporarily but permanently in what early jurists designated as *dar al harb*, can they still rely on *darura* as a paradigm? The paradigm of *darura* enabled Muslims to make brief forays into *dar al harb*. Now that Muslims have permanently settled in what used to be seen as *dar al harb*, they have to transform necessity into law—bare life into canopy—and culti-vate nomos on an anomic space. As the examples I give later will clarify, the movement from canopy to anomie is always temporary: it inevitably ends with arrival at a new canopy. Canopy construction, which is the construction of new reality, is similar to dwelling and has a temporal character. In plain terms, a guest who stays for too long is no longer a guest but a lodger. Whether temporal or spatial, the anomic liminality of *darura* expires with either a return to the canopy or the emergence of a new one.

So far, in my discussion of *darura*, the zone of exception, I have touched upon the relationship between *darura* and law and its manifestations in time and space. Before concluding this section, I shall briefly explain the reason it came to prominence and the type of ethos *darura* engenders.

As a space of unenforceability of law or dispensation from the application of law, *darura* implies the impossibility of experiencing a given place as a fully justified home. Thus, it works as a temporary protective juridical shield (like a raincoat) for limited exposure to *dar al harb*. *Darura* gained jurisprudential prominence in modern times as a result of the processes that caused (dis)placement of Muslims into non-Muslim lands. These processes include colonialism in the past and globalization and Muslim immigration in contemporary times.

A juridical term designating the condition of "crisis times" and "unhomely places," *darura* has a particular ethos. This ethos is a "deficient mode of care" in the Heideggerian sense.[10] In other words, the ethics of *darura* is negative. It demands avoidance, minimal involvement, and unsettlement. It thus corresponds to the condition and experience of sojourners who do not feel at home. In a more strict sense, this ethos is a diasporic ethos, where home/land is elsewhere and the heart is there. In the next section, I give a quick overview of some prominent topoi of Muslim diasporic culture. Each topos tells us about a certain aspect of the experience of Muslim immigrants.

Topoi of Muslim Diasporic Imagination

Under the conditions of immigration, Muslims are displaced and disembedded from their original national environments. With immigration, they find themselves in a diasporic condition and interstitial location. For example, they are in American society but not (yet) *of* it. To explore how "Muslims in America" become "American Muslims" we need to first understand the consequences of displacement (immigration). Diasporic conditions trigger the release of some Muslim idioms from their otherwise marginal status and pull them to the surface of Muslim imagination. There are several prominent root paradigms (V. Turner 1974, 67) that immigrant Muslims in America employ in making sense of their experience. These include *hijra* (Prophet Muhammad's migration from Mecca to Medina), *ummah* (the universal Muslim community), *dawah* (mission or propagation of Islam), and *jihad* (struggle, just war).[11]

Hijra: When Prophet Muhammad and his followers were persecuted by the pagan Arab establishment of Mecca, he migrated to the nearby city of Medina in the year 622 CE. This event occupies such a central place in the Muslim imagination that it marks the starting point of the

Muslim calendar (called the Hijri calendar). *Hijra* as a movement from Mecca to Medina represents a flight from chaos and oppression to a place of freedom that represents "the city" and "civilization" all at once.[12] The Prophet's *hijra* thus constitutes the primary referent for the Muslim topos of *hijra*, migration. There is also a second event from the early days of Islam that contributes to the term's symbolic meaning: the migration of Muslim refugees to Abyssinia (present-day Ethiopia) in 615 CE. Fearing that the Meccans' hostility to his teachings might lead to the destruction of the nascent Muslim community, Muhammad sent a group of his disciples to seek refuge in the Christian kingdom of Abyssinia. The Meccans sent their own emissaries after them, asking the king to hand over these "insurgents" for punishment. The king instead questioned the refugees and discovered that their "subversive beliefs" differed little from his own Christian doctrine. He granted them amnesty, much to the disgruntlement of their pursuers. For Muslims this historical moment has become a touchstone of solidarity among Ahl ul Kitab ("Peoples of the Book," i.e., followers of revealed scripture) and an emblem of the potential benefits of *hijra*.

Hijra is the primary idiom for Muslim immigrants who seek to frame their displacement—voluntary or not—in religious terms. It is not only the movement from one place to another or departure from one's native land that makes these historical events relevant to contemporary migrants but also the fact that the destinations were in both cases non-Muslim. Thus, *hijra* gained prominence among Muslims in the United States because it provided a framework for their contemporary experience as immigrants (Haddad and Lummis 1987, 156). African American Muslims even interpret their exit from slavery with reference to *hijra* and call *hijra* "The Greatest Migration" (Dannin 2002b, 59, 2002a). At the other end of the spectrum, a fringe radical group of Muslim immigrants based in Britain employs the self-identification Al-Muhajiroun (the emigrants) (Wiktorowicz 2005).

Ummah: This concept designates the global community of Muslims (Mandaville 2003; Roy 2004). It also refers to the community of followers of any prophet. Some Muslim scholars link *ummah* to the concept to *shahada* (witnessing). "The greatness of the Islamic *ummah* is to be understood in the fact that it is a community of the middle path which must bear witness to the faith before all mankind" (Ramadan 2002, 158–59). A nonterritorial concept, it allows Muslims to transcend their ethnic, linguistic, and racial differences. In this imagined community, the members of which are tied to each other through exposure to the scripture and belief in one God, Muslims relate to each other across time and space. In the words of Benedict Anderson:

The strange physical juxtaposition of Malays, Persians, Indians, Berbers and Turks in Mecca is something incomprehensible without an idea of their community in some form. The Berber encountering the Malay before the *Kaaba* must, as it were, ask himself: "Why is this man doing what I am doing, uttering the same words that I am uttering, even though we cannot talk to one another?" There is only one answer, once one has learnt it: "Because *we* . . . are Muslims." (1991, 54)

Muslim experience in America is often compared to the Muslim experience in Mecca because Muslims discover and feel the extreme diversity within the Muslim community both during their pilgrimage in Mecca and upon their arrival in America. It is at that moment that the concept of *ummah* gains prominence as a way of acknowledging and overcoming differences. The appeal of the concept of *ummah* comes from both the diversity of Muslim communities and their minority status vis-à-vis non-Muslim majority society and consequent need for solidarity.

Dawah: *Dawah* means religious propagation, fulfillment of the religious obligation of representing the faith to outsiders. *Dawah* is the primary mode of relating to the outside of the Muslim community. *Dawah* is not limited to proselytizing but can include charity work and participation in community service. As much as it targets outsiders, the more immediate motivation for its deployment in the foreign setting is the protection of the identity of insiders. As such it becomes a means of preserving religious identity and authenticity. It is an internally articulated means of engaging with the social environment. This sense of *dawah* is particularly relevant, for instance, for members of the branches of the Muslim Student Association (MSA) on university campuses. A female undergraduate Muslim student at the University of Michigan once told me, "I am Muslim. I wear my Muslim identity wherever I go. Every action I make publicly is an act of *dawah*. It is especially important to me because I know that everything I do, every stance that I take, reflects the entire Muslim *ummah* whether I want it or not."

Jihad: Of all the terms discussed here *jihad* looms largest in the American psyche. It is a contested concept for both Muslims and non-Muslims. *Jihad* refers to the constant structuration of the self and the world along the lines of Islam. It literally means struggle; it is the equivalent of self-discipline in Protestant cultures. The concept covers a variety of struggles, ranging from spiritual self-restraint to the collective execution of a just war. Recent uses of the term in ethnic nationalism and global terrorism have, however, undermined its legitimacy in the eyes of non-Muslims.[13] Muslims themselves, in turn, employ the term increasingly reluctantly and uncomfortably. Yet they cannot do away with it, since it is part of Islam.

These key idioms have almost nothing to do with America per se as a destination for Muslim immigrants. They are root paradigms that help Muslims make sense of their mobility/movement. The prominence the terms enjoy in America is absent in Muslim majority lands except for those places where colonialism has had a disproportionate impact and thus induced the feeling of being a minority, if we accept a definition of minority in terms of power and not numbers. For a very long time, the Muslim idea of *ummah* was quite marginal and would be felt explicitly only during the once-in-a-lifetime pilgrimage to Mecca. Globalization has altered this fact, but only recently. The power of *ummah*—and, for that matter, *hijra* and *dawah*—as primary topoi derives entirely from the diasporic moment. Therefore, although American Muslims have used these topoi since the earliest period of their immigration, they are like a certificate that authorizes their departure but does not deal with their destination. These topoi are extensions of old homelands; they hardly touch America.[14]

Before proceeding any further we need to remember the relationship between law and *darura* (necessity). Law is generated out of necessity and experience, but when it becomes alienated from its ever-changing source (*darura*, charisma), the law faces suspension. Its hardened layer has to be cracked or thinned so that the experience beneath can manifest itself.

What appears beneath the melting layer of law itself will soon become a new hardened layer. This means that just as anomie is temporally limited (transitional) and has to disappear, so does charisma, which is always *in statu nascendi* (Weber 1946, 246; Shils 1972, 110). One person's charisma or anomie is someone else's rationality or reality. In other words, a foreign reality and rationality will always seem anomic and, depending on taste, charismatic. It is always a matter of time and location for the charisma and anomie to (routinize or fade away and thus) become rationality and reality, that is, to become a new canopy—whether one calls it a "sacred canopy" (Berger 1969) or a secular "iron cage" (Weber 1946; 1992, 181).

Therefore, we cannot rely on ideal types without bringing in the freshness of experience. We cannot conceptually understand habitus without understanding dwelling, rationality without charisma, or law/nomos without *darura*/anomie. It is this linking of binaries that allows us to lay bare the dynamics and origin of social constructions whether they are of home, homeland, or the world or of law and rationality. The question is how concrete experience, practices of lifeworld, face-to-face interactions, and everyday experience in general congeal and theoretically sediment into ideal types, abstract images, and common sense. The understanding of experience and ideal types as mutually embedded in each other in an ever-expanding net that encapsulates us in the form of "the world" allows us to historicize the cultural objects of our analysis.

Changing Muslim Discourses on America

The immigrant Muslims' encounter with America starts well before their arrival, because America has already entered the minds of Muslims as a phenomenon. The portrait that Muslims have of America is usually based not on direct experience but on powerful images or ideal types that are unchallenged. Those images are not necessarily negative, but rather range from positive to neutral to negative. Furthermore, not every Muslim who arrives with negative views of America ends up developing a positive one and vice versa. Nevertheless, one thing is certain: in their own national cultures, Muslims have very little ground for knowing America and rely almost exclusively on ideal types supplied by globalized American popular culture and stereotypes. When the question is posed from a religious-juridical point of view, the status of America becomes even more problematic. America is a non-Muslim and arguably a Christian country. Is America *dar al harb*? And if so is it religiously permissible to stay in America for an extended period of time or even permanently? Under what conditions are Muslims allowed to live in such places?

Some Muslims ask these questions; others do not. Not all Muslims are interested in religious justification of their presence in America. Some might not even be aware of the juridical terms discussed below. Moreover, some of them might be aware yet choose to ignore them in the face of some incongruity between the terms' implications and the reality of their own lives. People can choose to place themselves outside this particular juridical question by rejecting its relevance or avoiding it altogether as a theoretical nuisance. Whether they embrace the relevance of the question or not, however, all Muslims engage in interpretation and produce a certain perspective on America (Haddad 2004, 32; Leonard 2003a, 154).

These questions have come to occupy a central place in American Muslim discourse. Especially after 9/11, according to an American Muslim pundit, such questions create a moral dilemma that needs to be solved:

Many Muslims who see Islam and the U.S. in a state of conflict have enormous problems in beginning to think of themselves as American Muslims. They want the prosperity and the freedom of America, but not its foreign policy or its liberal culture. And Muslim leaders who oppose political assimilation without opposing [legal] naturalization inadvertently place Muslims in a morally delicate situation. There are no simple solutions to this moral dilemma. It will have to be resolved at the theological level. Changes in American attitudes and policies toward Islam and Muslims will also be helpful in this transition to citizenship within the mind of each American Muslim. The theological discussion will have to take American Muslims beyond the *dar-al-Islam* (house of peace) and *dar-al-harb* (house of war) dichotomy. (M. Khan 2002, 10)

Early Muslims considered living in American society a dangerous venture. It meant the risk of assimilation and moral decay. The students who constituted the kernel of American Muslim identity in the 1960s and 1970s wanted only to avoid the negative influence of American society (Schumann 2007, 11). This perception, however, changed over time (Mattson 2003, 203).

The terms or, rather, juridical tools available to Muslims for making sense of American space have outflanked the binary of *dar al Islam* versus *dar al harb*. The dichotomy, which existed for so long because it was not challenged by direct experience, becomes problematic and insufficient when Muslims are actually in America. Reality interferes. The alternative or complementary concepts that were historically marginalized in the production of this binary are remembered, reappropriated, and even possibly invented.[15] Therefore, in addition to *dar al harb* and *dar al Islam* Muslims in minority settings have brought back several notions, the most important two of which are *dar al dawah* (abode of call, propagation, mission) and *dar al ahd* (abode of treaty, contract). In place of the *dar al harb–dar al Islam* dichotomy, we now have a continuum of abodes: from *dar al harb* to *dar al dawah* to *dar al ahd* to *dar al Islam*.

This continuum, of course, implies no teleology. It is rather a spectrum of juridical terms providing religious meaning or justification for different discourses Muslims develop with respect to America. In this part of the chapter, I shall highlight what is specific to each of these categories and the relationship between them as phases of a possible process of settlement. This process or spectrum can be both temporal and spatial.

Table 3.1 Stages and juridical tools of Muslim cultural settlement in the United States

Darura (exception/negative)		Law (rule/positive)	
Abode of war (*Dar al harb*)	Abode of mission (*Dar al dawah*)	Abode of accord (*Dar al ahd*)	Abode of Islam (*Dar al Islam*)
War/chaos	Mission/visit	Peace/accord	Home/Islamic
External	Frontier	Neighbor	Home
1970s	1980s	1990s	2000s
Visitor	Newcomer	Resident	Citizen
Diasporic		Settled	

There are two broad paradigms under which we can classify the major juridical tools. They are either mobilized under the paradigm of *darura* or construed as part of an existing legal order or as products of a newly articulated code that caters to the needs of Muslims in the minority status. The first two categories (*dar al harb* and *dar al dawah*), which fall under the paradigm of *darura*, are diasporic with respect to the American setting. The last two (*dar al ahd* and *dar al Islam*) come under the paradigm of law and are employed by Muslims in their postdiasporic moment, those who see or want to see America as home. A more comprehensive juxtaposition of the four categories is provided in table 3.1.

In the following sections, I shall discuss the specifics of each of these categories. What are the consequences of perceiving America as an abode of war (*dar al harb*)? Who sees it as such and when? Such questions will be answered for each of the four categories used by Muslims as juridical tools or, to put it in Ann Swidler's (1986) terms, as part of their juridical "toolkit." These juridical terms can be interpreted as symbolic stations in the cultural settlement of Muslims or moments of their internalization of America as a habitat.

Abode of War: An Impossible Homeland

From the perspective that sees America as an abode of war (*dar al harb*), America is *external* to Islam and, as such, is a source of anxiety and cultural threat.[16] This perception is based on a lack of knowledge about what goes on inside America. America, in this view, is a monolith—it is completely profane and without legitimately perceptible nomos. It has to be avoided unless there is emergency (*darura*, exception). America is a black box that can be treated only in its totality since it can be grasped—in this understanding—only from without.[17] The ideal type for this conception is a visitor; it can be said to represent the common understanding of Muslim immigrants in the 1970s.

Changing immigration policies in the 1960s and Cold War politics opened the door for Muslim immigrants and students. Interestingly enough, the students from Muslim countries who came to America to study not only created the nucleus of a Muslim community but also laid the groundwork for the formation of a number of major organizations, including MSA and later the Islamic Society of North America (ISNA). Those Muslims who happened to be in America in this period believed that they were there under *darura*. They saw themselves as an outpost of Islam inside American space. In keeping with this view, they had no connection to the space except for being in it for a short time of necessity. They were geographic and cultural orphans, people out of place. Their plans to go back home kept them always in a precarious position, unsettled. *Dar al harb* (abode of war) characterized the perception of those Muslims, mostly students from Muslim countries, who either were religious or became religious due to diasporic pressures during their studies at American institutions of higher education in the 1960s and 1970s. They set out to acquire American science and technology without getting contaminated by its culture. Their plan to return home after the completion of their studies and their desire to avoid the influence of American culture were two defining features of their attitude toward American space. These students relied on funding from their home countries and were oriented toward their homelands.[18]

America was simply a meeting ground for Muslims from various countries. Within the framework of a Heideggerian conception of space, their "American space" did not fully exist. To the extent that care and involvement produce space (the world) for the situated subject, their American space was very small; their primary *concern* was political and cultural solidarity with the Muslim world and its rehabilitation through the acquisition of American scientific and technological knowledge. The institutions built in this era catered to students and were concerned almost exclusively with the preservation of Islamic identity against the corrosive influence of American society. Publications of the time, such as *MSA News* and, later, *Islamic Horizons*, depicted the American environment as an undifferentiated culture having nothing to do with Islam (Schumann 2007, 16). America was technologically superior but morally bankrupt, a perception that echoed Sayyid Qutb's image of America.[19] In the eyes of these identity-centric, diasporic Muslims, America was an undifferentiated mass. It was at worst an impure place, at best a neutral space for the encounter and education of Muslim activists from Islamic countries.

Their orientation was thus overseas, toward the Islamic world. Their American location gave them extra space and allowed them to mobilize technical and ideological resources for what Benedict Anderson calls "long-distance nationalism" (1998, 58), which in this case meant long-distance Islamism. Even the notion of *dawah*, which was activated in response to displacement—its temporariness notwithstanding—was an *introvert dawah* directed at students themselves. The purpose was to have "an impact on homelands by educating Islamic activists and preparing them for their future return" (Schumann 2007, 18). Inspired by the Islamic revivalist movements in Muslim countries, they interpreted their own experiences in terms of mobility, movement, or mobilization. The idea of returning home turned their stay into a prolonged transit. America was not a place to dwell; it was not home. Therefore, the ethos of living in America was a "deficient mode of care."

Today, most Muslims would reject the idea of America as an abode of war and might even contest the applicability of the term altogether. The culture of "America as *dar al harb*," survives, therefore, mostly in old community literature and biographical narratives about "Muslims then." One would expect the culture of *dar al harb* to have disappeared entirely over the last couple of decades, since today almost every Muslim sees Muslim presence in America as permanent. But it has not. I discovered this persistence when I talked to the imam of a mosque in Detroit in 2007.[20] This mosque, which has an Arabic name, describes itself as *salafi*.[21] The congregation appears to be predominantly Yemeni. Imam Talib, also from Yemen, is on a long-term visa and has been here for a few years. One of the striking things about this mosque is that the imam does not speak any English at all and delivers his sermons in Arabic. He does, however, use a translator. I interviewed him through one of the people who helps translate his sermons and weekend classes. The following exchanges are selections from the interview.

I started by asking his opinion about the English language, since we were not able to communicate in it.

Question: When one immigrates to America, a lot of things change. For example, here all the Muslims speak English. What do you think about the English language?

Answer: English is good for giving *dawah*. When I came here, there were some brothers who could speak both languages [English and Arabic]. That made it easy for me to do my own Islamic studies. If I go to English-language classes, it will take a lot of driving. Also, you know, classes are mixed, men and women. . . . Muslims should learn this language, of course. If you do not know the language, it is going to be hard. We should give *dawah*.

There are a lot of *masjid*s [mosques] which claim to be *ahlul sunnah* [Sunni], but they actually are not spending enough time on *aqeedah* [creed]. Kids in this country get very little Islam. Here in this *masjid* we try to focus more on Islam so that kids don't get *shirkiyat* and *khurafat* [violations of monotheism and deviation]. We want them to stay away from *shirk* [worshiping things other than the one God]. This is our focus.

Q: What do you think about the *dar al harb* and *dar al Islam* distinction? What is America in your view?

A: America is a *kuffar* country [the land of disbelief, *dar al kufr / dar al harb*]. It is a matter of who is dominant. The dominant identity in this country is *kuffar*. If we can have *dawah*, that is the most important thing. We need to show the people what Islam is. We should teach them.

Q: But Muslims have more freedoms here than in Muslim countries. Think of *hijab*, for example.

A: It is true we have more freedoms, but it does not mean this country is better than the Muslim countries.

Q: Since you have plans to return to Yemen and won't stay in this country, what do you say to Muslims here, those who are going to stay.

A: I say, if they can go back, it is better for them. The future seems very hard here. It is hard to live as a family. It is hard. If something happens, that will be good: if the government *puts all the Muslims in one place* [my italics], that will be good. Then we can live without mixing.

Q: So you would like Muslims to be more isolated and by themselves?

A: Well, we can mix with them to give *dawah* but we should not lose our kids. They should not lose their *deen* [religion].

I left the mosque with some degree of bewilderment in that even though I had observed a whole spectrum of Muslims in the American context, this was a truly *extraordinary* case. Even though many American Muslims believe that they live in "electronic internment" since 9/11, I had never met one who considered internment—be it electronic surveillance or physical imprisonment similar to what Japanese Americans endured during World War II—to be desirable. Here was a Muslim who was "in" America and believed that the best thing that could happen to Muslims living in this country was to be placed in a ghetto or camp. Interestingly enough, the Detroit-Dearborn area is currently the only place in America that approximates a ghetto (Abraham and Shryock 2000). Yet the significant concentration of Arab Muslims in the area still seemed insufficient to this imam, as far as the protection of Islamic identity was concerned. The only justification for Muslims to stay in this country was *dawah*; otherwise, America was a *kuffar* (infidel) country, *dar al harb*, and to protect their religion, Muslims should leave as soon as possible. America was an insecure place and could never qualify as a homeland. This insecurity was not so much about civil rights and liberties—concerns shared by many Muslims—but about religious reproduction and spiritual purity.

To inquire further into his mosque's relationship to the American environment, I asked if they were involved in any interfaith activities. He replied: "No interfaith activity here. All our information [about Islam] is on the website. I say, go to call them to Islam but not to listen to them. Those who go and say, 'We are the same, no difference,' they are wrong. Call them to Islam."

According to this introverted view of Islam and the Muslim community, America had to be avoided, and when that was not possible, then the only legitimate form of involvement was *dawah*, which for this imam meant conversion. Any other form of involvement should be shunned. "Interaction" with the outside world was thus not a two-way street.[22] It is not surprising that this was the only mosque in my research area where they try to convert visitors, even Muslim ones, to their form of Islam. Other colleagues who visited this mosque told me that they were approached with an intention to convert even though they had made it clear that they were there for research alone.

Most past Muslim immigrants had and some Muslims in the early stage of their immigration today still have a slightly tamer view of the American environment and the role of Muslims in that they perceive themselves as an outpost of Muslim geography in an alien land. As long as their presence is temporary, they comfortably continue to hold the view that America can be an abode of war. This ideal typical perception of America as abode of war/chaos changes only under the influence of direct experience, interaction, and the recognition of dwelling that is usually outside the control of the subjects. The concept of *dawah* (mission, call to Islam), which together with *darura* (necessity) is one of the two justifications for being in America, eventually outgrows the juridical category of abode of war and becomes the point of reference in itself. Limited engagement in the form of *dawah* ultimately leads to a perception of America as an open field for unlimited *dawah*. *Dawah* is no longer directed at other Muslims but at non-Muslim others. This change of orientation also marks the transition to the next stage where America is perceived as a land of mission.

Abode of Mission: An Outpost in the "Land of Possibilities"

As an abode of war, America represented the absolute outside and an an-
tihomeland. As an abode of mission, while still external to Islam, America
is recognized as an adjacent space. As such, it becomes a *frontier*. It is a
target of concernful interest or a destination of risky spiritual venture. In
this conception, America is a field of exploration that is at once dangerous and potentially beneficial. The most significant change in the perception from the earlier one is that America is no longer a monolith. Weak
signs of differentiation emerge as the newcomer withholds his or her
final judgment about America while approaching it with caution. The
newcomer's presence is most likely temporary or in its early stages.

In the stage of abode of mission, the notion of *dawah* (mission) under-
goes a shift in terms of orientation: now it explicitly targets non-Muslims.
The introvert conception is replaced by an extrovert one as some involvement with America becomes possible. The primary concern is still
the preservation of identity *through* a narrowly defined engagement with
American society. Even though America is still viewed as a place of moral
decay, Muslims are now seen as capable of contributing to its positive
transformation, and reluctant involvement becomes a desirable partial
participation. A shift also occurs from activism that targets Muslim students to activism aimed at changing an otherwise-threatening environment. In this transformation, the Qur'anic idea of "promoting good and
preventing evil" becomes a touchstone.[23]

If previously the Muslim world and America were polar opposites, in
this stage even though they are still largely monoliths, they each acquire
negative and positive aspects—the problems of the Muslim world and
some virtues of America are acknowledged. The Muslim world or past
homelands now lose their sharpness and complexity in the mind's eye
of the immigrant, and this distancing from the past homeland is accompanied by the development of a comparably limited "nearness" to the
American environment. In terms of community development, this approach characterizes the 1980s. Early signs of recognizing America as a
"nation of immigrants" emerge, and the possibility of somehow fitting
in becomes imaginable for the Muslim immigrant.

Yet even though the beginnings of settlement are observed, America
is still diasporic: this settlement has not yet fully disengaged itself from
a movement that began elsewhere. Muslims who were in transit are
now settled into "mobility" and outreach. In the process, *darura* (excep-

tion) becomes a conditional "stay." One can stay, but only to perform *dawah*! That is, a shift occurs from conditional visit to conditional stay. A necessity-based risk has become an opportunity-based one.

As a consequence of the shift, calling America an abode of war becomes increasingly difficult and the term itself is seldom employed. As Mustapha, a young Muslim I interviewed, stated, "If America is *dar al harb*, what does that add to you? What matters more is whether you as a Muslim change yourself and your environment." The formerly monolithic and impure surface of America is now seen as receptive to the inscription of Islam. Along the same lines, an essay published in 1985 in *Islamic Horizons* claims, "We cannot continue to throw out the baby of *dawah* with the bathwater of our disaffection towards this government and society. For clearly we have been placed here with a purpose. . . . If we plan to leave tomorrow, we still have today to work, to do our share in remodeling what has been called a *dar al harb*—a home of hostility—into a *dar al Islam*—a home in which all Muslims can seek shelter. For wherever we are, our Home is Islam" (Omar 1985, 10, quoted in Schumann 2007, 21).

So either Muslim institutions change their orientation, or institutions with a new orientation emerge in their stead: institutions oriented toward "non-American" Muslims in America and the Muslim world are replaced by a "global Muslim" discourse with some localization. The Islamic Society of North America (ISNA), established in 1982 in response to the fact that more and more of the students who had planned to return to their homelands ended up staying and forming families in the United States, is a perfect example of this new transformation. Now a Muslim community occupying North American space came into existence with early and small signs of localization and settlement. For instance, the essay quoted above and published in *Islamic Horizons* was titled "Participation of Muslims in America as a *Land of Possibilities*" (my italics).

In addition, the Muslim community is no longer identified with students but with their families: ISNA catered to this emergent community, which was still diasporic but was now inclined toward settlement. In this stage the community's institutions begin to engage the American environment, but only on the grounds of ideology and self-interest aimed solely at the dissemination of Islam. Still, this reluctant settlement and narrow involvement transform the nature of the Muslim community from being a thin "outpost" of Muslims in an alien land to a "thicker" extension of the global Muslim community at large. To sum up, the ideological transition from the 1970s to the 1980s was one from students to families, from MSA to ISNA, from avoidance to protectionism through partial involvement.

Though this mind-set had its heyday in the 1980s, it can still be found in Muslim communities in the United States. I saw it reflected in some of my conversations with Muslim community leaders. One such example was Imam Haroon of Masjidun-Nur (Mosque of Light) in Detroit. Established in 1978, this inner-city mosque is at present predominantly African American. The imam himself is from the Caribbean (the island of Granada) and is ethnically South Asian. He had been serving as imam at this mosque since 1984 when I asked his opinion on several issues. Although very conservative and introverted, his views about the American setting were more nuanced than those of the previous imam in that—at least on a few registers—he thought that the American context was unusual. "Sometimes *ulama* [religious scholars] overseas do not know the life here. They do not know how America is different. There are some necessities. You cannot say that women should not drive. If she is Muslim and her family is non-Muslim and against her, how can she call her brother to drive her to the hospital? Like this there may be necessities in America."

When asked about the distinction between abode of war and abode of Islam, he preferred to avoid the binary and emphasized instead the perception of America as "a land of possibilities" in the following manner:

I have been able to pray at the airport, at the mall, or at the bus station. Since I've been here it has been very easy to live Islam. I don't know what category America fits, but we are free to live Islam and do *dawah*. Sometimes people are more welcoming. Once there was a non-Muslim woman; she invited us to her house when she saw that we were going to pray on the grass. She did not know us, but she invited us to pray at her house.

[America] is Allah's country. We're here to invite people to Islam. We are here for the guidance. Some scholars say it is not permissible to stay in a non-Muslim land. But what about those who are from here? Where will they go? The earth is vast, and for making a living, anywhere is OK. Some *sahabas* [companions of the Prophet] did both living and *dawah*.

When asked how he views the future of Islam here, he noted, "I see a great future because of the saying of Prophet Muhammad, 'Islam will dominate and not be dominated.'" Despite the relative openness to and appreciation of the American environment, his response to my question on interfaith activism, which I use as an index of involvement with the social environment, revealed the striking ambivalence produced by the perception of America as abode of mission:

No, we don't do interfaith activities. My personal opinion, I don't feel the need for it. They stay their way and we stay our way. We respect but don't talk. . . . I think it became more difficult after 9/11. But some non-Muslim African Americans started to wear *kufi* [Muslim skullcap] and say, "as salamu alaikum," to support us. We have no hostility with others. . . . The main thing is *dawah*; I don't want to use that word, but we work for *dawah*; it is an imperative for us.

Dar al dawah basically takes Muslim immigrants to the threshold of settlement, and as such marks the limits of diasporic orientation. The negative connection with the environment (through the juridical device of *darura*) is now replaced by a narrowed yet positive connection (based on a redefinition of *dawah*). At this point, the neat division "anything Muslim is good, anything American is evil" starts to erode. Yet the Muslim subject is still mentally located in another homeland and has only a limited justification for his presence in America.

Abode of Accord: From Mission to Dialogue

As *dar al ahd* (abode of accord) America is *neighbor* to Islam and a party to an accord; it is a source of mutual benefit. America is religiously justified and protected by religious laws such as the injunction that Muslims must obey the law of the land wherever they live. America thus becomes even more differentiated and emerges as a peaceful space of opportunity for Muslims, but one that has not yet been fully internalized or naturalized. The benefits and opportunities now supersede the risks. This conception's ideal type is a resident: his presence is permanent, with the reservation that one day he might have to leave. The stage represented by the concept of abode of accord entails a cautious embrace and the early phase of settlement. Many Muslims interpret abode of accord with relative comfort due to its resonance with the social contract theories of American society. Abode of accord, therefore, symbolizes the first cultural encounter of the immigrant Muslim with American citizenship. While for abode of war and abode of mission, the Muslim just happens to be in America, in the conception of abode of accord he begins to see himself as part of a larger society in which he, too, has a stake. It thus allows Muslims to imagine a place of their own inside American society, creating the possibility of an American Muslim cultural "ghetto"—in the positive sense of the term—within a liberal society. More specifically, abode of accord represents a communitarian understanding of membership in American society, where private autonomy is slightly expanded and buttressed as an adequate domain for the survival of Islamic identity. The sense of belonging that abode of accord generates is located in the spectrum between a protected subject and a full citizen.

Muslims who see their new environment in this way no longer hold themselves apart from majority society but still preserve their distinct identity. They share with the rest of the society a culture in which Islam seeks a place. The idea of abode of accord therefore lends itself to a spectrum of existence from reluctant participation to hopeful and safe engagement with the American environment.

In 1999 the Mauritanian shaikh Abdallah Bin Bayyah was invited by the Zaytuna Institute, a neotraditional center of Islamic learning based in California, to speak to American Muslims in the Bay Area. He delivered his lecture in Arabic, translated by an American convert, Shaikh Hamza Yusuf. After examining the needs and conditions of Muslims in diaspora, Shaikh Bin Bayyah discussed the problem of the status of lands where Muslims are minorities. He criticized the dichotomy of abode of war and abode of Islam:

Most people think that the world is divided into two abodes, the abode of peace and the abode of war. The abode of peace is the land of the Muslims, *dar al-Islam*, and the abode of war is everywhere else. In [former president] Nixon's book that I read a translated version of called *Seize the Moment*, Nixon wrote a long chapter on the Islamic phenomenon of the modern world. One of the things Nixon said . . . is that they view the world as a dichotomy of two abodes: the abode of peace and the abode of war. So, the central aspect of international relationships with the Muslims is aggression; it is one of war. This idea is wrong. There are three abodes: there is the abode of peace, the abode of war, and then there is the *abode of treaty* where there is a contractual agreement between two abodes. (Bin Bayyah 1999)

The shaikh explained the relationship between immigrant Muslims in America and their country of immigration by referring to his entry into the country. His personal border crossing became an illustration of entry into abode of accord/contract:

For instance, when I came into this country, they issued me a visa, and I signed something. In the issuance of the visa and my signing of it, a legally binding contract occurred. It was an agreement that when I came into this country, I would obey the laws and would follow the restrictions that this visa demanded that I follow. This was a contractual agreement that is legally binding according even to the divine laws. In looking at this, we have to understand that the relationship between the Muslims living in this land and the dominant authorities in this land is a relationship of peace and contractual agreement—of a treaty. This is a relationship of dialogue and a relationship of giving and taking.

The shaikh also articulated the conception of America as an abode of treaty:

The first essential thing is that you respect the laws of the land that you are living in. . . . In this country, the ruling people are allowing you to call people to Islam. They are not prohibiting you. . . . It is necessary for us to show respect to these people. Islam prohibits us from showing aggression towards people who do not show aggression towards us. . . . We also have to be good citizens because an excellent Muslim is also an excellent citizen in the society that he lives in.

Muslim discourses, including those of the Zaytuna Institute, which hosted Shaikh Bin Bayyah in 1999, have changed since then in response to the aftermath of 9/11. Zaytuna's change of orientation can be traced through the writings of its leaders, among them Imam Zaid Shakir.[24]

As far as Muslim community leadership is concerned, the idea of abode of accord appears to have been the dominant conception in the 1990s. Since 9/11, it has been criticized by Muslim public intellectuals who urge a complete transition to the conception of America as an abode of Islam. Muqtedar Khan, a Muslim professor of political science who became prominent after 9/11, finds the idea of abode of accord an inadequate and morally problematic position for Muslims in the United States (M. Khan 2002, 8). From another perspective,[25] Tariq Ramadan, a European Muslim intellectual, finds the same term untenable due to its dependence on the old dichotomy of abode of war–abode of Islam. Instead, he proposes *dar al dawah* (abode of mission)—using a sense different from my own discussion above—and he even calls for a total abandonment of the idea of abodes: "At a time when we are witnessing a strong current of globalization, it is difficult to refer to the notion of *dar* (abode) unless we consider the whole world as an abode. Our world has become a small village and, as such, it is henceforth *an open world*." The whole world, according to Ramadan, is therefore an abode of call/mission. We should "stop translating the notion of *dar* in its restrictive meaning of 'abode' and prefer the notion of *space*, which more clearly expresses the idea of an *opening of the world*, for Muslim populations are now scattered all over the world." This global space is *dar al dawah* (space of testimony/mission), where Muslims "bear witness before all mankind" (Ramadan 2002, 147).

Abode of Islam: "Thinking without Accent"

Encouraging Muslim political participation, Agha Saeed, Muslim political activist and president of the American Muslim Alliance, wrote that Muslims need generations who "not only speak without accent but also think without accent" (2002, 55). To him "thinking without accent" means changing the orientation of Muslims in America from preoccupation with the Muslim world to taking an interest in American domestic issues. Criticizing immigrant generations for being too much invested in goings-on in their countries of origin, Saeed finds hope in new generations of Muslims who instead regard America as both home and homeland.

In the conception of abode of Islam or abode of peace, the ideal type is a citizen, a person who feels at home in America and thereby achieves equilibrium or symmetry between the subjective culture (Muslim identity) and the objective culture (American culture). America no longer remains a mismatched habitat for a Muslim habitus developed elsewhere. Rather, it becomes an American Muslim habitus in an American habitat. As such, even immigrant parents who might not consider America their homeland would not hesitate to call it the homeland of their children.

When I asked a Bangladeshi imam in Hamtramck, Michigan, what he thought of America as a new home for Muslims, he replied, "There is no return; we have settled here." When I said, "But you know there are Muslims who have reluctance because of the distinction of two abodes," his response came very quickly: "Oh no, no. I take one poet; he said, [quotes first in Bengali, then translates freely] 'China is mine. Arabian Peninsula is mine. Japan is mine. America is mine. I'm a Muslim. All the world is my country.' That is my understanding. I decided to live over here; I'm a citizen of this country; this is my country. It is my children's country."

In the three previous perceptions of America, Muslims had remained in their prepolitical state in relation to American politics. It is only with the conception of America as abode of Islam/peace that membership in American society begins to translate into active citizenship and political participation. If "abode of accord" (*dar al ahd*) designates an American environment not incompatible with Islam, "abode of peace" (*dar al Islam*) designates an American environment that is perceived as Islamic.

Muslims who regard America as an abode of peace actually consider American values to be lost or alienated Islamic values. As Ingrid Mattson, the current president of ISNA, notes:

Among the most interesting efforts to permit Muslims a full embrace of American identity is the attempt to show that the constitutional democratic structure of America is almost equivalent to the political structure of an ideal Islamic state—in other words, a dialectic in which a redefinition of Islam meets a particular definition of America so that American democracy is identified with Islamic *shura* (consultation) and freedom of religion is identified with the Qur'anic statement "there is no compulsion in religion." (2003, 207)

The legal structures of democratic society become an extension of Islamic political order, if not an unnoticed embodiment of it. On the European front, Tariq Ramadan argues that abiding by the law of the land is an extension of following Islamic law:

Implementing the Sharia [Islamic law], for a Muslim citizen or resident in Europe, is explicitly to respect the constitutional and legal framework of the country in which he is a citizen. Whereas one might have feared a *conflict of loyalties*, one cannot but note that it is in fact the reverse, since faithfulness to Islamic teachings results in an even more exacting legal *implantation* in the new environment. *Loyalty to one's faith and conscience requires firm and honest loyalty to one's country*: the *Sharia* requires honest citizenship within the frame of reference constituted by the positive law of the European country concerned. (2002, 172; italics in original)[26]

The perspective identifying Islam with American values tends to emerge among American-born children of immigrants (i.e., the second and third generations) and among convert Americans seeking harmony in their double identity. For example, Robert Dickson Crane, a former adviser to President Nixon and convert to Islam, writes in his *Shaping the Future: Challenge and Response*, that "the basic principles of Islamic law are identical to the basic premises of America's founding fathers, but both Muslims and Americans have lost this common heritage" (1997, 45). This was the implicit theme of the keynote speech that Hamza Yusuf of Zaytuna Institute delivered in 2007 in Chicago at the annual convention of ISNA. He argued that not only are Muslim and American values aligned, but American Muslims are the true inheritors and present-day bearers of "old-fashioned American values," which otherwise have been lost in the modern world.

Similarly Mirza A. Beg, a Muslim freelance writer, wrote the following in an essay that was posted on several Muslim websites and that advocated Muslim participation in American democracy:

America has been a land of immigrants ever since the founding of the Republic. Though European in the beginning, in the last few decades, it has welcomed all, irrespective of color, ethnicity or religion. . . .

As Muslims, Islam enjoins us to be just and truthful, in thought, works and deeds; as well as be respectful of other religions while practicing the tenets of Islam. As Americans we cherish the constitution and the bill of rights. *America is our home* [my italics] and our children's future.

Democratic norms are embedded in Islamic heritage. . . . The only way for a peaceful religion to flourish is in a democratic setting, without coercion. Freedom is a yearning of all human souls. The quest of centuries for equality and justice led to the realization, that the only guaranty of individual freedom is to guarantee freedom for all, within a constitutional framework. It culminated in the pluralistic American democracy. (Beg 2008)

This new "Muslim homeland" can be considered more Islamic than most, if not all, Muslim countries. A land of freedom (especially religious freedom) and democracy, America is a heterogeneous arena of good and bad, right and wrong. Just like historically Muslim lands, America also has its share of bad things. But it is up to Muslims to live Islam. They can contribute to its culture and society not only by their faith but also through their hard work and service. America is no longer an opportunity space or a land of possibilities; it is a privilege for Muslims. As such it places them in a special status with regard to both America and the Muslim community at large. American Muslims see themselves as having a special location and a historical responsibility—indeed, a number of contemporary Muslim intellectuals have called it a "manifest destiny" (M. Khan 2002, 1). American Muslims could even come to lead the Muslim community at large (the *ummah*).

Muslim writers publish articles with such titles as "Life, Liberty, and Pursuit of Happiness are Islamic Values." The pursuit of happiness (which had been regarded by Qutb, under the paradigm of abode of war/chaos, as antithetical to Islam) is now seen as part of Islam. Islam becomes an *American religion*, part of the landscape of American civil religion in the minds of Muslims themselves. Interfaith consciousness matures and interfaith activism intensifies. At the 2007 ISNA convention, Victor Ghalib Begg, a local champion of interfaith activism and board member of the Muslim Unity Center in Bloomfield Hills, Michigan, asked, "Where is Muslim ecumenicalism? Protestants and Catholics had their 'ecumenical' moment and are now well past it; this is a stage we Muslims should also go through, both among Muslims and with the non-Muslims."

Now America is home and the Muslim world is the target of outreach. At the stage of America as abode of Islam, the shift of perspectives is complete. Muslims see things from the "point of view" (i.e., location) of their new home/land, America. They are now set to make strategic incursions into the Muslim world, seeking to derive benefits from it (in the form of cultural resources) while avoiding its problems (corruption, authoritarianism). Whereas previously only converts had behaved in this way, it now becomes common practice among the children of American immigrants. New generations of Muslims often criticize the "cultural Islam" of their parents, which they see as immigrant confusion of culture with religion. They want to dissociate Islam from its Middle Eastern or South Asian "baggage" and make it an *American* religion. Often they ignore the fact that America also comes with its own "culture," that "pure Islam" without a local culture is nowhere to be found. What had once been approached with suspicion (i.e., America, the abode of war/chaos) is now naturalized, and what was natural for their parents (i.e., overseas culture) has now become an object of suspicion.

The signs of a more autonomous Islam can be seen in the words of Maher Hathout, a Muslim community leader, who spoke at a Muslim conference in the early 2000s, stating: "As much as we can make clear that Muslim-American identity is not a natural extension of the Middle East, the better off we will be."[27] As American Muslims gain relative autonomy vis-à-vis other Muslims, America becomes in their eyes an increasingly complex entity. America presents manifold eidetic appearances while the Muslim world shrinks to a few ideal types. The process of autonomization of American Islam is best illustrated in a piece that Imam Zaid Shakir of Zaytuna Institute wrote in response to the Danish cartoon crisis that broke out in September 2005.[28] In "Clash of the Uncivilized: Insights into the Cartoon Controversy," Shakir criticized the Muslim protestors in the Middle East and elsewhere for ignoring the consequences of their irrational behavior for Muslims living in the West:

One of the most disturbing aspects of the current campaign to "Assist the Prophet," for many converts, like this writer, is the implicit assumption that there is no *dawah* work being undertaken here in the West, and no one is currently, or will in the future enter Islam in these lands. Therefore, it does not matter what transpires in the Muslim East. Muslims can behave in the most barbaric fashion, murder, plunder, pillage, brutalize and kidnap civilians, desecrate the symbols of other religions, trample on their honor, discard their values and mores, and massacre their fellow Muslims. If any of that undermines the works of Muslims in these Western lands, it does not matter. If it places a barrier between the Western people and Islam, when many of those people are in the most desperate need of Islam, it does not matter. If our Prophet, peace and blessings of God upon him, had responded to those who abused him in Ta'if with similar disregard, none of the generations of Muslims who have come from the descendants of those transgressors would have seen the light of day. (2006)

Shakir's critique of "Muslims in the East" represents a threshold moment in the separation of American Islam from its imagined origins in a Muslim world that is growing increasingly unrecognizable in the eyes of American Muslims. And as he goes on to note, this symbolic separation is truly remarkable:

As Muslims in the West, we may be approaching the day when we will have to "go it alone." If our coreligionists in the East cannot respect the fact that we are trying to accomplish things here in the West, and that their oftentimes ill-considered actions undermine that work in many instances, then it will be hard for us to consider them allies. . . . No one from the Muslim East consults us before launching these campaigns. We have a generation of Muslim children here who have to go to schools where most of them are small minorities facing severe peer pressure. Their faith is challenged and many decide to simply stop identifying with Islam. Is that what they deserve? We have obedient, pious Hijab wearing women, who out of necessity must work, usually in places where they are the only Muslims. Should their safety, dignity, and honor be jeopardized by the actions of Muslims halfway around the world? (2006)

The process of autonomization of American Islam is accelerated by second- and third-generation American Muslims who make fun of their immigrant parents and Islamophobic non-Muslim compatriots. The rise of Muslim comedians, especially in the post-9/11 era, amply attests to this transformation.[29] The emergence of an American Muslim ethos and the development of a sense of being at home in America reverse the relationship between the abode of peace and the abode of chaos. America becomes the land of order and pure reality, while the homeland of immigrant parents retreats into chaos and anomie. Now, the Muslim world is seen through an American lens and judged *from* that location.

Conclusion

This chapter has examined the way in which immigrant Muslims eliminate their sense of homeland insecurity and gradually come to see

America as a new homeland. As Muslims begin to dwell in America, either the American nomos becomes legible to them, or they introduce a new Islamic nomos to the American surface. Often the two possibilities converge.

Phenomenologically speaking, our situatedness creates nearness and distance. Muslim views of America are shaped by their relative exposure to American space and the degree of their involvement with it. This chapter has traced the transition from the paradigm of exception (*darura*) to the construction of legal order on a previously anomic space. As we have seen, the abode of chaos–abode of peace binary faces an irruption of experience and is shattered into a plurality of new categories—and, as a consequence, the Muslim lifeworld in America becomes religiously legitimate and meaningful. Examination of the stages of this process reaffirms that there is no such thing as a blanket Muslim perception of America, a salient reminder at a time when Muslim loyalty to the American nation is viewed with increasing skepticism.

This discussion of the juridical tools that help immigrant Muslims feel at home rests on the concept of "cultural settlement," which highlights the dynamic relationship between habitus and habitat. Bourdieu's notion of habitus is often construed as a tool for understanding the persistence of past forms of symbolic violence. My study shows the dialogical rearticulation of habitus through settlement, that is, through the inhabitation of a new cultural environment. The gradual character of this process, which entails a "digestion" of the new environment on both the politico-communal and the psychic level, requires attention to issues of temporality and space. Furthermore, unlike legal inclusion and naturalization, which focus on the role of sovereign or disciplinary apparatuses of power in integrating the newcomer, cultural settlement pays attention to the agency of the displaced subjects, who are seen to appropriate their new homeland, even as it appropriates them.

Taking a phenomenological approach to the immigrant experience sensitizes us to particular aspects of the settlement process: the way displacement causes disequilibrium between the subjective culture of the individual and the objective culture of their environment; the terror and anomie they experience at this loss; the way their dwelling in a new space generates, over time, a new canopy, a new ethos, and a new common sense. The human being and the world he or she inhabits are much less dissociable than our liberal conceptions of citizenship tend to suggest. In an important sense, the immigrant does not move from one part of the world to another. He moves from one world to another. Truly "being" in that new world, as Heidegger reminds us, demands an unmaking and remaking of self, a shift from a deficient mode of care, which is a disposition of nonattunement toward the new environment, to an attitude of involvement, openness, and attunement. A proper phenomenology of the immigration experience—that is, of the processes of dissociation from the past and *there* and reassociation with the now, the *here*—reveals a transformation from chaos and confusion, from life as a constant state of exception, to attention, receptivity, and nomos. This is creative work, both on the part of the immigrant and on the part of the society that receives him. Immigration, with its discordance between habitus and habitat, ceases to define a person only when concordance is established between habitus and new habitat in a gradual process of mutual appropriation.

PART TWO

Citizenship Practices

FOUR

Awakening Citizenship: Rights Meet Bearers

The best criteria by which to decide whether someone has been forced outside the pale of the law is to ask if he would benefit by committing a crime. If a small burglary is likely to improve his legal position, at least temporarily, one may be sure he has been deprived of human rights. For then a criminal offense becomes the best opportunity to regain some kind of human equality, even if it be as a recognized exception to the norm. The one important fact is that this exception is provided for by law. As a criminal even a stateless person will not be treated worse than another criminal, that is, he will be treated like everybody else. Only as an offender against the law can he gain protection from it.   ARENDT 1973, 286

Writing on the philosophical meaning and historical consequences of statelessness in interwar Europe, Hannah Arendt depicts it as the most radical form of exclusion and dehumanization. Statelessness is a condition where human rights and civil rights are de-linked, where bare life is detached from the law that assigns it a place and a voice. In Foucauldian language, subjectedness to the law is what produces human beings as subjects. A stateless person falls outside the pale of the law: he lacks nomos. Because he is metaphysically unformatted, it becomes impossible to commit a crime against him—there are no boundaries to be transgressed. Modern-day prisoners at Abu Ghraib and Guantánamo fall into this category; we see them stripped of their clothes, toyed with and humiliated, piled into pyramids of bodies. People of this category, says Agamben, "may be killed but cannot be sacrificed" (1998, 8). When law—the metaphysical mantle that produces human beings—is lifted from over them, they lose their "right to have rights" (Arendt 1973, 296; Somers 2006, 35–63).

The conditions I am going to discuss here are by no means that severe, but a similar logic applies. Statelessness certainly reduces human beings to what Arendt calls "the scum of the earth" (1973, 269). Arendt's reasoning, I believe, also implies that there are varying degrees of being "within the pale of the law." Even for those within the compass of the law, there are varying degrees of protection (Bosniak 2006, 4).

Let me turn now to the relationship between Muslim life and American law. If Muslims inside America were in some sense "legally neglected citizens," the crime of 9/11, although connected to them only very tenuously, imposed on them a variety of new legal forms. I will touch briefly on a few of these accidents of citizenship here, before turning to the real meat of my discussion.

The tragedy of 9/11 has transformed noncitizen, non-American Muslims (in Iraq, Afghanistan, and elsewhere) into objects of American sovereignty, differentiating them into enemy and friend or good Muslim and bad Muslim (Mamdani 2004). Those who were outside the scope of American law were nonetheless touched by its sovereignty. Those who were encompassed by the law, however, experienced a tectonic shock. And a few of them fell into the abyss. Some citizens were designated as "enemy combatants" and removed outside the pale of the law, albeit temporarily. John Walker Lindh (the so-called American Taliban) and Yasser Hamdi (another an American citizen accused of fighting for the Taliban) are two famous cases (Cole 2005, 4). The metaphysical mantle of the law was lifted from over them. Actually, the receding boundary of law landed squarely between them: while Lindh was eventually brought back into the legal fold, Hamdi was forced to renounce his American citizenship as a condition of his deportation to another country. From the beginning, Hamdi's citizenship was treated as "accidental" (Nyers 2006, 22).

As you trace the receding shoreline of the law, you begin to come across new categories of people. Some are citizens whose connections with foreigners seem to have been used to implicate them in crimes. In this group are two Muslim members of the US Army, Ahmad Al Halabi and Chaplain James Yee, both married to Syrian nationals, who were accused of espionage while stationed at Guantánamo. The story of James Yee, in particular, is reminiscent of the Dreyfus affair. The government was finally compelled to drop all charges against him, but only after much legal posturing and expense. Others are illegal immigrants—many of whom have lived here peaceably and productively for years—who, caught by the immigration authorities, seek only to return to their countries of origin but find themselves stuck between the law and extralegality. Osama Siblani, the publisher of *Arab American News*, a Michigan weekly, said in a public lecture on March 23, 2007, "I receive letters from prisons. Lebanese, Iraqi, Pakistani . . . all kinds of people who need to be deported but can't because they don't have passports. They beg to be helped." Legal scholars like David Cole argue that sacrificing the rights of immigrants and aliens for the security of citizens will eventually lead to the loss of the rights of citizens themselves (2005, 17). Arendt observed a similar phenomenon: "Once a number of stateless people were admitted to an otherwise normal country, statelessness spread like a contagious disease" (1973, 285).

Having crossed this littoral of fractured and receding citizenship, we reach the body of mainstream Muslims who are full legal citizens. They are protected by the law but, unlike their non-Muslim fellow citizens, are under intense scrutiny and surveillance. Many of them believe that they are seen as "guilty until proven innocent."

The impact of 9/11 on this final and largest group of Muslims, I would like to argue, has been ambiguous. It includes the distress of exclusion and surveillance but also, counterintuitively, the benefits of recognition. Though painfully, the gap between American Muslims and the law has been narrowed. A law that was not particularly sensitive to them has become much more so. This close encounter between Muslim citizens and the law has produced the category of "victim citizen." Victimhood is the price the immigrant pays to become a citizen.

In what follows, I engage in a discussion of the relationship between victimhood and citizenship as it is articulated in the work of a Muslim advocacy group, the Council on American-Islamic Relations (CAIR). I begin with a brief history of CAIR and then move on to the ways in which CAIR mediates and strives to establish fluency between rights (American law) and their bearers (Muslims). I conclude with a discussion of the cultivation of civility and an argument on negative incorporation.

American Muslim Organizations in the 1990s

The history of Muslim institutions in the United States at the national level is not very long. The Islamic Society of North America (ISNA), today the largest umbrella organization for Muslims, was started in 1982 when the members of the diasporic Muslim Student Association (founded in

1963) realized that their stay in America was not temporary after all. In the naming of those institutions, Muslims treated America as an undifferentiated entity. Foreign Muslim students, reflecting their experience as outsiders in America, and Black Muslims, for whom Islam was then an oppositional identity, all defined themselves in an external relation to America. When the Lost-Found Nation of Islam in the Wilderness of North America was transformed into an orthodox Islamic community under the leadership of Warith Deen Mohammed, black American Muslims named their new organization the World Community of Al-Islam in America.

Over time, however, Muslims began to recognize differentiation in America, and consequently the institutions dealing with the complex entity called America became more specialized. At the same time there was also a change in focus from overseas to domestic affairs. This shift is discernible in the character of organizations launched in the late 1980s and early 1990s. The 1990s, in particular, saw a real explosion of Muslim institutions. This was partly in response to a growth spurt on the part of the Muslim community. Formation of civil rights advocacy groups and professional associations in the 1990s marked the transition from diasporic orientation to cultural settlement. CAIR is one of the many organizations launched in this period. Others include the American Muslim Council and the American Muslim Alliance. By the end of the decade, despite their youth, American Muslim organizations were celebrating their first concrete achievements. The first stamp celebrating Muslim holidays (Eid ul Adha and Eid ul Fitr) was released in 2001, shortly before 9/11. The Clinton administration and the State Department hosted Ramadan *iftaar* dinners with American Muslim leaders. The year 2001 was also a threshold year in Muslim political participation. An umbrella organization of various Muslim political affairs committees endorsed George W. Bush in exchange for his promise to repeal the Secret Evidence Act. Over the objections of African American Muslim organizations, most immigrant Muslims voted Republican in expectation of the greater recognition promised by Bush.

The 9/11 attacks brought this string of successes to a screeching halt. The American Muslim Committee, perhaps the most active Muslim lobbying organization, fell into obscurity. One of its officials told me in 2003 that the White House was no longer answering their phone calls. The organization became practically defunct. CAIR was perhaps the only Washington-based Muslim advocacy organization to survive the fallout of 9/11.

Development of CAIR

CAIR was established in 1994 by Omar Ahmad, Nihad Awad, and Ibrahim Hooper. Ahmad is currently a board member, Awad is executive director, and Hooper is communications director of the organization. Ahmad and Awad are students-turned-activists and naturalized immigrants, while Hooper is a journalist and a convert to Islam. As Awad writes in an essay that he gave me, when they opened a two-person office on K Street in Washington, "We inherited two great challenges. The first was the negative image of Islam and Muslims in the American media, and the effects of that negative image on public perception and public policy. The second challenge was the lack of interest and motivation among Muslims themselves to do anything about it."

Awad is an ethnic Palestinian who came to America from Jordan in 1984. While pursuing his studies in engineering, he also became active in Muslim community affairs in Minnesota, but he grew somewhat disillusioned with their efforts. "We had annual conventions held by ISNA-like organizations for Muslim students and their families since the 1960s, but their focus was on spiritual development, internal affairs and the problems of Muslims abroad." What was lacking was engagement with the larger society and public institutions. Awad believes that his awakening to the need for a Muslim institution oriented toward improving the image of Muslims and promoting their engagement with American society happened at the time of the Gulf War. "Though tragic for the Middle East, it proved catalytic for the Muslim community in America." Muslim Americans were in a sense forced out of their lethargy when they became targets of anti-Arab sentiment.

In the first year of its establishment, CAIR organized a few antidiscrimination campaigns. In September 1994, a Muslim woman reported an offensive greeting card to the CAIR office. The card depicts a veiled woman with the words "Rather than confront her morbid fear of germs, Millicent changed her name to Yazmine and moved to Tehran." Inside, the card read: "So you're feeling like Shiite. Don't Mecca big deal out of it." The campaign against the postcard company, Recycled Paper Greetings, lasted for two months until CAIR persuaded the company to apologize and stop producing the card.

The real turning point in CAIR's young life, however, came with the Oklahoma City bombing. When Timothy McVeigh bombed the Alfred Murrah Federal Building in Oklahoma in 1995, there was an immediate backlash against Muslims. When I asked Awad about CAIR's response, he said, "When that happened we had less than a thousand dollars in our account. I got a ticket and borrowed a cell phone. A reporter got me inside the area closed for investigation. Ibrahim sent a news release that we'll have a press conference on the spot. That press conference was historic. Later we met with the governor of Oklahoma and gave a check from the local Muslim community in Oklahoma to help the victims."

The same year, CAIR published its first civil rights report, "Rush to Judgment," and started to raise more funds. CAIR owes its rise to a series of crises that have led to backlash against American Muslims. Each crisis becomes an opportunity for CAIR to establish itself as the legitimate voice of the American Muslim community. In Awad's words, "one success led to another," and CAIR emerged as the main civil rights group for American Muslims.

CAIR is involved in a range of advocacy work. Among other projects, the organization has tackled survey research (producing "The Mosque in America: A National Portrait") and grassroots mobilization (a voter registration drive), condemned acts of terrorism (declaring a "fatwa against terrorism" in cooperation with the Fiqh Council of North America), protested and preempted media stereotypes (the villains in *The Sum of All Fears*, a film by Paramount Pictures, were changed to neo-Nazis following objections from CAIR about stereotyping of Muslim characters), and mediated cases of commercial- and employment-based discrimination (Nike was prevented from selling sneakers emblazoned with "Allah" in Arabic script; Liz Claiborne was discouraged from producing pants with Qur'anic verses printed on them).

During the summer of 2003, I spent two months working as an intern at CAIR's national headquarters in Washington. In a way, CAIR became my entry point to the world of Muslims in the United States. CAIR provided me with the exposure to the flows of people, ideas, and practices that I needed to familiarize myself with the community and its national-level institutions.

I was assigned to the research department, where my task was to update a database of Muslim institutions in several states. I would place phone calls to those institutions to verify the contact information listed in the database. I was struck by the fact that, even though I introduced myself as calling from CAIR, a significant number of the contacts were reluctant to give information about their institutions. Around this time the government crackdown on Muslim charities was intensifying. A second lesson I learned from my otherwise-boring phone job was the degree of mobility of American mosques. Many *masjid*s (mosques) were no longer to be found at their old phone numbers. Small mosques—which tend to have informal congregations—were even more mobile than established ones. I wondered if this had to do with the 9/11 backlash and growing sense of insecurity within the community. Even large mosques' answering machines would sometimes say that they could not give directions to the mosque because of security concerns.

I would occasionally have informal conversations with the people at the other end of the phone. Some of the respondents told me that they "had never heard of CAIR"—a neat confirmation of the idea that communities and ethnic identities are mostly group-making projects (Brubaker 2004, 10) or an effect of the representations made on their behalf—a nuance captured nicely by Bourdieu's famous phrase "the mystery of ministry."

Although not everybody had heard of CAIR, most were eager to find a channel to express their feelings and grievances. A Bangladeshi respondent explained how there are "more liberties in America than in Muslim countries"—a statement you can hear from many Muslims. The tone of another respondent's comments was different. He was the representative of a Muslim charity in the Midwest. He said that their organization had been visited by the FBI. Since then, "the name of our organization is on the news. This has a negative impact. People are scared about donating." When I asked what it meant to be an American Muslim, his response was: "You live by the laws of the land. You expect protection and equality. There should not be any difference."

He went on to complain about "some media outlets show[ing] Islam as evil. We need to inform people about Muslims. Muslims are regular folks who eat, drink, etc. . . . We want to educate our children. . . . Americans are nice, open to learn. They want to listen. We should build bridges."

Since CAIR was located two blocks from the Capitol, we attended numerous congressional hearings. On the second day of my internship I found myself in the halls of the capitol building attending a public forum organized by the American Civil Liberties Union (ACLU). The forum, "Justice for All: Selective Enforcement in Post 9/11 America," took place before Senators Edward Kennedy and Patty Murray. The testimony discussed mandatory detention, lengthy detentions without charge, holding immigrants who had been ordered deported, selective enforcement of obscure immigration infractions, secrecy in immigration detention, and eroding accountability. It also touched on the alienation of immigrant communities, including "voluntary" interviews of Arab and Muslim males and the recently imposed requirement of Special Registration for Arab and Muslim males.

The ACLU presentation was accompanied by the stories of four victims of detention and discrimination. One of them, Asif Iqbal, was a New York Muslim who found himself on the "No-Fly List" because he shared the name of a terrorist suspect held at Guantánamo Bay. After being repeatedly denied boarding or interrogated by law enforcement authorities prior to boarding, Iqbal sought assistance from CAIR. He gave spoken testimony that day. It is a long quotation but a useful illustration of the post-9/11 challenges some citizens and civil rights groups face.

I have been repeatedly discriminated against at airports across America solely because of my name, "Asif Iqbal." I think it is important to note that in Pakistan, my name is as common as John Smith is here. Since the initial implementation of the "No-Fly List" by TSA [Transportation Security Administration], passengers like myself have been denied boarding simply because our names are the same or similar to that of a suspect on the No-Fly List. Let me describe to you what it is like for people like myself to go through the routine process of checking in at the airport. Every time I check in for a flight, the airline computer terminal locks up because my name matches a name on the No-Fly List. I am then asked to step aside while they contact local law enforcement. Upon their arrival, I am questioned, often in front of a whole line of passengers and eventually given clearance from them. Unfortunately this isn't the end of it. After I'm given clearance by local officers, the airline representative is then prompted to contact the FBI and other government agencies for further clearance. In some instances, the FBI has responded by coming to the airport to further interrogate me. Finally, after a tedious run of questions and answers and clearance from the appropriate persons, I am allowed to board my flight. The sense of relief I feel when finally cleared for boarding is quickly diminished when I remember that I will have to repeat this whole process again on my return flight. On several occasions this process has caused me to miss my flights and in some instances has forced me to lose a day's work.

My travel goes well beyond vacation travel once in a while. I work for BearingPoint Inc. as a Senior Consultant out of the Manhattan office. My job requires 100% travel and therefore I hold Elite Status with Continental and US Airways. I typically travel every Monday morning to my client's site and fly every Thursday evening to my home in Rochester, NY. Like many other Americans, I had my own apprehensions about traveling after the September 11 attacks and I must admit that initially, seeing the extra security helped to lessen my feelings of anxiety. While I understand the need for some of the vigorous measures taken by airport security, I feel there must be a better way to handle this situation. Being stopped the first time was acceptable, but each and every time I travel? Not to mention the fact that each and every experience has been extremely humiliating and emotionally draining. Since February of 2002, I have been trying to get some kind of relief from the government so that I do not have to be subjected to this when I travel.

CAIR and ACLU have been consistently following up with TSA to get updates on when a new procedure would be implemented, however, as yet, no definitive timeline has been given. Instead, TSA and other government agencies involved passed the buck when questioned about the implementation of a relief procedure. Which leaves me today wondering when, if ever, a new system will be activated to give me relief and allow me to travel as freely as other Americans?[1]

After we came back to the office, I asked Laurie, a CAIR staff member, about Iqbal's case. Laurie said she was frustrated with the lack of progress in this case despite her prolonged efforts. "There are multiple [No-Fly] Lists," she complained. "They keep shuffling everything around. Bureaucracy is expanding and moving. I think it is part of the strategy so that people would not know where to go."

Even when we cannot solve the problem, she said, "it makes a difference for any Muslim to have the support of an organization like CAIR. I have several people who we never worked on their case at all but they call me once every two months to let me know that they're still OK, they are still alive, and that they haven't been deported. Knowing that someone else is paying attention and watching out what is happening to them is huge. Especially in areas where you are the only Muslim, the only one dealing with this thing."

Laurie works on issues related to government affairs, the FBI, and Homeland Security. She once told me about the case of a young American Muslim who had been court-martialed. She attended the hearing and said that people pay more attention and act differently when someone is observing the proceedings:

The minute they notice there is an outside organization watching, they've changed. Alhamdulillah [thank God], it ended positively. I have no doubt if we were not involved it would be negative. At the time we were involved his attorney was telling him to plead guilty. We fired the attorney. . . . When you say, "Council on American-Islamic Relations" in DC, they pay more attention, a little bit more. . . . They said, "We didn't think it would go that far."

Victimhood and Citizenship

On July 15, 2003, CAIR held a press conference for the release of its 2003 Civil Rights Report, "Guilt by Association." Journalists from the Associated Press, CNN, C-Span, and many other news outlets were present. There were four speakers. Ibrahim Hooper made the introduction and

Nihad Awad gave a brief speech. He said that old violations of rights were perpetrated by individuals and were due to ignorance and bias, but that new violations are the result of government policies. When the government is the problem, the government has to be the solution. Civil rights are central to our lives, he said, "But this administration let down the community." He added that civil rights cannot be sacrificed for security. The Muslim community must defend its rights by being more politically involved. After Awad's speech, CAIR's research director presented his statistics on the rise in violations of the rights of Muslims across the country. He also mentioned nine successful hate-crime prosecutions. The fourth speaker at the press conference was a Muslim woman, Aysha Nadrat Yunes, who claimed that her civil rights were violated. Federal agents broke into her house, handcuffed her, forced her to remove her headscarf, and took her picture. She said, "I chose to become a citizen of the USA for liberties. I voted for President Bush."

The events of 9/11 generated a polarized response from Muslims in the United States. They either withdrew from a visible Muslim identity or decided to reclaim it through mobilization and participation. Some of those who took the first tack chose to disappear into the larger society by renouncing their Arab, Pakistani, or even Muslim identities. Some chose to dissociate themselves from the community to avoid risks that might be caused by other members. Some have even changed their names to avoid discrimination in employment and other interactions with the rest of the society. In short, a significant segment of the American Muslim community has been culturally and psychologically inhibited.

The alternate trajectory—the one the majority of American Muslims are in the process of taking—is to fight for equality and legitimacy. The search for ways of expressing and facilitating an American Muslim identity has resulted in an increasing emphasis on advocacy work. In this climate, organizations like CAIR attract a great deal of interest and support from the community.

Some members of CAIR's staff are direct victims of post-9/11 civil rights violations. Laurie, for example, told me that she used to be a high school teacher. She decided to work for CAIR after her house in Virginia was raided in 2002 by federal agents (her husband is an Arab Muslim).

When our house was raided . . . it was March 2002. That was the day when I decided that I needed to come and work for CAIR full time. You know, it was shocking that this kind of thing could happen. Even though you read about it here and there, when it actually happens to you, then you get out and talk about the issue, and you start hearing other people's stories, and they are devastating, I mean really. To see what people were going through. And you know, then I decided I would. I called Ibrahim back in April, and you know, I said, "If you have any opening, I am interested." And we talked and I ended up in the civil rights department.

Victims of civil rights violations tend to become active citizens with an enhanced appreciation for the values surrounding civil and human rights. In a sense, as victims Muslims become sensitized to civil rights work. Of course, this does not happen automatically. If immigrants who lack cultural means of expressing themselves and of dealing with events are victimized, their victimization may not translate into activism and participation. Furthermore, the link between victimhood and active citizenship holds true only for those who are fully protected by the law.

CAIR and the American Muslim Public Sphere

There are two historical moments in the formation of a national Muslim public sphere in the United States. They are the founding of the Muslim Student Association in 1963 (which marks the diasporic moment) and the launch of the CAIR-NET e-mail list in 1996 (the postdiasporic moment). For a religious minority dispersed across the country, collective spaces of interaction and spheres of representation are crucial for the development of codes and standards that define the group. This is particularly important in the case of American Muslims, who are divided along many lines. Hundreds of thousands of Muslims receive e-mails from CAIR on a daily basis. In each dispatch, one typically sees news about Muslims across the country and about CAIR's activities and "Action Alerts" calling on Muslim citizens to react to a particular incident. The reaction requested can be positive or negative and often takes the form of asking subscribers to write to public officials commending or criticizing them for some recent action or statement. Muslims also learn about the media coverage of Muslim communities across the country through these e-mails.

Occasionally you'll hear Muslims say, "You're on the CAIR list, right?"—much as a certain group of liberal, educated Americans is apt to say, "Did you hear the other day on NPR . . .?" Through this e-mail list Muslim Americans learn about goings-on in Muslim communities across the country. In an interesting way, CAIR's e-mail list has become an internal clock, an agenda-setting device. It is not that Muslims are told what to do, except in Action Alerts, but that they are exposed to stories about Muslims in other parts of the country that they probably would not hear about otherwise. These are not always stories about hate crimes. They can be about a lawsuit won by a Muslim employee or an award won by a Muslim high school student. In Ramadan the list fills up with stories from what feels like every small-town newspaper in the country, all titled "Local Muslims Share Fast-Breaking Meal with Non-Muslim Neighbors." In short, CAIR-NET has created a virtual American Muslim public sphere within which the triumphs, fears, and hopes of the community circulate. It also appears to be a popular source of material for Friday sermons. The list, moreover, has contributed to CAIR's image in the minds of American Muslims by giving it relevance and continuity. CAIR's pan-Muslim advocacy work also places it above the Shia-Sunni divide. As such it has become an important avenue for articulating a *common* Muslim identity in the United States. One can observe this characteristic of CAIR in the successful outreach of its Michigan chapter. The executive director of the Michigan chapter, Dawud Walid, has been devoting a great deal of work to overcoming sectarian differences, especially when it comes to issues of civil rights and communal solidarity.

Crises and Citizenship Capital

If, at the individual level, being victimized leads to greater participation in the struggle for civil rights and internalization of the values associated with it, being victimized generates a different kind of benefit at the collective level: citizenship capital. Crises open space for displays of Muslim identity, allow Muslim leaders access to network television, and force government to recognize Muslims as a particular American community. It is almost surprising now to remember that President George W. Bush has indeed said positive things about Islam. Immediately after 9/11 he visited the Islamic Center of Washington, DC. After meeting with the Muslim leaders, including CAIR representatives, President Bush said, "The face of terror is not the true faith of Islam. That's not what Islam is all about. Islam is peace" ("A Decade of Growth" 2004).

Every crisis that involved Muslims placed CAIR in the position of interlocutor with both the government and the media. Every crisis has inadvertently made CAIR into a partner for coalition building and public recognition and a source of information on the Muslim community. Let us consider some of these crises and CAIR's response to them.

On April 30, 2005, *Newsweek* published a piece by Michael Isikoff claiming that interrogators at Guantánamo had flushed a Qur'an down the toilet in an effort to demoralize the prisoners. *Newsweek* later retracted the story because its main source, a government employee, changed his story. But subsequent Pentagon investigation turned up several instances of Qur'an "mishandling."

The report triggered anti-American riots at various places in the Muslim world, most notably in Pakistan and Afghanistan in May 2005. On May 11, CAIR issued a statement urging President Bush "to initiate an open probe of the incident, make public its findings and punish those responsible." The following weekend, CAIR sponsored a conference, "Islamophobia and Anti-Americanism." On May 18, CAIR issued another press release, urging members to call their representatives in support of a House resolution authored by Representative John Conyers of Michigan that recognized "that the Qur'an as any other holy book of any religion should be treated with dignity and respect."

In response to this crisis, CAIR launched its "Explore the Qur'an" campaign. Posters and brochures were printed and ads placed in various media outlets, offering copies of the Qur'an to anyone who requested one. In the meantime, CAIR initiated a major fundraising campaign, asking its members to support the production and distribution of the holy books. Thousands of copies of the Qur'an were sent to interested citizens. Later, when the controversy over the Danish cartoons escalated into a full-blown crisis, CAIR launched another campaign: "Explore the Life of Prophet Muhammad." Among the distributed material were Karen Armstrong's influential book on the Prophet (2006) and a DVD of a recent PBS documentary by an American convert, Michael Wolfe, entitled *Muhammad: The Legacy of a Prophet* (2002).

On a similar front, in response to the growing interest in Islam after 9/11, CAIR launched the Library Project ("Bring Islam to Your Library"). The aim was to send a package of books and audiovisual material to every public library in the country. The package included eighteen items, ranging from the PBS documentary *Islam: Empire of Faith* to the book *Idiot's Guide to Understanding Islam*. The project was intended to reach out to more than 16,000 public libraries in the United States. CAIR's Library Project is one of its few purely "proactive" undertakings. CAIR generally responds to events and crises, although the organization has become more inclined to proactive work since 9/11.

CAIR used each of these crises as an opportunity to inform the wider public about various aspects of Islam (e.g., the Qur'an, Prophet Muhammad, Islamic perspectives on torture) and to increase its publicity. At the same time, CAIR called on government institutions to acknowledge and recognize the rights of Muslims. CAIR's varied civil rights work includes frequent media appearances, collection of data on cases of discrimination against Muslim citizens, coalition building, and lobbying.

"We Did Not Reinvent the Wheel"

The Muslim encounter with American civil rights discourse is relatively new but is evolving fast. Muslims began to appreciate the civic contributions of earlier generations of mistreated communities. Nihad Awad told me that when they first started they got a welcoming message from the Anti-Defamation League. "We expressed our willingness to work together on issues of common interest," he said, but noted that not much has developed out of this initial contact. Awad also said, "We used the experiences of other groups and the civil rights movement of the 1960s. Today, Muslims are at the forefront of defense of civil rights. We've built coalitions with different civic groups. We need to fill in the information gap between Muslims and non-Muslims. The system in this country works for all. Muslims are learning how to communicate and work with the system." Awad concluded his words with "we did not reinvent the wheel."

In 2005 CAIR named a scholarship after Rosa Parks. The award is offered to students who are studying in fields that promote civil rights, social justice, and conflict resolution. Muslims increasingly draw on the legacy and experience of African American, Jewish, and other communities. In May 2008, a group of Muslims in Los Angeles joined the Thirty-Ninth Annual Manzanar Pilgrimage in recognition and remembrance of the suffering of Japanese Americans who were put in internment camps during World War II. CAIR–Los Angeles executive director Hussam Ayloush told those gathered at the event: "We know now what it feels like when people look at you with suspicion or treat you like you are a second-class citizen. Our presence here today isn't meant to suggest Arab Americans are facing the threat and the loss of freedom of those Manzanar internees, but we want to stand with our Japanese American citizens wishing to ensure this could never happen again. Like them, we want to remember the past and to learn from it."

Muslims today not only learn from earlier cohorts of the civil rights movement but also help newer cohorts learn from them. Nihad Awad once told me that "people from New Zealand, Germany, Australia are learning from CAIR's experience. We are a model to be emulated around the world." American Muslim organizations like CAIR have started to offer help and mediation to other Muslim minority communities in Europe and elsewhere. And it is not only Muslims who are learning from CAIR. "After 9/11," Awad told me, "Sikhs started to get organized and CAIR helped them. Their organization is called SMART."

Dissemination of "rights" vocabulary and sensitivity is an important task for CAIR. In this pedagogy of civility, there is a call for a civic asceticism. Training Muslims, especially immigrants, about their rights is a call for appropriation and ownership.

"Know Your Rights"

What if the FBI comes to visit you at your home or at your workplace, what can you do, what are your rights? We have seen cases where the FBI has come to Muslim homes. The man's gone to work. They know, they know the schedule of the person they are going to see. They wait for the man to go to work. They come to the home, knowing there will be only the wife. They knock on the door. They say we are the FBI, can we ask some questions. Normally they are smart enough to bring with them a woman officer because they know that a woman would not just let them in. They know the community. So they come with a male officer and a female officer. And then she does not know her rights. So she is scared. She opens the door. So they start asking questions about, "your husband's trip to Pakistan and your son went to Karachi this and that. You don't mind if we take a look at your books, etc." The woman or even the husband doesn't know their rights. If the FBI comes to speak to you, you have the legal right not to say anything to them. One word. Irrespective if they are accusing you of something or they are asking you about someone else. You can respectfully say, "I don't mind speaking with you but I would like to do that in the presence of a lawyer." This should be the response. Even if you have nothing to hide. . . . Most people don't know their rights, so they take advantage.

Muslims in the United States have lately become students of civil rights. This thought crossed my mind as I listened to a lecture at the Ann Arbor mosque on August 24, 2007. The program was titled "Know Your Rights"; the speaker was Dawud Walid, the local representative of CAIR. He had a lot of issues to cover that night: the crackdown on Muslim charities and the rights pertaining to charitable donations; new regulations made by the transportation department with respect to traveling; citizenship delays; employment-related rights; body search procedures for female travelers; and so on. The audience was large and lively. Afterward they peppered the speaker with anxious questions about airport experiences, awkward encounters at their children's schools, and obnoxious comments in the local media. Such lectures are common these days at mosques around the country.

Through these presentations Muslims, most of them immigrants, learn about the Civil Rights Act of 1964, the experience of Japanese Americans who were put in internment camps after the attack on Pearl Harbor, the laws pertaining to religious expression in public schools, and the cultural codes of how to act if you are pulled over by the police. CAIR is one of the institutions playing a key role in this *learning* process. In this process African American Muslims often share their knowledge with the immigrants.

That evening at the end of the lecture, those in attendance were given a tiny laminated pamphlet called *American Muslim Civic Pocket Guide: Your Rights and Responsibilities as an American Muslim.* In minuscule type, the accordion-folded page covers a surprising amount of citizenship know-how: sections include "Writing a Letter to the Editor," "Communicating with Congress," "Your Legal Rights as an Employee," "Your Legal Rights as a Student," "Reacting to Anti-Muslim Hate Crimes." Through this pedagogical work, organizations like CAIR and activists like Walid engage in awakening citizenship in Muslim immigrants. Some of these immigrants come from societies where they never voted or where the only state or police they knew were to be feared. When in America, they are reluctant to participate in the political process or may panic in encounters with law enforcement agents. Raising the spirit of citizenship within the alien body of the immigrant is a matter of cultivation. It is not that an existing citizenship is awakened. Rather, it is that the immigrant awakens to a new self as citizen.

We should remember that this project of teaching the Muslim community its civil rights is only half of what CAIR does. The other half is to sensitize corporate/legal structures (in both the public and the private sector) to the existence of Islam and to Muslims as members of those structures.

CAIR offers a variety of publications addressing the needs of Muslims and the public at large. Those publications include practical handbooks such as the *American Muslim Civic Pocket Guide, The U.S. Congress Handbook, An Employer's Guide to Islamic Religious Practices, Law Enforcement Official's Guide to the Muslim Community, A Correctional Institution's Guide to Islamic Religious Practices, An Educator's Guide to Islamic Religious Practices, A Health Care Provider's Guide to Islamic Religious Practices, Muslim Community Safety Kit, Ramadan Publicity Guide, Hajj/Eid Publicity Guide,* and *Voter Registration Guide.*

The "Islam in America" Ad Campaign

CAIR's role with respect to government and the private sector complements its position in the Muslim community. It aims to teach each side the necessity of the other in the language that each understands. In 2003 CAIR launched an expensive ad campaign called "Islam in America."

4.1 CAIR's "Islam in America" ad campaign. The text of the ad on the right reads:

> My name is Dr. Aisha Simon. I attended the Medical College of Virginia, completed my residency at Georgetown University and I'll be attending Harvard University to earn a master's degree in public health. I'm a family physician, a wife and a mother. I'm also involved in international relief work, traveling to places like Bosnia and Africa, and coordinating medical volunteers to serve in Guatemala. I was previously a regional coordinator for an anti-tobacco education campaign for elementary school children and I've served as an advocate for domestic violence survivors.
>
> I'm an American Muslim woman and I believe in the importance of charity and service to my community.
>
> The values I learned from my family and my religion while growing up in America have led me to a life of service. Islam calls upon us to strive with one another in hastening to good deeds, and to care for the less fortunate as we care for ourselves. The Prophet Muhammad taught us that when we serve our brother and sister, we are serving God.

Published in the *New York Times*, these ads depicted American Muslims as normal, regular citizens with mainstream American values (see fig. 4.1). Although CAIR could not keep up the campaign for long due to financial constraints, the ads were later made available for local use by Muslim communities. The common message of the ads is the normality of being both Muslim and American. One of the ads is entitled "I'm an American and I'm a Muslim." It provides a good example of how the profile of a Muslim professional woman can be presented as the perfect embodiment of the compatibility between American and Muslim identities. (Other ads in the series featured an image of a Muslim Girl Scout Troop from Santa Clara, California, and a profile of a Muslim American family of Puerto Rican descent.)

According to CAIR the campaign was "designed to foster greater understanding of Islam and to counter a rising tide of anti-Muslim rhetoric." One of the ads starts with a question: "We are all Americans . . . but, which one of us is a Muslim?" The ad features pictures of three people from different ethnic and racial backgrounds—a white man, an African American schoolgirl, and an East Asian man (fig. 4.1). Their warm smiles are accompanied by a text explaining the ethnic composition of Muslims in the United States (and of course the answer is that they are all Muslim).

Digression: An Anecdote from the Field

It is my last night in Washington, DC. My flight back to Michigan is the next day. A box of field material including books, documents, and other heavy stuff needs to be shipped back, but I am not able to take them with me due to limitations on the number of bags I can check in. One alternative is to have it sent through the publications department at the office. So I drive all the way from Fairfax to downtown DC, where my office—and research site—is located. It is very quiet. It is two blocks to Capitol Hill, after all, and you see hardly anybody there at night. I unload the box from the car and make sure that the address sticker is well stuck. I have already asked Joseph in the publications department to ship it as soon as he can. My days in DC are over. The next day I fly back to Michigan. The material I collected while in Washington arrives a week later. The news from the field, however, just keeps coming. Several weeks later, I am startled to read on CAIR-NET (in a story reprinted from the *Charlotte Observer* titled "Ballenger Grouses about Muslims"):

U.S. Rep. Cass Ballenger blames the breakup of his 50-year marriage partly on the stress of living near a leading American Muslim advocacy group that he and his wife worried was so close to the U.S. Capitol that "they could blow the place up." . . . Ballenger, a Republican from Hickory, called the Council on American-Islamic Relations—whose headquarters are across the street from his Capitol Hill home—a "fund-raising arm" for terrorist groups and said he reported CAIR to the FBI and CIA.

The nine-term Republican made those comments during an interview discussing his legal separation from his wife, Donna. He told the reporter that the couple's proximity to CAIR after September 11 "bugged the hell" out of his wife.

"Diagonally across from my house, up goes a sign—CAIR . . . the fund-raising arm for Hezbollah," said Ballenger, 76, referring to a Lebanese militia group the United States has labeled a terrorist organization. "I reported them to the FBI and CIA." Ballenger said in the post 9-11 environment in Washington, his wife, a homemaker, was anxious about all the activity at CAIR, including people unloading boxes and women "wearing hoods," or headscarves, going in and out of the office building on New Jersey Avenue. "That's 2½ blocks from the Capitol," he added, "and they could blow it up."

I was amused by Mr. Ballenger's comments but CAIR handled it differently. Reading Ibrahim Hooper's press release made me feel a bit less guilty: "Unloading boxes is no crime." In response to Ballenger's statements, CAIR filed a defamation lawsuit against the North Carolina congressman and called on national Republican leaders to repudiate his bigoted statements.

I would like to conclude this chapter with two important points: (1) the overall role of CAIR-like actors in the process of appropriation of Muslims as citizens and (2) an overall thesis about inclusion in liberal democracies.

A Pedagogy of Civility: Opening Routes and Deepening Roots

The institution of citizenship is maintained through the practices and right-claims of members of a given society. But what if rights and their bearers are separated—or, even worse, are unaware of each other?

A major implication of the story of CAIR is that Muslim interaction with law and legal structures has taken on a new density. Despite the fact that the cause of that interaction is, for the most part, negative, the mere fact of being close and dealing with the law has had a transformative impact on both Muslims (by pushing them toward the discovery and exercise of their own rights) and legal and administrative institutions (by pushing them toward recognition and accommodation of Muslim needs and sensibilities).

Drawing on the rational-legal discourse of inclusion, CAIR brings both violators of rights and their Muslim victims into equality before the law. Opening them up to the action of law (and public opinion) has the consequence of correcting both parties' discordances and making them both civil (i.e., exposed) and civic (city-bounded). With lawsuits against non-Muslim legal persons, CAIR seeks to sensitize and correct those who have ignored or injured Muslims. It rectifies their sense of limits and teaches them a "lesson" in the existence of Muslims as bearers of rights. By encouraging the reporting of instances of discrimination, CAIR draws in injured Muslim bodies. With these paired acts—eliciting the testimony of victims and calling to account the violators of their rights—it fosters equality and solidarity. The social fabric is strengthened against future violations. CAIR constantly mediates between private and public, individual and communal, and it is the intensity of this flow that generates equality before law—a more pleasant formulation of the leveling effect of citizenship.

Hence, CAIR plays two very important roles. On the one hand, it unifies the Muslim community around discourses of victimhood and solidarity. It hails them into the form of citizenship and asks them to inhabit the formally designated shape of the American citizen. CAIR makes Muslims the bearers of rights that are theoretically theirs but have not been made their *own*. CAIR, as it were, searches for Muslim bodies that have been "injured" in the dark by those who saw them as aliens and then makes their private pain a public issue. The story enters the public domain, as well as the minor domain of the Muslim community, which in turn makes the injury of the victim its own. Like all other advocacy groups, CAIR in effect distributes pain and collects solidarity. To harvest solidarity, the scattered Muslim individuals need to be connected and wired. That is the task of CAIR-NET, a listserv that operates like an ethnic nerve, sensitizing cells to each other and knitting them into solid tissue. The result is a pan-ethnic, nonsectarian, civic Muslim identity. Domestically CAIR demands and facilitates a space where all Muslims stand for one and each Muslim stands for all. Here we see the cultivation of Muslim community out of a plurality of Muslim persons and their sufferings. Through representation and advocacy a Muslim community is born. It is not that it was fully present before and CAIR merely represented it. Rather, the act of advocacy or representation by CAIR is partly what brings the community into being.

On the other hand, CAIR sensitizes the government, the law, and corporate culture to the existence and rights of Muslims. The 9/11 attacks gave CAIR the necessary publicity, raw material, and community support to accomplish this mediating role. CAIR spreads the knowledge and sensitivities of Muslims into the interior of American legal, political, and bureaucratic bodies. Knowledge of and sensitivity to the existence of Muslims as a community open up a space for Islam to trickle into the interior of American society, making it something familiar and sensible. In other words, standing between two foreign (alienated) bodies, CAIR spreads America into the interior of Islam and Islam into the interior of America, a work of exposure that shapes their dispositions. Muslims learn about and participate in the maintenance of the law, and America learns about Muslims and respects their rights. Organizations like CAIR extend the nerves of each into the body of the other. They (often painfully) open Muslim veins to the circulation of American civic blood—and American veins to the circulation of awareness of Muslim members. To generate such an attunement, knowledge needs to penetrate into the opaque interiors of the two parties. Making them receptive to this circulation of knowledge requires the opening of new lines of transmission—a process captured by the word *asabiyya*.

The law as endower of rights demands a bearer. The challenge is to reach the status of bearer. Once that is achieved, the rights deliver themselves. Once the alien being becomes a bearer of rights, he puts on the clothing of equality. To the extent that law is formal and universal, there is indeed only one citizen, only one civic body. That is why the discourse of civil rights (or human rights) inevitably resorts to the logic of "all for one, one for all." This requires media such as CAIR to stand between "one" and "all," constantly transmitting signals of pain and joy.

Recent in-depth studies of post-9/11 Muslim experience (Bakalian and Bozorgmehr 2009; Baker and Shryock 2009; Cainkar 2009)—even when they start with painful accounts of discrimination, violation, and exclusion—acknowledge that 9/11 had some positive consequences in terms of integration. The story of CAIR in a sense illustrates the nature of this outcome. While most works recognize this fact, not many have fully conceptualized it. One exception is Shryock's perceptive notion of "disciplinary inclusion." By way of building on their conclusions, I would like to offer here a further interpretation of the phenomenon and introduce the notion of *negative incorporation*.

As I have argued elsewhere, being targeted means being recognized, and being recognized opens the path to incorporation. In liberal democratic societies, when a crisis like 9/11 happens, it forces the rest of the society to acknowledge the existence of Muslims (whether as a threat or as an ingredient of diversity). The fear and vigilance of the broader public bring the minority group to center stage. Recognition, whether positive or negative, is the crucial raw material for cultivation of citizenship. Only those who exist can become members of society. One has to be first caught up in the "category" to be protected by the "imperative" that comes with it. That is why the full citizenship envisaged by liberal political culture is "active" citizenship—a citizenship of "presence." Silence and invisibility are luxuries that can be afforded only by members of the majority culture. Their existence is collectively registered and institutionalized. But for minority groups, silence and invisibility amount to nonexistence, even political death. Therefore, any kind of noise that forces mainstream institutions (whether of government or of public opinion) to register the existence of a particular group aids in its incorporation (Bilici 2010, 137). This is the rule of law: it holds and protects even its own violators, but lets down those who stand in a relation of indifference to it.

FIVE

Seeking Kinship through Abraham: Muslim Interfaith Activism

I found myself in the most ecumenical environment I had ever experienced when I walked into Christ Church in Cranbrook, a big church located in a northern suburb of Detroit. The event was the World Sabbath of Religious Reconciliation, also known as the Sixth Annual Interfaith Holy Day of Peace among the Religions of the World. The evening was a mix of music, dance, and ritual. After seven "calls to prayer" by Muslim, Jewish, Buddhist, Sikh, Christian, Native American, and Hindu representatives, a rabbi, two pastors, and an imam were scheduled to give brief speeches. Though on the program, Imam Hassan Qazwini of the Islamic Center of America in Dearborn was not back from hajj and therefore was represented by his spokesman, Eide Alawan. The talks were very general—all about love, peace, and tolerance. Eide Alawan, however, took the opportunity to invoke the tragedy of 9/11 and the difficulties Muslims faced. He spoke about his work on the interfaith coalition and then read a prayer written by Imam Qazwini about not blaming the innocent for the tragedy, coming together, taking hatred from our hearts and ignorance from our minds, and making our country a safe haven and the earth an oasis of peace. He ended with "May God bless America," repeated three times.

I noticed that Eide Alawan was the only one at the World Sabbath of Religious Reconciliation to specifically mention

America. But he was not the only Muslim at the event. Two other Muslims were given Peace Awards for their contributions to interfaith dialogue: Imam Abdullah El-Amin of the Muslim Center of Detroit, for his work in the production of the Children of Abraham Project (more on which below), and Najah Bazzy, a nurse who specializes in transcultural health care and is known for her social service and interfaith work. The evening ended with the participants signing a Call to Peace and the entire congregation joining together in prayer.

Ecumenical events like the World Sabbath are now quite common in the Detroit metropolitan area and across the country. There has been an explosion of such events since 9/11, and American Muslims are increasingly becoming visible on the ecumenical scene. They participate in interfaith dialogue as new partners, a process that started before 9/11 but took on a different quality after it. Contemporary Muslim vocabulary draws heavily on the shared origin of the three monotheistic religions and can be safely summarized as Abrahamic discourse. Interfaith dialogue constitutes a significant part of the work of Muslim citizenship in the post-9/11 era. In this chapter, I explore the background against which such activities are carried out, the actors involved in this work, and the discourses they develop. I also ask why Muslims resort to Abrahamic discourse/language rather than to that of liberal pluralism.

To explore the nature and meaning of interfaith activism for American Muslims, I talked to leading Muslim practitioners of interfaith work in the Detroit metropolitan area. In the following pages, I first describe the kind of misconceptions that exclude Muslims and deny Islam a place in the American religious landscape. Next, I discuss in detail how Muslim activists reconstruct Islam as an American religion through interfaith dialogue. Taking a close look at the profiles of interfaith workers, this section provides a detailed picture of Muslim involvement in Detroit's local interfaith scene. The final section is a rethinking of interfaith work as a citizenship practice.

Islam as the Religion of the Enemy

For many Muslim Americans the greatest damage caused by 9/11 is that it seriously undermined the legitimacy of their religion. They often note that 9/11 was an attack on both their country and their religion. Seen as the religion of the terrorists, Islam and its associated culture became a liability in public life. Even nonpolitical, mundane concepts of the faith became subject to contestation and controversy. By way of illustration, let me describe three instances where the legitimacy of Islam as a faith has become an issue.

Allah: An American God?

One aspect of the 9/11 backlash has been an amplification of the belief that Muslims worship a god different from the God worshiped by Jews and Christians. In 2003 Lieutenant General William Boykin, a deputy undersecretary of defense, made headlines by suggesting that Allah is "not a real God." He told church audiences that he is in "the army of God" and claimed that Muslims worship an "idol" (reported by CNN on October 17, 2003). Similar remarks have been frequently made by some evangelical Christian leaders. Pat Robertson has on various occasions claimed that today's world conflicts concern "whether Hubal, the moon god of Mecca known as Allah, is supreme, or whether the Judeo-Christian Jehovah, God of the Bible, is supreme."[1] Boykin's and Robertson's statements, in particular the moon god libel, belong to a genre of stereotypes that date back to medieval times. They depict Muhammad as a Christian schismatic and idolater. After his statements became public, Boykin faced pressure from civil rights groups and the media. On August 26, 2004, a *New York Times* editorial called for him to be fired. Donald Rumsfeld, secretary of defense at the time, rejected all such calls.

Lieutenant General Boykin's perception of Islam is clearly not shared by the majority of Americans. Nevertheless, it reflects a growing tendency to see Islam negatively. According to a Pew Forum on Religion and Public Life survey (2003), the number of Americans who believe their own religion to have a lot in common with Islam is declining. In 2003, 22 percent believed so, compared with 27 percent in 2002, and 31 percent shortly after 9/11. The same survey also revealed that in 2003 44 percent of Americans believed that Islam encourages violence.

Even though the idea that Muslims worship an idol is clearly wrong, Muslims suffer the consequences of such statements. In January 2007 the old mosque complex of the Islamic Center of America in Dearborn was vandalized. The perpetrators spray-painted hateful graffiti on the front of the mosque: "You Idol Worship[ers], Go Home 911 Murderers" (fig. 5.1). The Islamic Center of America is one of the oldest mosques still active in the Detroit area. Ironically, members of this mosque are among the earliest Muslim immigrants, some of them third-generation Americans, and it is an institution that champions dialogue with other faith groups. (A more detailed description of the mosque and its community will be presented later in this chapter.)

5.1 Hate graffiti painted on the front of the old Islamic Center of America in Dearborn, Michigan.

Boykin's remarks, nevertheless, caused both journalists and Muslim community leaders to discuss whether the word "God" should take the place of "Allah." Journalist John Kearney, for example, wrote in an op-ed in the *New York Times* (2004) that "when journalists write about Muslims, or translate from Arabic, Urdu, Farsi or other languages, they should translate 'Allah' as 'God.'" He noted that those who think otherwise "might be surprised that Christian Arabs use 'Allah' for God, as do Arabic-speaking Jews. In Aramaic, the language of Jesus, God is 'Allaha,' just a syllable away from Allah." Kearney concluded his piece with a suggestion for the media: "Of course, there are distinctions to be made between religions, which the press shouldn't shy away from. But there is no need to augment these differences artificially, especially at the cost of an accurate understanding of the origins of the Abrahamic faiths."

Umar Faruq Abdallah, a convert Muslim intellectual and director of the Chicago-based Nawawi Foundation, wrote an essay that tackled the same question. He observed that not only do some non-Muslims insist that Allah is not God but also some Muslims insist on the exclusive use of "Allah":[2]

The fact that Allah and the Biblical God are identical is evident from Biblical etymology. From the standpoint of Islamic theology and salvation history, it is simply unacceptable to deem the Biblical God and that of the Qur'an to be anything but the same, despite the fact that, in recent years, many English-speaking Muslims have developed an ill-advised convention of avoiding the word "God" under the mistaken assumption that only the Arabic word "Allah" carries a linguistic guarantee of theological authenticity. (2004, 1–2)

After a detailed discussion of biblical and Islamic sources on different names of God and the need for Muslims to use the same word as Christians and Jews, Abdallah concludes his paper with the following remarks:

Use of "God" emphasizes the extensive middle ground we share with other Abrahamic and universal traditions and provides a simple and cogent means by which Muslims may act upon the Qur'anic injunction to stress the similarities between us. Failure to use "God" conceals our common belief in the God of Abraham and the continuity of the Abrahamic tradition, which are fundamentals of our faith. We must overcome our misgivings about "God" both because of the word's intrinsic, historical merit and because it empowers us to communicate with our Jewish and Christian, and other English-speaking neighbors in a meaningful way. (2004, 8)

"My American Jihad"

The second controversy involves a commencement speech. Zayed Yasin, then twenty-two years old, was one of the three students who made commencement speeches at Harvard University on June 6, 2002. When the title of his speech, "American Jihad," appeared on the list of speakers in the *Harvard Crimson*, a group of students started a protest against him. They asked for an explicit condemnation of violent jihad. A petition signed by his fellow students asked the university administration to withdraw his speech. He received hate e-mails and a death threat. In the meantime, experts and community leaders discussed the meaning of "jihad." The controversy soon spilled over into the national papers and wire services. Under tremendous pressure from his critics and parts of the university administration, Yasin agreed to change the title of his speech from "American Jihad" to "Of Faith and Citizenship" with the subtitle "My American Jihad." He also agreed to make references to the September 11 terrorist attacks. He told a reporter, "I am confronted with the assumption that because of my name I came from some other country, that I'm a foreign student, that I'm not American."[3]

When I talked to him over the phone on August 22, 2003, he described the attempts to depict him as un-American as a "dishonest abuse of patriotism." When he eventually made his speech, he started with a discussion of his personal experience as a Muslim and as an American:

I am one of you, but I am also one of "them." What do I mean? When I am told that this is a world at war, a war between the great civilizations and religions of the earth, I don't know whether to laugh or cry. "What about me?" I ask. As a practicing Muslim and a registered voter in the Commonwealth of Massachusetts, am I, through the combination of my faith and my citizenship, an inherent contradiction? I think not. Both the Qur'an and the Constitution teach ideals of peace, justice and compassion, ideals that command my love, and my belief. Each of these texts, one the heart of my religion the other that of my country, demand a constant struggle to do what is right. (Yasin 2002)

After affirming the compatibility between American identity and Muslim identity—or, as he put it, between his faith and his citizenship—Yasin discussed the meaning of "jihad" in an attempt to draw attention to what he sees as jihad's primary meaning.

I choose the word "struggle" very deliberately, for its connotations of turmoil and tribulation, both internal and external. The word for struggle in Arabic, in the language of my faith, is jihad. It is a word that has been corrupted and misinterpreted, both by those who do and do not claim to be Muslims, and we saw last fall, to our great national and personal loss, the results of this corruption. Jihad, in its truest and purest form, the form to which all Muslims aspire, is the determination to do right, to do justice even against your own interests. It is an individual struggle for personal moral behavior. Especially today, it is a struggle that exists on many levels: self-purification and awareness, public service and social justice. . . . So where is our jihad, where is our struggle as we move on from Harvard's sheltering walls?

By pointing out the alternative meanings of the concept of jihad, Yasin not only makes the concept familiar to non-Muslims but also translates it into universal terms. Jihad as determination to do right, to do justice, and as an individual struggle for personal, moral behavior is something that any American citizen would support. "My opponents tried to separate me from America. I wanted to give the opposite message: the harmony of values," he said to me over the phone. He also concluded his speech by linking jihad and the American Dream:

The true American Dream is a universal dream, and it is more than a set of materialistic aspirations. It is the power and opportunity to shape one's own life: to house and feed a family, with security and dignity, and to practice your faith in peace. This is our American Struggle, our American Jihad. As a Muslim, and as an American, I am commanded to stand up for the protection of life and liberty, to serve the poor and the weak, to celebrate the diversity of humankind. There is no contradiction. Not for me, and not for anyone, of any combination of faith, culture and nationality, who believes in a community of the human spirit.

Authenticating the Qur'an as an American Scripture

A similar controversy broke out in late 2006 when Representative Keith Ellison of Minnesota, the first Muslim elected to Congress, stated his intention to take the oath of office on the Qur'an instead of the Bible. In fact, the Qur'an was to be used only for a photo-op reenactment of the swearing-in ceremony. The official ceremony, where all newly elected members take the oath, is done collectively and without any books, but individual members are allowed to use their holy books later in reenactments. A conservative columnist, Dennis Prager (2006), attacked Ellison in an article: "Ellison has announced that he will not take his oath of office on the Bible, but on the bible of Islam, the Koran. He should not be allowed to do so—not because of any American hostility to the Koran, but because the act undermines American civilization." A congressman from Virginia, Representative Virgil Goode, also called Ellison's plan to use the Qur'an "a threat to the values and beliefs traditional to the United States of America" and added that "if American citizens don't wake up and adopt the Virgil Goode position on immigration there will likely be many more Muslims elected to office and demanding the use of the Koran" (reported by CNN on January 4, 2007). Such statements drew criticism from organizations such as the Council on American Islamic Relations (CAIR) and the Anti-Defamation League.

One of the first things Ellison did on the House floor was to shake Goode's hand and ask him out for a cup of coffee. He told CNN that "by reaching out to Congressman Goode I'm not trying to be accepted, I'm trying to build bridges. . . . In this world there are too many misunderstandings. I want to put a human face on things" (January 4, 2007).

Eventually, Keith Ellison took the official oath along with the other incoming members of the House. In the ceremonial photo-op he used a copy of the Qur'an that was once owned by Thomas Jefferson. Jefferson's copy of the Qur'an is a two-volume English translation that Ellison borrowed from the rare books division of the Library of Congress. The *Washington Post* noted that the holy book Ellison used had "an unassailably all-American provenance."[4] By using Jefferson's Qur'an, which has Jefferson's handwritten initials and notes in the margins, Ellison authenticated the Qur'an as a legitimate American scripture.

The above discussion of the controversies surrounding the words "Allah" and jihad and the Qur'an's status as a holy book illustrate the multiple ways in which the legitimacy of Islam as a faith is contested in post-9/11 America. A common Muslim response to the exclusion faced in such situations is to assert that the contested Islamic elements are legitimate. They do so by reformulating them as American. Muslims increasingly prefer the use of "God" over "Allah"; they redefine the stigmatized word "jihad" in relation to the ethos of the American Dream; and they frequently assert the compatibility of the Qur'an and the Constitution.

To make itself part of the landscape of American religion, Islam must prove its loyalty to the nation, a challenge faced by other faith groups in the past (Casanova 1994, 167). In the following section, I switch from examples of national controversies, which I believe are symptomatic of Muslim exclusion in the post-9/11 atmosphere, back to the efforts of local Muslim communities, whose representatives attempt to undo the exclusion through participation in the dialogue of faiths. What do Muslims do to make Islam an American religion?

Detroit-Area Muslims as Interfaith Partners

There are more than fifty mosques or Muslim community spaces in the Detroit metropolitan area.[5] The ethnic identity of Arab Detroit has been extensively studied (Abraham and Shryock 2000). Not surprisingly, the city's emergent Muslim identity has gained greater attention after 9/11. I visited most of these mosques, some of them multiple times, some of them only once.[6] Most of these mosque communities engage in some sort of interfaith dialogue, since it has become hard to avoid such encounters. Even when Muslims may not be interested in participating in such activities, they have to respond to the demands coming from non-Muslim groups and individuals who seek to reach out to Muslims as a gesture of solidarity. This structural push toward such participation, however, in itself does not tell us much about how Muslims themselves feel about their involvement in the interfaith world. While the demand for and intensity of interfaith activities have risen dramatically, participation is still the work of a few individuals. I have talked to these people and also observed them on multiple occasions as partners in interfaith events. Some of the most active Muslims in the ecumenical scene in the Detroit area are Eide Alawan (Islamic Center of America), Najah Bazzy (Islamic Center of America), Victor Begg (Muslim Unity Center), Imam Abdullah

El-Amin (Muslim Center of Detroit), Dawud Walid (CAIR–Michigan), and Imam Achmat Salie (Muslim Unity Center).

While these six individuals do not exhaust the list of all Muslim interfaith activists, they are the most visible ones. They have also institutionalized their involvement in interfaith work to a certain degree. Their mosques provide the infrastructure for them to work as a network. For the sake of contextualization, I shall briefly describe these mosques, which deserve to be highlighted because their engagement in interfaith activities often goes beyond brief neighborhood encounters.

Islamic Center of America: This mosque was mentioned earlier as a victim of vandalism and hate graffiti. The Islamic Center is a Shia mosque serving both third-generation, well-established Lebanese and first-generation Iraqi immigrants. It is one of the three oldest mosques still active in the area. Unlike most of the mosques in Detroit, the Islamic Center was built as a mosque and opened its doors in 1963. (Its history, however, goes back even further, since it was an offshoot of the Dix Mosque, which was established in 1937.) In 2005 the Islamic Center of America moved to its new complex. Now one of the largest mosques in North America, the new building is located on Ford Road and includes a large auditorium, a social hall, and offices and can accommodate thousands of believers. While the congregation includes many new immigrants from Iraq and other places, the founding generation of Lebanese still control the board. The Islamic Center also attracts some African Americans and white converts. The imam of the mosque, Sayyid Hassan Qazwini, also active in interfaith dialogue, gives his sermons in both Arabic and English. Most of the immigrant members of the congregation prefer Arabic, while some older and American-born members prefer English. Eide Alawan, who is part of the center's outreach committee, comes from a Lebanese-French family and does not speak Arabic. While he is a very visible face on the interfaith scene, his profile seems to be an exception rather than typical for his congregation. Now in his late sixties, Alawan is not satisfied with the level of Muslim participation in interfaith work: "Most of the time I try to get my community to participate in the same things that I'm doing so they see that I'm participating within the community as well as connecting to the outside community. But it's very difficult to get our Muslim community involved."

Another active member of the Islamic Center is Najah Bazzy, a nurse who specializes in transcultural health care. In her late forties, Bazzy is a third-generation Arab American and is a senior adviser to the Islamic Center's youth organization, the Young Muslim Association. A local celebrity, she makes many media appearances and frequently lectures about Islam to non-Muslim audiences. She wears *hijab* and does culturally sensitive nursing. She says it took some time and several crises—such as the Iranian Revolution and 9/11—for people like her to rethink their ethnic and religious identity. During a lecture on a college campus on March 22, 2005, she told her audience that "when I decided to wear *hijab*, my family was opposed. My mother was against it. They wanted me to assimilate. But I did it." She also points to a shift in her tripartite identity from "Arab-American-Muslim" to "Muslim-American-Arab." She thinks that religion is an easier way of relating to American society than ethnicity, given the commonalities Islam has with the values of this society. Her involvement in interfaith activism bears the mark of her professional work. She wants to put interfaith dialogue and diversity to work in the social services and institutional settings such as hospitals.

Muslim Center of Detroit: Established in 1985, the Muslim Center is an inner-city African American mosque that is part of Imam Warith Deen Mohammed's community. After the transition from Elijah Muhammad's Nation of Islam to orthodox Islam, the community's self-identification has changed several times: it is currently called the Muslim American Society. Not far from the Muslim Center is Masjid Wali Muhammad, the main mosque that follows W. D. Mohammed's teachings more closely. While sharing a lot of history with Masjid Wali Muhammad, the Muslim Center is a more active and diverse community. The Muslim Center is located on Davison Avenue in Detroit in a building that used to be a bank and that has recently been expanded. The chairman of the Muslim Center, Imam Abdullah El-Amin, is an active leader on various fronts. In addition to his work at the Muslim Center, El-Amin is one of the publishers of the *Muslim Observer*, a weekly Muslim newspaper based in Detroit but with a national readership. El-Amin also runs a funeral home.

Imam Abdullah El-Amin converted to Islam in the mid-1970s. He is now in his fifties. "I became Muslim about a year after Imam W. D. Mohammed came. I wasn't part of the Nation of Islam back with Elijah Muhammad and that group. I didn't take part in that, actually." Unlike mosques that exclusively serve African Americans, the Muslim Center has a large immigrant African membership, mostly from West Africa. It is also not unusual to see immigrant and European American Muslims during the Friday prayers. In many ways, the Muslim Center represents the middle point between indigenous African American mosques and immigrant ones. El-Amin says that "this mosque is universal. As a matter of fact, we were thinking about changing our name to the Universal Muslim Center." The Muslim Center has various social programs that also attract non-Muslims in the neighborhood. "The block association meets here. We have a group of Narcotics Anonymous that meets here. . . . We have a soup kitchen where we feed the neighborhood around here every Saturday, and there's also a free clinic, a medical clinic that we have here."

Another prominent African American interfaith activist is Dawud Walid. He is currently the executive director of the Michigan chapter of CAIR. The youngest on my list of prominent interfaith activists, Walid has the rare combination of interest in civil rights and social justice issues and a cleric's knowledge of Islam. He used to be an assistant imam at Masjid Wali Muhammad. Walid thus can easily claim both elements of authenticity. In his speeches he comfortably recites the Qur'an and other religious sources in Arabic, while at the same time quoting leaders of the American civil rights movement. I have heard him speak on many occasions. He has increasingly become interested in Muslim intrafaith dialogue. The main theme of his campus lecture to members of the Muslim Student Association at the University of Michigan on February 2, 2006, was the notion of *ummah* (community). Walid's speech emphasized the need to bridge the gaps between the African American and immigrant Muslim communities, as well as between the Sunni and Shia communities. He referred to a well-known occurrence at the time of Prophet Muhammad, when the Prophet paired the indigenous people of Medina with newly arrived immigrants from Mecca: the partners were to look out for one another's spiritual and material well-being, with the locals helping the newcomers to adjust to their new environment. Walid went on to make the analogy that today's Muslims in the suburbs (immigrants) and Muslims in the inner city (African Americans) should pair up and engage in closer dialogue. He concluded by underlining the post-9/11 reality that "we should realize that we are all in the same boat. We either sink together or swim together."

Muslim Unity Center: The Unity Center was founded by Victor Begg in 1993 in Bloomfield Hills, an affluent suburb in the north of Detroit. Begg is originally from India and has been living in Detroit for decades. A successful businessman who used to attend services at the predominantly Indo-Pakistani Islamic Association of Greater Detroit, he became dissatisfied and decided to start a mosque that was nonethnic and nonsectarian. Together with other Muslims, he decided to buy a school building and expand it into an Islamic center. When they purchased the building from the Pontiac School District, they faced opposition from the neighbors. After much furor and media attention, they managed to convince the neighbors "that they were not terrorists." Among those who supported their case at the court hearing were Christian and Jewish clergy. Speaking at the Interfaith Symposium at Wayne State University on April 15, 2006, Begg recalled this experience in speaking about how far they have come as an interfaith community: "Back in 1993 we wanted to have a mosque in Bloomfield Hills. We bought the school property. As you know, the neighbors thought 'terrorists are moving in' . . . and we did a pretty good job working with the city and school district but forgot the neighbors. So we had problems. . . . Back then many neighbors thought that we are some kind of Satan worshipers."

Victor Begg's dream of having an ecumenical mosque that would reach out not only to different Muslims but also to non-Muslims is today a reality. The Unity Center serves more than two hundred and fifty families. Its inclusivity is reflected in the sermons, which always strike me as unusually ecumenical. The congregation is mostly affluent and professional. Ethnically diverse and open to all schools of thought, the Unity Center has also become a hub of interfaith work. The signs of this conscious engagement with faith groups in the larger society are everywhere to be seen. The official description of the center says it all: "Established in 1993 as a center open to the ethnically diverse Muslim community in the area, the Unity Center is a place where families and individuals from all backgrounds can feel comfortable praying, learning about Islam, and socializing. The center is also a place where non-Muslims are welcome and can come and learn about Muslims and Islam."[7]

The Unity Center often celebrates its dual achievements of internal (pan-Muslim) ecumenism and external (interfaith) ecumenism. As visitors approach the entrance of the center, the first thing they see is a rock inscribed with a verse from the Qur'an. This verse is an explicit statement of Islam as an Abrahamic religion (fig. 5.2): "Say, 'We have believed in God and in what was revealed to us and what was revealed to Abraham, Ishmael, Isaac, Jacob and the Descendants, and in what was given to Moses and Jesus and to the prophets from their Lord. We make no distinction between any of them, and we are Muslims submitting to Him'" (Qur'an 3:84).

The religious leaders of the Unity Center—both Imam Musa, the principal imam, and Imam Achmat Salie, who is affiliated with the center— are always strikingly broad-minded. The availability of resources informs the roles that spiritual leaders of places like the Unity Center take. After Imam Salie left another mosque and joined the Unity Center, I observed something of a bifurcation in the orientation of the two imams. While Imam Salie, who is from South Africa and has both native mastery of English and greater familiarity with Christianity, focuses on outreach activities and often seems to speak in the jargon of New Age Chris-

Say, "We have believed in God and in what was revealed to us and what was revealed to Abraham, Ishmael, Isaac, Jacob and the Descendants, and in what was given to Moses and Jesus and to the prophets from their Lord. We make no distinction between any of them, and we are Muslims submitting to Him."

Quran - Al-Imran 84.

5.2 The text that greets visitors to the Muslim Unity Center, Bloomfield Hills, Michigan.

tianity (self-actualization through spirituality), Imam Musa, who is an immigrant from Egypt and has a more authoritative knowledge of Islam but lacks comfort with the English language, has become more reserved. He is increasingly interested in the preservation of Muslim identity.

Who Becomes an Interfaith Worker?

Although they are a small group, Muslim interfaith workers are very diverse. Of the six individuals, two are African American (Imam El-Amin and Dawud Walid), one is a woman (Najah Bazzy), and only two are professional clerics (El-Amin and Achmat Salie). They are overwhelmingly American born. Najah Bazzy, for example, always tells audiences with pride that she is a third-generation American. Victor Begg is an immigrant (he migrated in the 1960s), but he is the one with the largest financial resources and strongest social standing. They come from both upper-middle-class suburban communities and lower-class inner-city communities. What they all have in common is American *cultural literacy*, which includes the English language and mass communication skills. They collectively respond to a demand for the presentation of Islam to members of other faith groups. Andrew Shryock (2004a) provides a fascinating discussion of the strategies of community representation in his discussion of the "double remoteness" of Arab Detroit.

In an article published on an Islamic website, an American Muslim community organizer, Altaf Hussain, asks whether Muslims are up to the challenge of interfaith dialogue. After discussing the various levels at which Muslims find themselves engaged in interfaith dialogue, he points to several challenges:

One of the major challenges we face as Muslims in such discussions is agreeing on a common language for communication. In America, our imams and representatives must be well versed in the English language—in terms of possessing both a solid grasp of the English vocabulary and an understanding of American idioms. Too often, we minimize this element, and push for people to represent Islam in such discussions who are non-native English speakers. Although they possess the Islamic knowledge, they often have a difficult time trying to explain fundamental Islamic beliefs in plain language using phrases and expressions common to Americans. What happens is the speakers end up confusing listeners, and leaving them with more questions afterwards than before the dialogue. (2001)

Adding that the ideal representative in an interfaith dialogue has to understand the religious perceptions of non-Muslims, Hussain points out the need for the Muslim community to develop standards for the uncharted area of interfaith encounters. For example, should Muslim clergy shake hands with the opposite sex? Which rituals of other faiths should they participate in within the framework of interfaith dialogue? When Jennifer Granholm, the governor of the state of Michigan, visited the old Islamic Center of America after her election in 2002, she stepped into one such gray area. Before the visit she was advised by her staff (and representatives of the Islamic Center) that she should not shake hands with men at the mosque. During the visit she was confused to find herself surrounded by the men of the congregation, all wanting to shake her hand.

Most Muslim communities have yet to fully articulate a language of interaction with the outside world. An important form of that interaction, interfaith dialogue, remains the domain of just a few individuals. As the public faces of their communities, these individuals mediate the images and information presented to the wider public. As Shryock points out, their task is similar to our task as ethnographers—except that theirs is performative, while we rely on writing. When Eide Alawan says that he feels more comfortable with Christians and Jews than Muslims, he partly reveals what he is usually expected to keep hidden: that some aspects of his community (especially the immigrant elements) embarrass him. Their "cultural intimacy" (Shryock 2004b; Herzfeld 1997) instills in these individuals—whose tastes and life trajectories often diverge significantly from the communities they represent—both a fierce protectiveness and a certain degree of embarrassment. Meanwhile, people lacking cultural literacy (e.g., those who speak with an accent) are usually not put on display, even when they are more representative of the majority of a given community. Unlike the average members of their congregations, the public mediators are more Americanized and have the time and resources to devote to outreach activities.

Interfaith Dialogue: Before and after 9/11

Muslim involvement in interfaith dialogue certainly has a longer history, but all activists agree that 9/11 had a tremendous impact on their level of engagement. Some Muslim commentators describe the new era as "a silent revolution" (Takim 2004, 343). I asked Eide Alawan in 2005 about the impact of 9/11. He said,

Prior to September 11, it was more of a low-key situation. The occasional visitation, the occasional discussion. But after September 11, because of the curiosity about Islam, really people wanted to know: is Islam a thing we should be fearful of? What is this religion? Although we've been here over one hundred years in this country, one hundred and fifty years. September 11 accelerated our interfaith work and it was a positive situation. Most Muslims will feel that it was a negative situation. It wasn't negative as far as I was concerned. There was a positive situation. The occurrence that happened was a bad thing, there's no question about it, but what developed from that was a positive situation. The Jewish community, the Christian community came in and said, "Look, we've got to do something. We've got to understand that these are people of faith just like us. We all come from the same stem." And this is how it all started to evolve. Victor Begg the very next day got together Jewish and Christian and Muslim friends and said, "We've got to do something. We can't just continue to hold hands; we have to dialogue. Instead of Christians just with Muslims and Christians just with Jews, we have to all three get together." And this has been occurring the last four or five years. It's nonstop.

Alawan's views on the impact of 9/11 are echoed by the experience of other interfaith workers. Najah Bazzy, for example, observes that "before 9/11, I was pushing doors open for dialogue. After 9/11 doors were opening and I was walking in and that was the difference. 9/11 as well as tragedy, the end result was that it gave many of us an opportunity to dialogue, to teach, to collaborate. Muslims were no longer forgotten at the table anymore." She also comments on the increase in her appearances in the media and at public venues, where she assumes the role of a mediator who represents a legible image of Islam. She believes her gender makes her particularly fit for this role:

And in terms of post-9/11 I will tell you that I have spoken at more Christian pulpits than I have at Muslim mosques. So what that's allowed, it's allowed a visual, a female—which breaks the stereotypes—it allows a visual of a woman in *hijab*. It allows an auditory of a woman who is born and raised in this country, who really does not have an accent, so breaks that stereotype. And it allows the beauty of the faith to really flow. And to really talk about peace and justice and reconciliation and conflict resolution and all of those things that America is afraid to really believe about us. So it's trust, and humans need ambassadorship. And that's what I've really found post-9/11.

Activists like Najah Bazzy think the importance of the work they do cannot be exaggerated as far as the recognition and integration of Muslims are concerned. Yet they usually have difficulty mobilizing more Muslims for the task. Muslim scholars such as Suleyman Nyang argue that interfaith work can very well be treated as an index of Muslim acculturation in America (J. Smith 2004, 167).

Most of the interfaith activities Muslims participate in are initiated by other faith groups, primarily Christians and Jews, and therefore, Muslims participate as "guests" while other faiths remain "hosts." But Muslims are increasingly recognizing the need to be involved in the dialogue on an equal basis as hosts, and one can observe that American Muslims have been undergoing a transition where their roles as participants of interfaith dialogue change from being guests to being cohosts. Writing in the early 1980s, Muslim American thinker Ismail Raji al-Faruqi recognized this problem in his *Trialogue of the Abrahamic Faiths* when he wrote "no dialogue can succeed where one party is 'host' and the others are 'invited guests.' Every party must be host and feel itself so" (1982, ii). Muslims who engage in sustained interfaith activism are not diasporic immigrant communities but rather postdiasporic individuals and communities.

Detroit-area Muslims have been involved in organizations such as the National Conference for Community and Justice in Michigan. Whereas before 9/11 Muslims were merely newly joined members in most of the interfaith organizations, since 9/11 they have begun to take part in the *creation* of new initiatives and organizations. Interfaith Partners is one such organization. A subgroup under the umbrella of the National Conference for Community and Justice, it was formed on September 12, 2001. Interfaith Partners has been organizing annual interfaith symposiums since 9/11. I attended one on May 4, 2006, at Wayne State University, where a number of workshops were held. Among the interfaith work done under the umbrella of Interfaith Partners is something called the Children of Abraham Project.

"We Are All Children of Abraham"

Interfaith encounters elevate one element of Muslim identity to a central position: the idea of Abraham as father of the three monotheistic religions. Muslims like Victor Begg often emphasize that the Judeo-Christian tradition is more accurately the Judeo-Christian-Islamic tradition because all three are children of Abraham. They share a common belief in God, prophets, revelation, a divinely mandated community, and moral responsibility. While Jews and Christians trace their lineage to Abraham through Isaac, Muslims do so through Ishmael.

Many Muslim activists, as well as non-Muslim partners in interfaith encounters, imagine themselves as part of a family whose members have been alienated and dispersed over time and geography. Interfaith dialogue is a sort of coming together, a family reunion. The Children of Abraham Project grew out of this thinking. The project organizes retreats where Jewish, Christian, and Muslim students are brought together as a family to share their experiences. The project has also produced a play that bears the same title. Imam Abdullah El-Amin, who first introduced the idea, said, "This started with an idea I shared over lunch with my friend Brenda Rosenberg. We were talking about all the problems in the world that involve Muslims and Jews and Christians. And I said, 'If we would only remember that we all share the same father, Abraham, we might find ways to bring our family back together again.'"

After this conversation, Rosenberg went home and had a dream. In her dream she saw Isaac and Ishmael on a stage. She decided to put this idea into the form of a play. The play, *Children of Abraham*, would be a family reunification, the coming together of Ishmael and Isaac. The concept is to bring together teenagers from all three faiths, ask them to share their life stories, weave those stories into a play, then plan a short workshop to be held after the play to give audiences a chance to join in the discussion. I saw the play at Henry Ford Center for Performing Arts on February 28, 2005. Imam Abdullah El-Amin and Brenda Rosenberg received several community service awards, and their play was featured in a CBS network special on religious reconciliation.

I was told by Muslims who participated in the production process that both Jewish and Muslim creators of the play had to make sacrifices to reach a common language acceptable to both parties. Describing how the process was emotionally difficult for them, Alawan said: "So this has been a family relationship. We don't always get along. We argue, we disagree, we don't talk to each other a couple of days at a time because we're just upset, but this is no different than a family, we're treating it as a family." Alawan added that "these experiences basically go to show that families do differ, have disagreements, but they still can get along." In such situations often the best-equipped Muslims are convert Muslims who can navigate back and forth between the scriptures of the three faiths. The same dynamic that elevates the figure of Abraham to a central position also privileges convert Muslims in interfaith encounters. African American Muslims who were either themselves once Christian or have Christian relatives also find it easier to relate to Christians in interfaith dialogue (J. Smith 2004, 181). Imam Abdullah El-Amin once told me,

You see, by me having a Christian background, I can identify with American Christianity, you know. I have all that—Jesus, Mary, I know the Bible, the biblical scriptures that correlate with the Qur'an. Someone that's born in a totally Islamic environment wouldn't have that. Same with people here where it's all Christians, born in a primarily Christian environment. They know nothing about Qur'an and so they can't relate to it. But by me having this Christian background, I'm able to bridge the gap, speak the language, so to speak.

Muslim interfaith dialogue conspicuously clusters around a number of elements that Islam shares with Judaism and Christianity. Nor is this feature of American Islam limited to situations of interfaith dialogue. For instance, in 2006, when the California office of CAIR put out radio ads in recognition of the Muslim holiday of Eid ul Adha, they produced three spots highlighting three different themes: Abraham, Malcolm X, and "Mercy and Compassion." The radio ad focusing on Abraham had the following script:

This week, Muslims in America and around the world conclude the annual pilgrimage to Mecca, "the Hajj," with Islam's most important holiday, called Eid-ul-Adha or "Festival of the Sacrifice." The central figure in this religious celebration is Prophet Abraham. Muslims believe that Abraham built the first House of Worship to God, known as Kaaba. The Hajj commemorates Abraham's prayers at the Kaaba. The Qur'an, Islam's holy book, states: "Who can be better in faith than one who submits his whole self to God, does good and follows the way of Abraham, the true in faith?"

This fact offers an excellent opportunity for all of Abraham's children—Muslims, Christians and Jews—to recognize and cherish their shared religious heritage and to promote a harmonious future as people of faith.[8]

From Judeo-Christian to Abrahamic?

Muslims' emphasis on Abraham allows them to establish a relationship of kinship with the dominant religious identity in the United States. Whether such a genealogical language is the best way to overcome the exclusion remains to be seen. Muslims are partly responding to an Islamophobic trend that was already started by evangelical Christian movements and political God-talk but that intensified with 9/11. When individuals like Pat Robertson pit Allah and the biblical God against each other, Muslims are forced to prove that Allah is indeed the God of Abraham.

Muslims frequently note that Judeo-Christianity is not an adequate framework to express America's religious diversity. Their Abrahamic language can be read as an argument on behalf of the expansion of boundaries to encompass themselves as a newcomer faith. Such potential boundary shifting can be compared to the shift from Christian to Judeo-Christian, which took place relatively recently in American history.

Although the idea of a Judeo-Christian tradition was not new, America continued to be seen up until the 1950s (and perhaps is still seen by some) as a "Christian nation" or a "Protestant country." Widespread cultural and political acceptance of Jews under the rubric of Judeo-Christianity came shortly after anti-Semitism in the United States reached its height at the end of World War II. In response to the Holocaust and Cold War pressures to diminish differences among Western peoples, Jews (together with Catholics) were effectively "Christianized" in the public culture (Mart 2004, 116; Zolberg and Woon 1999, 20). Starting with Will Herberg's classic work *Protestant-Catholic-Jew* (1983), there has been a rich literature on the way immigrants are incorporated into the fold of American religion (Levitt 2007; Casanova 2007; Wuthnow 2005; Warner and Wittner 1998).

The analogy between the shift from Christianity to Judeo-Christianity and the shift from Judeo-Christianity to "Abrahamic faiths" has serious limitations, however, because Islamophobia, far from being a justification for acceptance of the Abrahamic framework, continues to haunt American Muslims. As Zolberg and Woon point out, in many Western nations "the boundary remains quite fixed in relation to Islam and, in some cases, became more clearly defined in the course of confrontations" (1999, 20).

Abrahamic versus Liberal Pluralism

American Muslims seem to be torn between two paths. At a time of resurgent nativism, they gravitate toward Abrahamic discourse, the language of kinship. This option gives them what can be called a "monotheistic advantage" over other newcomer religions. But they are also aware of the exclusive effects a closure at the level of Abrahamic faiths may have on other faith groups. Therefore, they also resort to the alternative path, liberal pluralism, which calls for de-emphasis of Judeo-Christianity. They recognize that this alternative is under attack by the very forces that operate to exclude Muslims.

I could see ambivalence with respect to the two paths in the responses of Muslim interfaith activists. Speaking to an interfaith audience, Victor Begg once said, "I always thought America should be Abrahamic, not Judeo-Christian. Or maybe Judeo-Christian-Islamic. But then we have other faiths that we need to think about." Similarly, Najah Bazzy thinks that the Judeo-Christian framework needs to be transcended:

The country seems to be understanding that this is a country of immigration and, you know, what is an American? Is it a Euro-American? And we're starting to understand that no, we are a tapestry. So I think because of our foundation we have to appreciate that. Where we run into the struggle, though, is because this country is also, also calls itself a Judeo-Christian country, that it's kind of stamped its level of acceptance. So the country itself, because of the identity it's given itself—although it's ethnically diverse, it's really not religiously diverse in its identity, in how it identifies itself.

While recognizing the need for transcending the current boundaries imposed by the Judeo-Christian identification, Bazzy remains satisfied neither with the Abrahamic model nor with its secular alternative. The ambivalence is most visible in her response to a question regarding whether the Abrahamic model will solve the problem of inclusion:

No one can deny that Isaac and Ishmael were both sons of Abraham. And Judaism came way after Abraham. So do I think this is a country that's going to be of Abrahamic faith? Yes, I do. Is that going to be a problem for Hindus and for Baha'i and for other people? I think so. And that I don't like, to be honest with you. I don't like that while you're creating space for some people, it's at the expense of other people, 'cause then to me what we've done is create the same thing that we had to fight against. What I fear, though, because of that, I fear that America is going to become much like France. I'm afraid of that. That it's going to lose its identity to really truly just a secular tapestry of all kinds of people in order to avoid conflict. And that scares me, because to me when you eliminate faith from the tapestry of your country, then what you're producing is a lack of moral authority, and then when you do that, you run into the kinds of problems we're running into already with crime and with lack of family values. And that's where 9/11 I think has been a wake-up call for America. Because it's brought people back to the question of God and spirituality and family values.[9]

External Ecumenism: American Civil Religion

As Muslims engage in interfaith dialogue, they step into the public square, where there is a specific form into which every particular religion is hailed by American culture. That form is American civil religion. Scholars of American culture have argued that American identity is no longer anchored in Christianity but rather in a more generic deistic civil religion (Bellah et al. 1985, 225). This religion is characterized by belief in God, respect for difference, and the belief that religion is a matter of individual choice. "If the primary contribution of religion to society is through the character and conduct of citizens, any religion, large or small, familiar or strange, can be of equal value to any other" (Bellah et al. 1985, 225). This conception of religion has produced a specific vocabulary, a domain of its own, independent of any particular religion. Entry into that domain and language is a sign of citizenship. For the most part, the interfaith conversation takes place through that language. When Muslims who participate in this language through their involvement in interfaith work go back to their own communities, they might be seen as speaking another language or they might find themselves alienated from their (immigrant) communities. Eide Alawan, for example, told me on multiple occasions that

I prefer to be with Christians and Jews more than Muslims. And what I mean by that is that there's dialogue. You know one of the difficult things I find in my lifetime—I've said this many years now—is that we can seem to dialogue with Jews and Christians and Buddhists and talk and feel as though we are brothers, but we have a problem between Shia and Sunni, and this is a barrier that I know that the American generation will overcome. . . . All I'm saying is, appreciate what both sides bring to the table. If you don't agree with someone, that's fine, it's OK to disagree. It's OK to disagree in a manner that's saying . . . it's just like between me and a Jew or a Christian.

On another occasion he said, "I've been in interfaith work for years. My interest has always been to promote Islam. Promote it in the sense of not conversion but promote it in the sense of understanding in the non-Muslim community. In fact, I feel much more comfortable being in a Christian or Jewish community than I do in a Muslim community." I would like to think of Eide Alawan as a believer in American civil religion. He is an American-born Shia, but most of his congregation at the Islamic Center of America are immigrants, some of them very recent. What he finds in interfaith environments is his Muslim identity deployed within American civil religion. He prefers being in environments where non-Islamic forms of American religion are present rather than in environments where non-American forms of Islam are present. In the former he is at home; in the latter he is a stranger.

I had similar thoughts when I attended an event in downtown Detroit. On the National Day of Prayer, Imam Abdullah El-Amin and Imam Achmat Salie lined up on a stage with representatives of other faiths (fig. 5.3). Prayers from the representatives of each faith were read. El-Amin made *adhan*, the Muslim call to prayer, in Arabic and then provided an English translation. When his turn came, Imam Salie read a long prayer in English. It started with "All praise is due to the God of all—of those who affirm and deny Him—the God of Adam and Eve—Noah, Abraham and Sarah, Moses, Jesus, and Muhammad, the Virgin Mary, Fatima and Aisha." He used "God," "Allah," and "Lord" interchangeably. The speech was colored by ecumenical language as well as by the self-help language of generic spirituality: "Beloved Lord, help us in our transition from bigotry to balance, . . . from corporate greed to selflessness." Imam Salie ended his prayer, just as he started it, by mentioning Abraham: "Lastly, we pray for the realization that compassion (not dogma) is the primary religious expression. Ameen—O Allah, Lord of Abraham, hear our prayers."

One way Muslim interfaith activists, consciously or not, make Islam an American religion is to adopt the ecumenical mode of speech. Islam is detached from its earlier forms (what most American-born Muslims disapprovingly call the "cultural Islam" of immigrants). The process of pouring Islam into its new mold, its American form, gives rise to two kinds of ecumenism. Externally, it neutralizes the differences between Islam and the Judeo-Christian tradition. Internally, it undermines internal divisions along ethnic, racial, and sectarian lines. All the interfaith activists, Dawud Walid in particular, take extra effort to cultivate an Islam that is beyond *madhhabs* (juridical schools of thought). Of the impact of interfaith work on *intra*faith Muslim life, Alawan says, "I think one of the

5.3 Interfaith National Day of Prayer in downtown Detroit. The Muslims on the stage are Imam Abdullah El-Amin (first on the right) and Imam Achmat Salie (at the podium).

things that interfaith is allowing me to see is that we should be doing this within the Muslim community."

Internal Ecumenism: From Interfaith to Intrafaith

Interfaith work encourages two types of ecumenism: internal ecumenism and external ecumenism. As Muslim practitioners like Eide Alawan and Dawud Walid frequently note, interfaith encounter leads to self-critique and demands internal solidarity. Internal ecumenism thus refers both to dialogue between Sunnis and Shias (what second- and third-generation college students call SuShi) and dialogue across ethnoracial divides (between various ethnic immigrant Muslims and indigenous African American communities). Interfaith activism allows Muslims to reformulate Islam as an American religion. The emphasis on commonalities with other religions is an important characteristic of American Islam because through interfaith work, American Islam gains autonomy from the rest of the Muslim world, where the need for interfaith work is either not felt or remains very small. Critique of overseas Muslim cultures is an important ingredient of American Islam. As Abdullah El-Amin remarked,

I think that's the only way that we can go here and now. We have the Shia and the Sunni in this area. We have a Sunni-Shia symposium, knocking down the walls between us. Because he's a Muslim just like I'm a Muslim, it's the same thing. We both believe in Allah, we both believe in the same Prophet, we both believe in the same Holy Qur'an, and so we have to look more to this than we do . . . many people mistake culture for religion. Take, for instance, in Saudi Arabia women don't drive cars. Well, did Allah say women can't drive cars, or did Saudi Arabian men say that women can't drive cars?

E Pluribus Unum: American Religious Diversity and Muslim Citizenship

It took some time for Muslims to develop interfaith consciousness. Muslim involvement in interfaith conversation evolved from a proselytizing, defensive mode of engagement (*dawah*) to a more self-confident style of interaction. The transition from *dawah* to dialogue and from conversion to conversation (Takim 2004, 343) is a milestone of Muslim cultural settlement in American society. Starting in the late 1990s, American Muslim institutions developed a more confident attitude toward their non-Muslim environment. A new appreciation of the universalistic "values" of the American Constitution and public culture in general began to claim the privileged place previously occupied by the concept of *dawah* (Schumann 2007, 12).

Interfaith dialogue is practiced by Muslims who want to transcend ethnicity. Although there are still many Muslims who consider interfaith work a *dawah* opportunity (or engage in interfaith work under the rubric of *dawah* to legitimate it), there is no doubt that Muslim participation has widened and deepened. For some participants interfaith dialogue can be a survival strategy. In a time of exclusion and anti-Muslim discrimination, interfaith dialogue is both a means of making allies and a form of self-expression.

Interfaith work can also become a status device for the well-established. It is a marker of citizenship and social prominence. Take the example of Victor Begg, a wealthy businessman and founder of the Unity Center. In one sense, he is like the Aristotelian citizens whose activities are a "mixture of character building and public activity among well-bred gentlemen with plenty of free time" (Shklar 1991, 30).

Interfaith activism is linked to citizenship in several ways, not only for the well-established but for all Muslims involved in it. First, it is certainly an exercise of citizenship in the sense that it involves civic engagement and participation. Second, by granting status and positive public standing, it becomes an affirmation of equality. Third, it is a way of naturalizing Islam. By participating, Muslims remove a stigma that weighs heavily on them. If we are to follow Judith Shklar's analysis, not only issues of agency and empowerment but also those of social standing are central to citizenship: "The struggle for citizenship in America has, therefore, been overwhelmingly a demand for inclusion in the polity, an effort to break down excluding barriers to recognition, rather than an aspiration of civic participation as a deeply involving activity" (1991, 3).

While factors such as race, gender, religious sect, and the immigrant-native divide all play some role in which groups will engage in interfaith activities, the single most important variable appears to be what I call "cultural literacy." Cultural literacy includes a certain degree of fluency in English and—perhaps more important—familiarity with mainstream American culture and its religious landscape. It is the importance of cultural literacy that puts African Americans, women, and second-generation immigrants in the forefront of interfaith work. These individuals usually do not occupy the front line in the hierarchy of religious authority.

The figure of Abraham—who does not occupy a central place in Muslim cultures in their conventional settings—gains prominence in Muslim minority contexts. He is one of the few common threads through which Islam can enter the American (Western) imagination and find a foothold of legitimacy. A response to the exclusion generated by 9/11, Abrahamic discourse acknowledges the fact that (legal) citizenship alone is not enough to protect Muslims from public sentiment. If civil rights work is an appeal to the state, interfaith work is an appeal to the public. In the post-9/11 era, Muslims have gravitated more toward Abrahamic discourse than liberal pluralism. They rely on the tropes of genealogy and kinship to legitimate Islam as an American religion. As such, interfaith work becomes an emotional plea for inclusion in the nation. It draws on familial bonds to undo otherness. One reason Muslim interfaith activists are drawn to Abrahamic discourse, even though they are ambivalent about its merit relative to secular, liberal pluralism, is that they see secular pluralism as merely an extension of citizenship discourse, which in their eyes has proven inadequate for protecting Muslims. Abrahamic discourse, on the other hand, is a discourse that works on the "nation" rather than the "state." It is an attempt to erase differences in the public mind by assimilating Muslims into the category of "fellow Abrahamic believers." Therefore, if the post–World War II discourse of

Judeo-Christianity allowed the "Christianization" or normalization of Jews and Catholics, Abrahamic discourse in the post-9/11 era responds to a comparable Muslim demand for "Christianization" or normalization via inclusion, kinship, and commonality.

Conclusion

As a prominent citizenship practice of Muslims in the post-9/11 era, interfaith dialogue contributes to the inclusion of Islam as a legitimate "kindred" religion. Muslim claims to kinship and their quest for Islam to be recognized as part of an extended Judeo-Christian tradition represent a demand for the shifting of boundaries that presently leave Islam outside the fold of American religion. Interfaith dialogue also takes its Muslim participants into the realm of American civil religion, which as an empty form is open to all religious contents. Through acquisition of its vocabulary and style, Islam becomes a civil religion, a generic American religion with an emphasis on diversity, moral universalism, and toleration. Islam becomes one color among many. In this chapter, I have focused on interfaith dialogue as one type of Muslim response to 9/11 at the local level. Certainly race, socioeconomic background, and the immigrant-indigenous dichotomy shape the opportunity structure for interfaith activism. But in general terms, there seems to be a "confidence threshold" that has to be reached in order for Muslims to become involved in interfaith work in a sustained way. That threshold is reached mainly when both cultural literacy and a certain degree of social and economic comfort are secured. That is why the number of Muslim participants is still disproportionately small in Detroit, given the size of the area's Muslim community and the growing demand for Muslims as interfaith partners

SIX

Funny Jihad: Muslim Comedy Takes Flight

Fun and jihad? Many people are intrigued when they see the words "Muslim" and "comedy" in the same sentence. The very idea of "Muslim comedy" seems funny at least in one of the two senses of the word. When one says something is funny, people sometimes ask for clarification: "funny ha-ha or funny peculiar?" Reactions to the idea of Muslim comedy usually belong to the second category. And this is not so peculiar. In American society, the dominant image of Muslims and Islam is far from funny. You rarely see a smiling Muslim face on television. On the news and in the movies, Muslims look either angry or scared—when they manage not to be terrorists. The typical Muslim image is stern, foreign, and dangerous. Since the events that brought broad recognition to Muslim identity in American society are acts not of humor but of horror, Americans are likely to see a connection between jihad (or Muslims) and tragedy, rather than comedy. But in an interesting turn of events, there has been an upsurge of Muslim ethnic comedy since 9/11. More and more Muslim individuals and groups are appearing onstage with comic routines, and they are at-tracting larger and larger non-Muslim audiences. This para-doxical outcome raises two related questions. How can we interpret the phenomenon of Muslim comedy, and more specifically, what does it tell us about Muslim citizenship in American society? The following discussion of emergent Muslim ethnic comedy responds to these questions while proposing a new theoretical framework for the phenomenon of ethnic comedy.

The Tectonic Shock of 9/11

The impact of 9/11 on the surface of American society is in effect an ethno-quake: it opened a fracture on the surface of the social body.[1] This tectonic shock to the social landscape broke a formerly more or less unified surface (us, the citizenry) into two pieces. The crack separated a large piece, into which the sense of "us" receded, from a very small piece, where "not-us" remained. A nation that had been almost blind and certainly indifferent to the existence of this piece of itself (i.e., Muslims in America) now suddenly *began to see it* because now that piece had been externalized, objectified. Once the crack was produced, ethnic and religious stereotypes about Muslims began to proliferate.[2] In this process of hardening of stereotypes, the status of Muslims rapidly changed from *invisible strangers* to extremely *visible strangers*. I would argue that this status of extremely visible stranger is crucial to the question of why we have an upsurge of comedy right after a huge tragedy.

We have seen an explosion of Muslim comedy since 9/11 because it created the double conditions necessary for the deployment of ethnic comedy: *otherness* and *relevance*. The split between the nation and the Muslim alien not only turned the spotlight on Muslims as an object of scrutiny and source of danger but also turned the nation into an audience—an audience that came to the ethnic theater with a newly calcified stereotype of Muslims in mind, an audience constantly reminded to report any suspicious people and activities to the authorities. This is most evident at airports, where the relationship between Muslim identity and American sovereignty comes into the open. At the airport, Muslim visibility and difference reach new heights. Ethnic, racial, and religious profiling all assumed a new meaning after 9/11. Incidentally, Leon Rappoport, a scholar of ethnic comedy writing on the impact of 9/11, observed:

There are good reasons to argue that 9/11 has had a more fundamental impact on the general meaning of race and ethnicity. Traditional differences between most ethnic groups are fading because terrorist attacks make no such distinctions. All of us are in the same boat, equally and impartially threatened. . . . When any group of people, no matter how diverse, is facing a collective, life-threatening situation they invariably come together and set aside their differences. . . . The one exception has been Muslims and others with a Near Eastern background. (2005, 125)

This in a sense summarizes the reasons for higher circulation of Muslim humor in the aftermath of 9/11. With their newfound (*negative*) recognition, they moved to center stage as objects of suspicion, stereotyping, and wiretapping. Two instances in which Muslim identity and humor were associated with each other provide good illustrations of the post-9/11 milieu.

Looking for Comedy in the Muslim World, a movie released in 2005 and starring comedian Albert Brooks, takes off from the following premise: the American government sends a down-on-his-luck Jewish comedian to the Muslim world to find out "what makes Muslims laugh." Although the comedian visits only India and Pakistan—countries that, despite their huge Muslim populations, remain peripheral to most Americans' imagination of the Muslim world—the implication is obvious: Muslims may seem dour, but deep down they must have some sense of humor waiting to be discovered. Interestingly, the film presents its Pakistani characters as more dangerous, more "authentic," and much funnier than the Indians.

This almost optimistic view of Muslims' relation to comedy was overshadowed by the explosive controversy of the Danish cartoon crisis, which began in late 2005. Muslim reactions to offensive cartoons published in a Danish newspaper were perceived by Western publics as an example of Muslim intolerance for freedom of speech and lack of understanding for humor. Though some American Muslims felt obligated to comment on the film and on the cartoon fiasco, both events revolving around Muslim humor (and its lack) were in a sense external to the community. They both concerned Muslims outside America, and to the extent that American Muslims did wade into the issues, they frequently took them as opportunities to dissociate American Muslims from Muslims abroad. And as the issues became less acute, both the image of Muslims as lacking humor and the Danish cartoon crisis itself became the butt of jokes for Muslim comedians in America.

So, where does the comic come into the picture as this new epoch unfolds? If the tragedy of 9/11 contributed to the creation of certain "forms" (stereotypes about Muslims), comedy became possible when Muslims started to play with those forms. Mary Douglas's (1975) characterization of humor as "play on forms" helps us establish the link between tragic events and the emergence of Muslim comedy. Tragic events (crises) and the neuroses they trigger lead to the hardening of stereotypes (e.g., all Muslims are terrorists) and the objectification of ethnic groups. Some of the Muslims who see those incongruous forms thrown at them in the media and in personal encounters eventually decide to throw them back. The personal tragedy of being ethnic (an outsider, a stranger, different, stereotyped) is now made public through irony and comedy. And as has often been said, prejudice has no greater enemy than irony.

Muslim Ethnic Comedy: Space, Players, Forms

Ethnic comedy is intimately linked to the fortunes of ethnic communities. As my earlier discussion of the context points out, Muslim comedy is in a sense a form of "gallows humor" that "arises in a precarious or dangerous situation" (Koller 1988, 12). For Muslim communities in the United States, ethnic comedy grew out of danger. Islamophobia is what has made Muslim comedy a phenomenon of our times. The discrimination, prejudices, and stereotypes from which other Muslims suffer are a godsend for the Muslim comedian. Muslim comics thus represent the experience of most Muslims, but in an inverted way. They are perhaps the only beneficiaries of the *negative charisma* associated with being Muslim. Muslim comedy is the world of Islamophobia turned upside down.

The career of Muslim standup comedians resembles the story of Benjamin Disraeli, who in a totally different setting exploited the negative charisma that was associated with being Jewish in nineteenth-century Britain. Hannah Arendt (1973, 68–79) devotes part of her discussion of the history of anti-Semitism to Disraeli, who managed to float above its consequences. Far from being a disadvantage, he turned his Jewishness into a source of distinction and a privilege. This "potent wizard," says Arendt, recognized "how much more exciting it would be for himself and for others . . . to accentuate the fact that he was a Jew," for he "discovered the secret of how to preserve luck, that natural miracle of pariahdom." Despite the fact that he came from an entirely assimilated family and (according to Arendt) lacked any religious knowledge, he nonetheless exploited the negative charisma associated with being Jewish. "He knew instinctively that everything depended upon . . . an accentuation of his lucky 'strangeness.'" In Disraeli's own words, "what is a crime among the multitude is only a vice among the few." The crime of being Jewish "could be transformed at any moment into an attractive 'vice'" (Arendt 1973, 69). In a similar vein, Muslim comedians are exploiting a kind of "lucky strangeness." What makes other Muslims suffer becomes a career opportunity for them.

Muslim comedy is an emerging "market." Not only is its audience growing, but it is also a new career field for Muslim cultural entrepreneurs, mostly second-generation young people and converts. "The time is right," says Zarqa Nawaz, the Muslim producer of a popular Canadian sitcom; "the marketplace has never been this curious about Muslims." As cultural entrepreneurs, they claim the knowledge of both worlds: ethnic and mainstream. This is best illustrated in their ability to go back and forth between accented and normal speech.[3] As arbiters of a cultural encounter and as field guides to a contact zone, these stand-up comedians are situated in a unique position. They can practice simultaneously the *two ways of seeing* things: ethnic and majority. They can "leap" from one side to the other. This position is often a tragic one, in which a person belongs to both worlds and neither. The comic stands uneasily on the crack that separates the two, yet by standing there the comic becomes a sort of stitch that ties together the two sides of the divide.

Muslim comedy is produced and consumed in different ways. Take three recent products of popular culture. Between 9/11 and the time of the writing of this book, these comic enterprises gained national recognition.

First, a new TV sitcom, *Little Mosque on the Prairie*, started in January 2007. *Little Mosque* revolves around the daily experiences of a small Muslim (mostly immigrant) community living in Mercy, a fictional small town in Saskatchewan. It explores the funny side of adapting to life in post-9/11 North America. In the first episode, the community tries to establish a mosque in the parish hall of a church. A passerby, seeing the group praying, rushes to call a "terrorist hot line" to report Muslims praying "just like on CNN." In another episode the Muslim residents hire a Canadian-born imam from Toronto. He is a lawyer but he quits his father's law firm to take the job as imam. This, his father thinks, is career suicide. The young imam is detained at the airport while speaking to his mother on his cell phone because he is overheard saying, "If dad thinks that's suicide, so be it." Security staff rush in when they hear what he says next: "This is Allah's plan for me." As Neil MacFarquhar, *New York Times* correspondent for American Muslim affairs, observes, "that fictional moment is an all-too-possible occurrence as witnessed when six imams were hauled off a US Airways plane in Minnesota in November after apparently spooking at least one fellow passenger by murmuring prayers that included the word Allah."[4]

Though it began life with decidedly murky prospects, the show soon became the most-watched sitcom on Canada's CBC network.[5] During a visit to Detroit on April 5, 2008, Zarqa Nawaz, the Muslim creator of *Little Mosque*, explained why her show became so popular: "It is appealing because it shows Muslims being normal. It humanizes Muslims." She also added, "I want the broader society to look at us as normal, with the same issues and concerns as anyone else." Nawaz named her production company FUNdamentalist Films. When asked why, she said she wanted to "put the fun back in fundamentalism."[6]

The other two success stories are the phenomenal rise of Allah Made Me Funny: The Official Muslim Comedy Tour (AMMF) and Axis of Evil (AOE), two comedy troupes. In my discussion of Muslim ethnic comedy I will focus on these two groups, which have gained prominence and national recognition in the world of Muslim American popular culture and even made tentative steps toward crossing over into mainstream culture.[7] The AMMF troupe includes Preacher Moss, Azhar Usman, and Mohammed Amer. Perhaps we should start with the official description of the group: "*Allah Made Me Funny: The Official Muslim Comedy Tour* is the world's first and only organized standup comedy tour featuring America's top Muslim comedians. It is a community project centered around the promotion of shared core values. It simultaneously brings American Muslims out of their typical isolation to a mainstream comedy show and introduces mainstream American fans of standup to a uniquely Muslim perspective."[8]

The ethnic and cultural origins of comedians are also important. Preacher Moss, now in his early forties and from the Washington, DC, area, is an African American convert to Islam. He occasionally incorporates into his comedy his experience at his mother's Baptist church. Preacher Moss founded AMMF in 2004 and looked for companions. He was soon joined by Azhar Usman. Axis of Evil is not quite a trio: it consists of Ahmed Ahmed, Maz Jobrani, and Aron Kader, all from the West Coast, and Dean Obeidallah, their East Coast "guest member." While the larger social dynamics that brought both comedy groups to the stage are the same, they represent two different reactions. Therefore, one can see both overlaps and divergences in their primary identifications.

Several things can be said by way of a quick comparison. In terms of orientation, AOE could be called ethnic-ethnic, whereas AMMF is Muslim pan-ethnic. While it is hard to separate the Middle East from Islam in the popular imagination, it is important to note that many Muslims in America are doubly "ethnic": (1) ethnic in the sense of being Arab or Pakistani and living in America and (2) ethnic in the sense of being Muslim in America, regardless of their origin. Self-identifications like "Palestinian" or "Middle Easterner" correspond to the first sense of ethnicity, exemplified here by AOE. This type of ethnicity maintains strong (cultural) ties to an overseas nation of origin. The second sense of ethnicity, which I have called pan-Muslim ethnicity (or just "Muslimness"), characterizes AMMF. It functions similarly to Jewish American ethnicity. It is dissociated from any overseas ethnic origin, or acknowledges only a nominal link, yet still remains ethnic within the American context. In short, AMMF is Muslim first, ethnic second, while AOE is ethnic first, Muslim second.

This distinction can be seen in the naming of the two groups. Azhar Usman explains the rationale behind the naming of Allah Made Me Funny in the beginning of their first DVD: "Well, the word 'Allah'—which is a word that conjures up more negative images in the minds of non-Muslim Americans than any other word concerning Islam—is actually beautiful. And it is nothing more, nothing less than the Arabic word for God. So Allah Made Me Funny is the Muslim answer to God Made Me Funky."

Axis of Evil, on the other hand, draws on President Bush's famous 2002 State of the Union address, when he designated two Middle Eastern countries (Iran and Iraq) together with North Korea as an "Axis of Evil." The members of AOE are of Arab and Iranian descent, and their routine always includes mention that they are still looking for a North Korean comic to join them. Two of the performers were working in Hollywood (most often cast as terrorists) before they turned to stand-up in the aftermath of 9/11.

One thing needs to be clarified at the outset: Muslim comedy did not begin with 9/11. But it did take on a distinctive form and quality after it. In the history of American Muslim ethnicity as well as in the history of American Muslim comedy, 9/11 is a turning point. Preacher Moss of AMMF was a comedian producing primarily but not exclusively African American humor. He was writing for George Lopez (*The George Lopez Show*) and Darrell Hammond (*Saturday Night Live*). He was a mainstream comedian with an African American edge. As an individual comedian he was Muslim, but this was not the primary framework defining his work. Similarly, Dean Obeidallah of AOE repeatedly says that before 9/11 he was a white guy doing generic comedy. After 9/11 he says he lost his white status and became Arab. The neurosis was thus at work not only in the production of an American nation estranged from its Muslim members but also in the production of Obeidallah as an Arab and as an ethnic comedian.[9]

The ethnic backgrounds of the AMMF trio mirror the overall composition of the American Muslim community. The three major groups—South Asians, Arab Americans, and African Americans—are represented by Azhar Usman, Mohammed Amer, and Preacher Moss, respectively.

And the convert experience, an increasingly important part of the Muslim community in the United States, is also represented by Preacher Moss. This last element is absent from Axis of Evil, where the preferred identity is not Muslim but Middle Eastern.

After these general notes on the comedy troupes we can now take a closer look at the profile of each group and their comic routines. But it would be unfair to the standup comedians if I did not make one disclaimer about these jokes. I have noticed that when I write them down they lose a crucial element. Academic writing is just not the best venue for comedy. All I can do by way of giving due credit to the comedians is to say that I have seen audiences (myself included) laugh hard at most of these jokes.

Allah Made Me Funny

I had the opportunity to watch the members of both groups perform in various settings. The members of AMMF, in particular, appear almost every year at the annual convention of the Islamic Society of North America and frequently at local events organized by various branches of the Muslim Student Association. I had seen Azhar Usman perform at the Muslim Student Association's annual Eid dinner in 2005 at the University of Michigan, Ann Arbor. There was an audience of three hundred students, some of them with their families. One of my early conclusions about the nature of Muslim comedy was that it is a second-generation phenomenon. I saw the group most recently in mid-February 2008, when they performed at a fundraising event at Dominican University in the suburbs of Chicago. All the tickets were sold out. There were approximately fifteen hundred people, most of them young, most likely second generation. The audience was predominantly of South Asian Muslim background (Indian and Pakistani), reflecting the ethnic composition of the Chicago-area Muslim community. The audience also included Arab American and African American Muslims, as well as some non-Muslim Americans.

The first stand-up comedian to appear on the stage that evening was Mohammed ("call me Mike") Amer. He is ethnically Palestinian but was born in Kuwait and raised in the United States (Houston, Texas). Amer began his comic career at a young age (twenty) doing Arab ethnic and generic stand-up comedy. His jokes deal with issues of immigration, ethnic food and practices, and the symbolic burden of names like his own. That night, speaking of a recent trip to Europe, Amer said this:

I had such a good time in England. I am Palestinian American; I have been here seventeen years, almost eighteen. I am getting my passport next year. [*Applause*] Alhamdulillah . . . Alhamdulillah. . . . But I am still "homeless," you know, I'm still homeless. You know when it really got to me? In England there was this poster when I went through immigration. At the airport they have them everywhere. It is a poster with a dog. And he has a passport around his neck. A dog! It says, "Get your dog's citizenship today!" I am a human being and I have been waiting for seventeen years and (ruff ruff!) "get your citizenship." . . . And it's not even an English bulldog. It's a German shepherd!

Immigration is not easy, right? Immigration is not an easy process. Try to call immigration. It just does not work out. One time I called immigration for my uncle. It says, "Hello, you have reached INS, naturalization processing. Please hold." And then comes the hold music: "Never gonna get it, never gonna get it."

The comedy show that evening had a guest appearance by a thirteen-year-old comedian named Shaan Khan. Khan is an eighth-grader who is developing a local reputation for his impersonation of Azhar Usman of AMMF. One of the early skits that Usman no longer uses in his routine involves an Indo-Pakistani immigrant uncle (he calls him "Uncle Let-me-'splain-you") who fails to see how his broken English does more harm than good when he decides to act as a spokesperson for the local mosque in an interview on national television. As Khan says, commenting on Usman's character: "I don't care if you can't speak English. I don't mind. But why are you on TV?!!"[10]

Preacher Moss, an African American Muslim comedian whose real name is Bryant Reginald Moss, is in his early forties. He came up with the idea for AMMF and started the group in 2004. That evening Moss started his routine—as he often does—on a didactic note: "We have to battle stereotypes." He continued, "Like, you never see Muslim comedians on TV. Because all the Muslims they can put on TV for notoriety are Saddam Hussein and Osama Bin Laden. Neither of these guys is funny. Think about it. First you got Bin Laden but you can't find him. They can't find him, but he releases a DVD every month and a half. He is like the Muslim Tupac! They can't find him. They should change their name from Al Qaida to Al Hide-a."

Preacher Moss's jokes revolve around his conversion, issues of race (including his own interracial marriage to an Indian woman), and political satire. He frequently jokes about the double jeopardy of being black and Muslim. Back when John Ashcroft was attorney general, Moss said in an interview, "I am worried they're going to put race and religion on driver's licenses. . . . So when I get pulled over, I get two tickets."

179

One of the major themes in Muslim comedy is "immigrant time" in America. Moss wonders how Muslims can speed everywhere and still be late to everything. After poking fun at immigrant Muslims for always being late, he jumps to current events: "People are saying crazy stuff about Muslims. Sometimes people blame everything on Muslims. Some might even blame natural disasters on Muslims. [*Speaks as a reporter*] 'We are now in Orlando and we are waiting for Hurricane AbdulMalik. It was supposed to be here eight hours ago but you know how they are.'"

The last of the comic trio to appear that night was Azhar Usman. A native of the Chicago area, Usman is a lawyer turned comedian. He calls himself the Ayatollah of Comedy. He is a portly man in his early thirties and wears a full black beard and occasionally a *kufi* (skullcap). When on March 17, 2005, ABC's *Nightline* featured Azhar Usman as a Muslim comedian, after a brief introduction to the topic they cautioned their audience:

So far you have not seen the face of the man our story is about. He is an attorney. He was born in Chicago, raised in Skokie, Illinois. Now he is trying to make it as a stand-up comic, and he looks like this [*Pause, and then Azhar's image appears on the screen*]: Azhar Usman! He is a devout Muslim. Question: Does a guy who looks like this have any chance of making it in stand-up? Or when you first saw this did you think, just for a moment, "terrorist," "Taliban"?

The *Nightline* people were not totally wrong. Usman himself jokes that when he walks on the street, people who see him look shocked and whisper to each other: "Osaaama, Saddaaam, Talibaaan, Obama!" He goes on, "I am glad that you guys are laughing. Sometimes I am onstage and people are scared. People are looking at me as if I am responsible for 9/11. Can you believe that: Me, responsible for 9/11. 9/11? No. 7-Eleven? Maybe."

Usman's "Muslim shtick" pokes fun at both the Muslim community and the larger society. The second half of his routine that evening was devoted to jokes about various ethnicities. He would ask, "Any Malaysians in the house? Any Egyptians? Any Pakistanis?" and so on, and then poke fun at a cultural element specific to that group. His own ethnic background (Indian) informs a significant portion of his ethnic jokes. I have observed, however, that he tailors his ethnic jokes to his audience.

What looms largest in Usman's performance is his airport jokes. If Azhar Usman himself is the very model of a post-9/11 Muslim stand-up comedian, his jokes about the airport experience are the epitome of today's emergent Muslim comedy.

My least favorite thing about being a comedian is all the traveling. That's right. The moment I have to walk into the airport, heads turn simultaneously. The security . . . [*As though speaking into a walkie-talkie*] "We got a Mohammad at four o'clock." "Can I see your ID, please?" "We'll need to do an extra security check." Even worse is the moment I have to get onto the plane. That's right. People are shocked. They are in the middle of a conversation. "So where are you from . . .?" And then they suddenly see me. [*Slightly hysterical voice*] "Oh my God! I'm gonna die." [*Desperate whisper into cell phone*] "Honey, I love you. He is s-o-o hairy."

Here Usman takes a break from the drama and complains to his audience:

I don't really understand why these people are so scared of me. I don't get it. Just think about it: if I were the crazy Muslim planning to hijack the plane, this is totally not the disguise I would be in. [*Pirouetting his large, bearded self around the stage*] It doesn't exactly slip me under the radar.

He concludes his flight story with exaggerated relief:

Of course, once the plane safely lands, they are just looking over smiling. Ha ha ha. I am waiting for one real honest passenger to come up to me at the end of the flight. . . . He says, "Excuse me sir, I thought you were gonna kill us. Ha ha. Sorry about that. Ha ha. Remember when you got up to go to the bathroom? I was gonna stab you. Ha ha." That's what it feels like these days, man.

This joke provides a perfect illustration of the Muslim airport experience, where the negative charisma of being Muslim assumes full transparency. At the airport, those who have so far (i.e., in the city, at the ticket counter, etc.) been treated equally suddenly become suspect. Before they enter the airport, they may be outside the definition of the nation, but they are still protected by the law—that is, still inside the state. But when they walk into the airport—where internal and external meet and where external (state) borders are now internalized (Balibar 2004, 1)—they suddenly feel their protected status begin to evaporate. Now they risk falling outside both the nation and the state. Even those Muslims who do not consider themselves particularly profiled or discriminated against in everyday life suddenly begin to feel uneasy. They enter into *communitas* (V. Turner 1969), becoming occupants of an antistructure where they lack any status.[11] The metal detectors turn citizens into naked bodies, at least electronically. Strip search and other security rites of passage through the border show them the hard edge of the nation.

For Muslim citizens, the disjuncture between the nation and the state reaches its peak—at least psychologically—at the airport, because there they find themselves exiting the state at a time when they are already excluded from the nation. At that moment they become aware of the sovereignty beyond law, something experienced in its pure form in prison camps such as Guantánamo Bay. In short, at the airport, Muslims come face to face with the nation without the protections of the state. They fear and tremble.[12] This existential anxiety affects both sides: it brings extra security checks and profiling, on the one hand, and a sense of public and institutional discrimination, stress, and insecurity, on the other.

The fear a Muslim inspires is associated with the unpredictability of his behavior. What if he is a terrorist? What if he hijacks the plane? What if he is only pretending to be normal? All these questions that citizens are asked to consider by the airport authorities transform the Muslim passenger in the eyes of his fellow travelers into a source of unpredictability and danger. When a Muslim like Azhar Usman gets on the plane, faces fall. Danger is imminent. The anxiety reaches new heights when the plane takes off. Up until takeoff, the charisma and unpredictability of the Muslim have been contained in his body, but with takeoff, they contaminate the entire plane. The sense of suspense and anxiety ends when the plane safely lands. The relief from danger is reflected on the passengers' faces. People are laughing and almost thankful to the Muslim passenger for not doing what they feared he might do. Flying while Muslim thus becomes an extremely public event.

Much more could be said in the way of interpretation. Let me emphasize here one other dimension of this type of joke: its remarkable transparency and universality. Muslims and non-Muslims alike can understand and laugh at airport and airplane jokes. They are simultaneously ethnic and national, particular and universal. As such, these jokes represent the comic surface where Muslim and American experiences intersect most "dangerously" and with full intelligibility.

Axis of Evil

The Axis of Evil comedy tour started in November 2005 and gained national recognition with an appearance on the Comedy Central channel on March 10, 2007. The group also put out a DVD in 2007, which features Maz Jobrani, Ahmed Ahmed, Aron Kader, and guest member Dean Obeidallah. They perform on a stage festooned with nuclear warning signs, and each comedian is frisked by a tough-looking female security screener in full Transportation Security Administration (TSA) regalia as he steps onto the stage. Maz Jobrani is an Iranian American and jokes about the Iranian accent and the Iranian diaspora's tendency to call themselves "Persians" to distance themselves from contemporary Iran. In explaining his reason for becoming a comedian, Jobrani talks about how the only available roles for Middle Easterners in Hollywood are as terrorists. He says that after several such stints (including one with Chuck Norris) he decided not to take those parts any longer and began to do stand-up instead.

Ahmed Ahmed is an Egyptian American who also had an acting career in Hollywood. He was similarly dissatisfied with the parts available to Middle Eastern actors. Ahmed's routine typically revolves around the absurdities of the security check at the airport. He says that his name matches one of the FBI's most-wanted terrorists. So each time he goes to the airport he has to go through extra security checks. He says, "It is a bad time to be from the Middle East. I read a statistic on CBS.com. Right after 9/11, hate crimes against Arabs, Middle Eastern people, and Muslims went up over 1,000 percent. Apparently that puts us in the fourth place behind blacks, gays, and Jews. You guys know this? We are still in the fourth place. So what do we have to do to be number one in something?"

Ahmed Ahmed notes that people often do not believe that he is a comedian—especially the airport security staff who ask him what he does for a living. They always say, "So tell us a joke." He replies, "Well, I just graduated from flight school." Once on board, Ahmed looks around the plane. "Do you know who the air marshal is on the plane? The guy reading *People* magazine upside down while keeping an eye on me."

Aron Kader is a Palestinian American whose mother is Mormon. His jokes include impersonations of President Bush and accent jokes about his cousin in Jordan. He pokes fun at anti-American sentiment in the Middle East and uses relatively vulgar language. Unlike Jobrani and Ahmed, Kader looks more white than Middle Eastern. He also talks about how he is often thought to be Jewish because of his first name.

Dean Obeidallah is perhaps the most interesting member of the group. Growing up in northern New Jersey, Obeidallah had an Arab father and an Italian mother. Despite the fact that his father was an immigrant, he never considered himself a minority. Like Kader, he looks white, and his rediscovery of his ethnic identity is a post-9/11 phenomenon. He is another cultural entrepreneur who has used his newly found ethnicity to reinvent his comic career. In his routine, Obeidallah criticizes the backlash against people of Middle Eastern backgrounds. Referring to a recent movie title, he claims that these days the idea of "Middle Easterners on a plane" scares people more than snakes. "People are afraid of us because they don't know who we are. There are only two news stories about us. Bad story: We are terrorists. Good story: We are alleged terrorists. I see other minorities and I am jealous. They get a whole month that celebrates their heritage. Black History Month. Asian Awareness Month. Hispanic Awareness Month. What do we get? We get ORANGE ALERT!"

The No-Joke Zone: Airport as Stage

An interesting outcome of the securitization of society is the ban on jokes at the airport. Making jokes in the security check area at the airport is strictly prohibited and punishable by law.[13] This particular ban makes airports a unique place in the national space. Airports are the internal borders of the nation. As entry and exit points to the nation, airports provide a unique perspective on questions of sovereignty and identity. The heightened enforcement of no-joke zones at the airports after the tragedy of 9/11 is thus indicative of the paradoxical connection between the tragic and the comic.

An equally interesting development is the attempt by Muslim ethnic comedians to turn the stage into a symbolic airport space. They do so not only by drawing much of their material from their experiences at the airport but also by literally entering the stage in a mock ritual (antirite) of passing through the scanner and being frisked by mock TSA staff. AOE's famous performance on Comedy Central is the best example but not the only one. In one of their joint performances, comedian Rabbi Bob Alper and Azhar Usman patted one another down as they took turns at the microphone. (The two comedians have toured together across the country, doing shows on college campuses and at Muslim and Jewish religious centers. I saw them in Detroit at a Wayne State University program cosponsored by the Muslim Student Association and Hillel.)

The turning of airports into no-joke zones and the turning of the Muslim comic zone into a symbolic airport are two expressions of a single undercurrent. They are also symptomatic of the Dionysian continuum of fear and laughter and also the existential continuity between insecurity and relief. What links the no-joke zone to the comic stage is what links the tragedy of 9/11 to the emergence of Muslim comedy.

Themes and Audiences

The jokes that Muslim stand-up comedians make can be classified broadly into two groups: in-group jokes and out-group jokes. In-group jokes require some cultural literacy on the part of the audience. Such jokes are possible only when the out-group (mainstream culture) is used as a background. For example, a joke about Muslims' fear of being caught with one foot in the sink by their employer requires knowledge of Muslim ritual washing before the five daily prayers—but it would not be funny to Muslims living in Muslim societies. This joke is an in-group joke for Muslims who live in a non-Muslim society. The same can be said about one of the jokes by Azeem, another African American Muslim comedian. When he tells his grandmother, "Grandma, I can't eat that pork. I'm Muslim," his grandma says, "No you ain't! You ain't never been to jail." This joke would not be intelligible to most immigrant Muslims, although it is fully intelligible to indigenous Muslims and even many non-Muslim Americans. To make sense of the joke, one has to be familiar with the experience of Black Muslims or the Nation of Islam and their strong connection to prison ministries.

There is a difference between humor in front of an all-Muslim audience and humor in front of a non-Muslim audience. The latter has a narrower window of encounter (terrorism), whereas the former can exploit internal issues and differences (e.g., Azhar Usman's bit about the twenty ways of saying *as salamu alaikum*). The sphere of jokes that has maximum transparency for a general audience deals mostly with airports and terrorism. With such jokes the Muslim comic disappears into the laughter he or she generates in both Muslim and non-Muslim audiences. As one moves away from this sphere, the mutual transparency diminishes. For example, when Azhar Usman performed in one of Chicago's major stand-up venues before a large non-Muslim audience, many of his jokes failed to generate laughter. One can also speak of a certain "attention span" that determines the "shelf life" of a joke. Although with 9/11 Muslim comedians grabbed America's attention, they could not hold that attention for long. The window of opportunity for a Muslim comic is limited to a narrow range of issues, and as soon as he runs out of those jokes, the Muslim comic becomes opaque and falls back to the sphere of irrelevant otherness.

Part of the problem seems to be that Muslim comedy is all based on an appeal to commonality with an audience who is assumed to be "the other." The comics often start with a given difference (the stereotype of Muslims as radically different) and try to show similarity. Instead of saying, "Look, these people think I am this and that, so they are stupid," they usually say, "They did this and that thinking I am such and such, but look, I am really just like you." Because American society is accustomed to viewing him as outlandish, the "extraordinary" Muslim becomes funny when he does something ordinary (e.g., when the backyard explosion turns out to be a barbecue and not a bomb). This approach is certainly part of turning the symbolic order upside down, but it has a very limited scope.

Now that we have briefly surveyed the landscape of Muslim stand-up comedy, let us try to make theoretical sense of this comic phenomenon.

Theorizing Comedy

Most of the works on comedy, including extant sociological ones, tend to simply list various theories of comedy, humor, and laughter (Morreal 1983; Koller 1988; Berger 1997; Rappoport 2005).[14] In such theories, the role of the context within which ethnic comedy takes place is often neglected. Yet this aspect, I believe, opens the way for a distinctively sociological take on ethnic comedy. Sociological explanation and interpretation thus go beyond biological and psychological explanations.

There are several theories of ethnic comedy that in many ways complement rather than compete with one another. Nevertheless, one looks in vain to find a convincing integration of them that is distinctively sociological. One theory is known as superiority theory. I call this the political explanation. This ancient theory has been around since Plato and Aristotle and was most famously formulated by Hobbes as "sudden glory." Laughter is seen as a means of expressing superiority over other people. Such laughter can be aggressive and is certainly self-celebratory. For our purposes here, the main insight of the superiority theory of humor is the idea of *relationality*. Superiority theory acknowledges both power differential and relationality between two parties.

Another and by far more important theory is the incongruity theory. We can comfortably consider this a cultural theory. This theory, which has much greater explanatory power than the first, sees humor as an outcome of inconsistent, unexpected acts and conditions. For example, Pascal, one of the early proponents of this view, argues that "nothing produces laughter more than a surprising disproportion between that which one expects and that which one sees" (Morreal 1983, 16). Similarly, Schopenhauer describes laughter as happening in situations marked by "the sudden perception of incongruity between a concept and things themselves" (Schopenhauer 1966, 91). As Morreal puts it, summarizing Schopenhauer's perspective: "what causes laughter is a mismatch between conceptual understanding and perception" (1983, 18). Here a concept is general and lumps together unique and particular things as if they were identical instantiations of that concept. All concepts do violence to the uniqueness of the things they claim to represent. This is a problem intrinsic to any abstraction (Nietzsche 2006, 117; Simmel 1950, 63)—and it demands refutation or rectification. One way to accomplish this is through (comic) treatment. The discrepancy between our mental structures (theories) and the realities of the practical world (facticity) is bridged in the act of laughter. That is why, according to Kierkegaard (1982, 82), what lies at the root of the comic phenomenon is the discrepancy, the contradiction. Laughter, one may argue, is a product of the sudden recognition of this very gap. In this accidental encounter between *practice* (Bourdieu) or *experience* (Simmel) and *abstract metaphysics*, an everyday version of destruction of metaphysics (what Derrida calls *deconstruction*) takes place. Is not comedy nothing but a comic deconstruction?

The third prominent theory of humor is called the relief theory. A psychological theory, relief theory is best formulated in the approach of Sigmund Freud. Relief theory emphasizes the cathartic release from repression. In *Civilization and Its Discontents*, Freud explores the psychic cost of civilization (i.e., society) for individuals. He identifies the overwhelming power and expansion of *reality principle* over *pleasure principle* as the main cause for the unhappiness of modern man (Freud 1961, 22). In comedy the relationship is reversed. We revert to the pleasure principle, albeit temporarily. In his discussion of jokes, Freud also links jokes to the unconscious and draws attention to the economy of psychic energy in the repression of emotions (the id) by the superego. In *The Interpretation of Dreams* and *Jokes and Their Relation to the Unconscious*, Freud argues that the "manifest content of dreams and jokes yields pleasure through their disguised expression of unconscious wishes, resulting in partial lifting of repression and an economic expenditure of psychic energy" (Bergmann 1999, 3).

The closest to sociological perspectives on comedy are those provided by cultural anthropologists. Mary Douglas in particular draws attention to the importance of context in making sense of comic experience. The funniness of jokes depends on the context in which they are deployed (Douglas 1975). Both Mary Douglas and Victor Turner (1969), two prominent anthropologists working within the Durkheimian tradition, therefore rightly point to the margins and to liminality as the location of humor. Comedy is an anti-rite presented in a ritual, an antistructure imagined as an alternative structure. Let me clarify these two points. Comedy turns the world upside down by showing the audience the view from the other side. The majority's vision (structure) is temporarily and imaginarily relegated to the status of antistructure while the minority's vision (antistructure) is elevated to the status of structure. In this reversal of symbolic order, the minority is released from social classifications (e.g., stereotypes) and the majority is given the opportunity to feel like the minority (Douglas 1975, 103; Berger 1997, 72).

The idea of the reversal of symbolic order is of crucial importance for understanding the structural dimensions of ethnic comedy. Often perceived as a reversal of the relationship between the rational and the irrational, comic vision does indeed thrive on the discrepancies and interplay of two forces. For Nietzsche, these two forces were the Apollonian and Dionysian principles. The former is associated with structure, rationality, and seriousness and the latter with antistructure, emotions, and laughter (one cannot but remember Nietzsche's *Gay Science* as a revolt against rationalism). Both Plato in his cave metaphor and Nietzsche in his Dionysian language invite us to such a reversal of the symbolic order. This Dionysian element in Greek tradition was continued in the Roman festival of Saturnalia (Nietzsche 2006, 122) and extends into the present day in the many versions of Carnival. Mikhail Bakhtin famously observed that in carnivals and other rites of passage, the ordinary world is turned upside down (Bakhtin 1968; Brottman 2004, 150; Berger 1997, 21). Laughter is therefore "one of the essential forms of truth concerning the world as a whole. . . . It is a peculiar point of view relative to the world. . . . Certain essential aspects of the world are accessible only to laughter" (Bakhtin 1968, 20).

An important insight of the scholarship on the comic phenomenon is the idea that it is a particular *worldview*. Comic vision reveals a reality different from commonsense reality. It is thus a "worldview" in two senses: it reveals another world and it is the ability to see differently. The comic vision's ability to reveal reality is a theme that deserves further discussion.

In a famous piece, "On Multiple Realities," Alfred Schutz distinguishes between commonsense reality ("the paramount reality of the everyday life") and other realities ("finite provinces of meaning") (1962, 207). We leap from one world into another when we start to daydream, for example. Or we slip into another when we fall asleep.

Here, commonsense reality is objective in that it is shared by multiple social actors and is thoroughly sedimented in the language and everyday symbolic structures. Other realities, however, remain subjective and partial. The comic as an alternative reality transcends the reality of the ordinary and is capable of seeing things from a certain distance. What is crucial here is the relationship between *vision* and *distance*. Those who are in a condition of seeing things differently (the diasporic) are more likely to generate humor. Behind the large body of Jewish humor lies the Jewish experience of marginality vis-à-vis societies in which they lived (Rappoport 2005, 66; Berger 1997, xvii). Simmel's famous social type *the stranger* represents this ability to be both near and far and to be able to stay attached to the mainstream vision and withdraw back to the ethnic vision (1971, 143–48).

A Phenomenological Theory of Ethnic Comedy

As noted earlier, theoretical works on comedy—let alone ethnic comedy—are few and far between. The volumes upon volumes of popular books on ethnic comedy, not surprisingly, do not have a theoretical agenda (Lowe 1986). Unfortunately, the few sociological treatments of comedy that do exist (Koller 1988) are not particularly theoretical. John Morreal's alternative to existing theories (humor as "pleasant psychological shift") still remains psychological (1983, 38). Even Peter Berger, who is fully equipped with the insights of phenomenological sociology, somehow leaves the sociological dimension of comedy undertheorized in his otherwise very original and entertaining book (1997). As others have noted (Fine 1998, 383), a sociological discussion of comedy needs to combine the different theories of comedy that have been developed from nonsociological perspectives and then go beyond them.

In this part of my discussion, I propose a sociological theory of ethnic comedy. My aim is to build a structural framework for understanding the comic phenomenon. In this endeavor, I draw on Simmel's distinction between *subjective* and *objective* cultures. In his writings on the crisis of modern culture, he argues that in modern times we are experiencing a cultural crisis because the equilibrium between subjective culture and objective culture has been lost (1971, 227–34; 1997). What Simmel says about the relationship between the individual and modern society can be said as well of the relationship between (ethnic) minorities and (national) majorities. In the beginning, a minority group's subjective culture (an internal culture) has not yet been harmonized or synchronized with the objective culture, a culture that is external to them. The discrepancy between their subjective culture and the (objective) culture of the majority gives rise to incongruities and becomes a fertile ground for humor. Simmel's objective and subjective cultures correspond to Alfred Schutz's categories of "paramount reality" (i.e., everyday reality) and "finite provinces of meaning," respectively.

The relationship between the new minority and the majority, to use the terms of figurationist sociologist Norbert Elias (1994b), is the relationship between *the established* and *the outsider*. In the following outline of a theory of ethnic comedy I draw on the phenomenological insights of Simmel and Elias.[15] In addition to the relative *power* and *relationality* of parties that are central to the arguments of Simmel and Elias, one should pay attention to *location* and *temporality* as two indispensable elements in making sense of the rise and disappearance of ethnic comedy.[16] This rise and later disappearance of ethnic comedy is also an instance of the emergence of a group charisma and its later routinization.

Let me start with the most basic condition of possibility for ethnic comedy. Two different visions are necessary: the vision of the (ethnic or religious) minority and that of the majority. These are two visions emerging from two ethical conducts of life: the minority's communal ethos and the majority's social morality. They are not the same. If they were the same, we would not be able to speak of a minority and a majority, which are residual categories of each other. By "vision" here, I am referring to a situated perspective and a particular perception of reality. The space for stereotypes is opened by the discrepancy between these two visions or perceptions of reality. It is the difference between a group's self-perception and the way the group is perceived by others. Otherwise, prejudices would not remain prejudices but would become correct judgments. That is to say, when the gap between the two visions—between stereotype and reality—is fully bridged, both ethnicity and comedy disappear. This is when the merger in ethos (two ethics, two habituses) reaches equilibrium. If this is the case, when does ethnic comedy emerge?

People usually do not make fun of people about whom they know nothing (hence, there are no American jokes about Peruvians or Uzbeks). For ethnic jokes to emerge there has to be some *contact*. Real or imaginary, experiential or abstract, it is this contact that first opens the door for typification and opinion formation. But if the group is known too well and fully assimilated, we cannot speak of *ethnic* comedy either. Assimilation in this case means not the disappearance of group identity but the loss of "stranger" status. The temporality that flattens a joke (especially when it is told a third time) also flattens the ethnicity of a group as it gradually moves from outsider to insider position. Ethnic humor, therefore, is by definition an intracultural or subcultural phenomenon. We do not have German ethnic comedy in America any longer. Instead, we have jokes about Mexicans, Puerto Ricans, and Indo-Pakistanis. Such new ethnicities are usurping the visibility that once belonged to Italians, Poles, and the Irish. In short, ethnic comedy emerges when the ethnic group is like an iceberg in relation to the majority. The tip of the iceberg represents the zone of familiarity and contact. It has to be big enough. The part under the water represents the zone of unfamiliarity and exclusivity. In the beginning the iceberg is under the water and there is no ethnic comedy. When its tip surfaces (a form of intrusion) and catches attention, it generates comedy. But when its body is fully displayed, it loses its magic (i.e., ethnic and comic character) and, to continue with our metaphor here, starts to melt away.

Therefore, the ethnic group in question first of all has to acquire a relevant otherness. Irrelevant otherness does not generate jokes. It is the combination of otherness and relevance (the terrorists lurking among us, the Mexican worker in our neighborhood, the Pakistani computer engineer in the next cubicle) that generates jokes. Ethnic comedy is made across a boundary that separates us (majority) from them (minority). When that boundary is erased (including through comedy itself), otherness evaporates, despite continuing relevance. And so does the ethnic comedy that clings to it.

When both groups share the same vision, their comedy is no longer "ethnic." It is the gap between the two visions that makes each one funny *from the other's point of view*.[17] But when the object of comedy in one world (i.e., a minority's internal joke) lacks a counterpart or resonance on the other side, it will not appear funny. One can think of in-group jokes by Muslim comedians that fail to generate laughter among audiences unfamiliar with Muslim culture. All funniness is subjective and can exist only for and according to a particular point of view, situated in place and time. No joke is "objectively" funny. An act or joke, always situated in place and time, is comical only *to* someone. This is similar to the role of intentionality in phenomenological theory, which holds that consciousness is always consciousness *of* something. This directedness is part of the comic experience. Something that looks incongruous and thus funny from one vantage point might look congruous and unfunny from another. Our existential condition of being-in-the-world implies our ineradicable situatedness in time and space. Later expansions of horizon and accumulation of knowledge are pathways opened from that

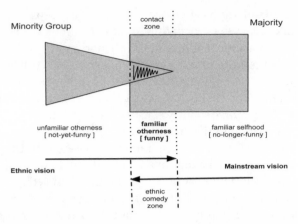

6.1 A model of ethnic comedy.

starting point. Comedy "occurs" as one moves along (i.e., opens up) that pathway. To the extent that different people's pathways overlap (in the form of common sense, *doxa*), they share a highway of everyday language and a collective attunement toward what might occur, be it comic or tragic.

The degree of humor diminishes as you move away from the overlapping areas or contact zones of mutuality and toward the exclusive domains (fig. 6.1). In that regard, comedy is similar to aesthetic experience. It introduces the unseen, the unknown, surprise. The performance of ethnic comedy onstage is a collaboration in routinization of the charismatic. The ineluctable, the strange and incongruous particular, is tamed, normalized, and neutralized under (and *toward*) the universal familiar. Ethnic comedy is unfamiliarity packaged in a box of familiarity, a glimpse of charisma before it is routinized. That is why its delivery must be partial and gradual, so that it can be digested mentally and perceptually. It is also why the creator of ethnic jokes himself does not laugh at them: they are not unfamiliar to him anymore. And for the same reason, most pieces of humor will have their full effect on an audience only once (because the joke exists only *in statu nascendi*). This rule holds not only for jokes but for ethnic groups as well. Length of stay in American society, for example, is important because those who come later are likely to be the butt of jokes. This is best illustrated in the thriving subgenre (among many ethnic communities, including Muslims) of "boater" jokes—humor at the expense of those "fresh off the boat."

The work of comedy is therefore aesthetic. In the aesthetic experience we come across a surface that has been experienced but not yet conceptualized. Let me explain this point using Heideggerian terminology, which, I am afraid, itself often begs explanation—but his writings on the work of art are of particular relevance here. Heidegger defines art "as the becoming and happening of truth" because "art is by nature an origin: a distinctive way in which truth comes into being, that is, becomes historical" (1971, 69, 75). Ancient Greeks used the word *techne* to describe craft and art. In their world, Heidegger believes, art (*techne*) and truth (*aletheia*) belonged together.[18]

The artist or comedian is someone who makes "truth as unconcealment" (*aletheia*) happen. As a form of art, comedy is similar to poetry. "Poetry proper is never merely a higher mode of everyday language. It is rather the reverse: everyday language is a forgotten [i.e., routinized] and therefore used-up poem" (Heidegger 1971, 205). As a result of this aesthetic incorporation of a foreign or new element, the language (i.e., culture) expands. Hence, the comedian is an artist, a Dionysian poet who brings forth new manifestations of being. The comic's magic lies in the ability to pull us into an experience that lies beyond our conceptualized world of familiarity. In short, like all aesthetic experiences, comedy has both otherness (unfamiliarity) and relevance.

Of course, one question that comes to mind is: why should the majority care about such comedy? Or to put it another way, what is it that links the two groups? The answer is *care* and *concern*. Here I use the concept of care in a Heideggerian sense, as the specifically human mode of being (Heidegger 1962, 225). It can be positive, as in love and care, or negative, as in fear and anxiety. Care and concern delimit the surface of relevance[19] and the zone of objects and themes. These objects and themes become the raw material for comedy. They can be taken up by an ethnic comedian to poke fun at the majority or by the majority to ridicule the minority. Fear and anxiety are similar to love and care in producing themes and objects of (selective) perception. Care and concern bring the other under our radar. The fear of the Muslim as a potential terrorist is precisely what creates room for him in the world of non-Muslims and thus opens the ground for Muslim comedy. Azhar Usman's description of his experience at the airport starts with the fact that as soon as he steps into the airport, "heads turn simultaneously." A Muslim who could otherwise be completely ignored takes on charisma, albeit a negative charisma. Even when other citizens fail to pay attention to the Muslim individual, the airport announcements invite them to turn their radars on and search for suspicious behavior.[20] In the face of such concern—whether naturally arising or artificially provoked—space is opened up for Muslims in the world of the average American.

Because the Muslim entered the American imagination (most force-fully, in both senses of the word) through the hijacking of planes, the most effective jokes that non-Muslim audiences hear from Muslim co-medians are jokes that happen to be about aviation and airport security. Such jokes are fully transparent and make perfect sense to the non-Muslim audience. They correspond to the tip of the iceberg (fig. 6.1).

In other words, in the mutually engaged routinization of the new ob-ject, each vision is influenced and transformed by the other. We can therefore speak of a comic "surrender and catch," a phrase Kurt Wolff (1991) devised to describe our immersion in experience and withdrawal to analytical objectification. This is also similar to the idea of precon-ceptual experience in Simmel and certainly the Dionysian element in Nietzsche. A specific experience (strangeness) is baptized into normality through mutual witnessing. At the very moment of linguistic expression of a life experience (what Wittgenstein [1997] calls *life forms*), language expands beyond its earlier limits. In his *Critique of Judgment*, Kant, along the same lines, defines beauty as the object of representation *without concepts* (1987, 53). It is the sighting of previously unseen surfaces that amazes and amuses us.

Taking in a stereotype and giving back a joke not only produce laugh-ter, which is a spark ignited by the merging of two visions, but also has a leveling effect on people and their understandings. The subjective and objective cultures that are expressed by the two visions approach a cer-tain balance, transparency, and correspondence under the jurisdiction of the comic operation.[21] Here the otherness is abolished and the other is released into the self.

In my theory of ethnic comedy, I attempt to integrate the three otherwise-separate theories of comedy: the superiority, incongruity, and relief theories. Here centrality goes to incongruity theory and it remains the backbone of the model discussed above. However, it is supplemented by the relational and cathartic insights of the other two theories. Further-more, my theory is phenomenological and pays particular attention to questions of time and space.

First, superiority theory provides the otherness necessary for the pos-sibility of vision from the other side. The incongruity theory posits two visions of reality in a structural relationship that produces comedy. Fi-nally, relief theory refers to the tension between these two visions. The comic relief is generated by the gradual fusion of these visions, which produces sparks of laughter. The integration of the three theories would not be sufficient for our model had elements of space and time not been included. Situated perspectives and different visions are absolutely central for such a theory building. Similarly, we have to recognize that not only a single joke but also the whole phenomenon of ethnic comedy is a temporal event. Muslim ethnic comedy is a product of a particular time (after 9/11) and place (in relation to the American mainstream).

As a temporal event ethnic comedy is a symptom of integration. The coming-closer that gives rise to jokes and the consequent attrition of otherness eventually lead to appropriation and incorporation. We are of course talking about domestic ethnic comedy and, more specifically, ethnic comedy in American society. (Comedy that pokes fun at external groups such as other nationalities has a different trajectory and as such is not part of this analysis.)

Ethnic Comedy and Cultural Citizenship

Muslim ethnic comedy in the United States is a symptom of the emergence of a Muslim ethnicity in America. One sees the signs of this process in the character of Muslim comedy. There is a Muslim in-group humor and a humor that is presented to outsiders or mixed audiences. The Muslim comedy that appears onstage has a very short shelf life. It is so perishable because the window of recognition for Muslims within the landscape of American society is still small and confined to terrorism and aviation. Over the last couple of years, my observation has been that Muslim comics are expanding their spectrum of jokes as they try to reach larger audiences. Presidential campaigns and national politics offer one such avenue.

Nevertheless, there is a more crucial point with respect to Americanization. As others have argued, ethnic humor is part of the Americanization process (Lowe 1986, 439). Muslim comedy existed as an immigrant ethnic comedy and as an in-group phenomenon prior to 9/11. However, pan-Muslim ethnic comedy, which is best illustrated by Allah Made Me Funny, is a by-product of 9/11, where the outsider audience is pulled into the theater of Muslim comedy. Such comedy also benefits from a trend triggered by 9/11 known as "Muslim first" (Naber 2005): being Muslim became the primary identification for many Muslim ethnicities. Muslimness provides a larger community and visible victimhood, which generate recognition. Pan-Muslim ethnic comedy addresses this new audience.

One of the functions of ethnic comedy is as a form of cultural mediation (Mintz 1985, 71). But it takes place within a "time bubble" (Collins 2004) and is closely linked to the life chances of the ethnic group in question. Not only an individual joke but also the entire ethnic humor of a particular group has a temporal character. If repetition of a joke blunts its power and newness, so too does prolonged encounter with an ethnic/religious group blunt ethnic comedy, because it saps its otherness and unfamiliarity. That which is familiar is no longer incongruent.[22]

Ethnic comedy or the comic operation as a form of interaction is a cultural *stitch*. What happens in ethnic comedy is that the comedian takes a stereotype (a synthetic form produced by the objective culture of the majority) and plays on it (adds to it his subjective culture, his concrete facticity) and finally gives it back to society through laughter. It is no wonder that ethnic comedy is often celebrated for its "healing" capacity. It soothes people. By undoing otherness, ethnic comedy lifts, albeit temporarily, the restrictive limits on the self and abolishes the gulf that separates the in-group from the out-group. It provides a relief from social classifications, which are often oppressive of the minority group. As such it is also a psychoanalytical operation: it makes one's own what was once perceived as external. It facilitates appropriation and inhabitation.[23] The self is redeployed in such a way that it now includes the former other. Boundaries are blurred. How does this inclusion happen? The ability of comedy to disclose the rock bottom of our identities as "human" plays a significant role in showing commonality under the surface of "difference." That comedy reveals our humanity is well illustrated by a statement by Jewish comic Rabbi Bob Alper, who said after his performance with Azhar Usman in Detroit on April 1, 2008, "You can't hate the person you've laughed with." One of the reactions Usman said he received from a non-Muslim audience member during his tour across America is similarly worth quoting: "I didn't see you as a Muslim, I saw you as a human being."

Conclusion

The tragedy of 9/11 focused America's attention on the Muslim minority. At the same time that it created unprecedented visibility, it also opened up the space for Muslim comedy. After all, Muslim ethnic comedy is exploiting that attention in a way that is beneficial to both parties. Laughing about the ways of Muslim people in America helps blur the lines that separate Muslims from other Americans. Its basic message is that we are all human. It shows that Muslims are not that different from the rest of humanity and therefore merit compassion and understanding.

The ironic humor that characterizes Muslim comedy "acknowledges certain de-humanizing, life-threatening circumstances and seeks to transform them into something human" (Koller 1988, 10). If humor is a distortion of reality, those whose reality is already distorted by stereotypes must resort to humor to rectify them. Humor becomes a means of undoing otherness. By rehumanizing Muslims in the eyes of non-Muslim Americans, Muslim comedy heals the effects of 9/11, which left Muslims outside the definition of the nation. The very crisis that cast Muslims away from the American mainstream becomes a means of reintegrating them. Muslim comedy provides another instance of what I have earlier called "negative incorporation." Finally, Muslim ethnic comedy is a symptom of Muslims' Americanization. It reflects the emergence of a distinct American Muslim ethnicity as a product of American experience.

On Appropriation
and Inhabitation

Imagine that I find an object on the street. I pick it up: a piece of cloth. As I look
at it and hold it, the thing starts to belong to me—to outsiders it looks like an
extension of me, something I hold. The smell and texture of my hand and of the
object begin to permeate one another. After a while, I realize that it is a glove.
Once I understand what it is, once I grasp it, my hand no longer holds the glove
but wears it. What had been present *at* hand now fits *to* my hand. And the more
it fits my hand, the less obscure and heavy it seems. The glove takes the shape
of my hand. It asks to be worn. I put it on and then move beyond it, occupied
already with other things. At first I still feel it, but gradually I become unaware
of it. It migrates from being something on my hand and in my sight to being
something like my hand itself, out of my sight. It becomes like my skin. Is this the
story of a glove? Yes, but in reality it is the story of my skin. The world around me
is my extended skin, a thick yet transparent body. The one who feels at home
wears the world like a garment.

When we find ourselves in a new place, we are overtaken
by it. We experience it as a Simmelian adventure, which
"has the gesture of the conqueror" (1971, 193). The event
of encounter is an *exposure* that in turn *disposes* us toward
the new place. It lays the ground for things to seem relevant
or irrelevant, familiar or strange, and so on. But often we
are still filled with the other places we have been, and those
past places partially eclipse our reception of the new place.
Whoever can transcend past places receives the new in a
more lively way. But at the same time the impact of those
past places is gradually being revised, transformed by the
arrival of the new. Thus, the migrant is often seen struggling

to complete the withdrawal from a past *there* and engage fully with the now *here.*

Immigration exposes Muslims to American space. This exposedness (being-in-America) breeds new dispositions (habitus). In a new land, immigrant Muslims are hungry for direction, language, and home. They cautiously swallow what is put in front of them. At first they poke it with the forks of cold reservation. Then once they get acclimated to it (if nothing else, this sizzling thing starts to smell interesting), they begin to make it their own. This hunger (we humans' innate desire to consume the world around us) makes possible the flow of objects into the empty interior of the subject. But digestion takes a great deal of energy; it is agonistic work. And as much as Muslims need to digest their America, America itself needs to digest its Muslims, foreign and domestic.

Muslim Inhabitation of American Forms

As we have seen in the first part of this book, when they find themselves in America, Muslim immigrants become disoriented. They want to face Mecca but the new land thwarts them. It is as though America itself blocks the view toward Mecca. Then gradually America gains transparency. Elucidated, it submits to the sway of directionality emanating from the Kaaba. The wild field becomes cleared ground. Properly appropriated, America withdraws as an obstructive object: Mecca is found in America. Now the hesitant prayer rug can take the form of a stable mosque. A few premature mosques still bear the marks of their earlier accents, but all the rest are fluent in their directionality.

Similarly, when Muslims first come across the English language, it is foreign to them. Halfway inside it, they feel it and carry its weight as an accent. When entirely inside, they feel English as their native language. With this gradual inward movement, they enter within the walls of the city and come to speak its language. Instead of grappling with English as an unwieldy object, they begin to float in it. The language bears the native speaker as the sea bears a boat. It becomes "equipment" (Heidegger 1962, 141).

Coming from another homeland, Muslims first perceived America as religiously opaque and morally dangerous. It seemed to show them nothing but darkness. They wanted to avoid it but were already too close to it. Then gradually they began to discover some scattered spots where the light came beaming in. With time, America moved from the periphery of the world to its center. It lost its object status, becoming part of the Muslim subject. As an object it had been a source of anxiety and concern, but as a part of the subject—like the eye that cannot see itself—it became invisible. Muslims came to talk and feel like Americans rather than talking about America from a distance. Muslims who once were anxiously aware of America as a foreign and dangerous place (a *dar al harb*) erased their insecurity and became "unaware" of the question of America's status as a Muslim land. For to ask such a question would be to question their own status, about which they feel no doubt. Since, as Muslims, they are American, America cannot be un-Islamic.

What initially appeared as a wound (disorientation, accent, homesickness) has now been healed. The difference that solicits attention is replaced by a sameness that resists it. By taking the shape of the new world's imposed borders, the subject releases itself from the burden of its edges. Unfelt and weightless, borders fall beyond the grasp of consciousness. They sink beneath consciousness—and not merely into the body.[1]

In the second part of the book we observed how the Muslim launches himself outward into American space (legal, religious, and personal). In this, we see the cultivation of courtesy, the replacement of terror with family, the transformation of warrior into courtier. The Muslim enters into the formal shelter of citizenship; the imam takes a seat at the ecumenical table, joining pastor, rabbi, and priest; and to celebrate the arrival, the Muslim comedian recounts their heroic struggle in comic poetry.

Citizens with Strong Faith and Good Humor

Muslims can now find the direction to Mecca, pass through and beyond the everyday wall of English, and build their new dwelling on this frontier land. By ascetic striving they latch on to the American surface. Their attachment is further reinforced by cultivating an awareness of the surrounding environment, by joining in networks of citizenship and neighborhoods of faith. At the end of this excruciating journey, the Muslim immigrant is finally released, as an individual, into the public sphere of Americanness. And relief from the tension of the marathon brings laughter. In the process, the Muslim immigrant, whose movement across the border was perceived as an intrusion, whose visage had seemed obscure and unsettling, now finally reaches a gestalt and acquires an American (i.e., human) face. This reassertion of personhood also comes as a relief for the onlookers, who have been looking for a face to rest their eyes on

Table C.1 Islamic Society of North America annual convention titles: Three thematic stages

Year	ISNA annual convention title
2000	Islam: Faith and Civilization
2001	Strength through Diversity*
2002	Islam: A Call for Peace and Justice
2003	Islam: Enduring Values for Daily Life
2004	Islam: Dialogue, Devotion, and Development
2005	Muslims in North America: Accomplishments, Challenges, and the Road Ahead
2006	Achieving Balance in Faith, Family, and Community
2007	Upholding Faith and Serving Humanity
2008	Ramadan: A Time for Change
2009	Life, Liberty, and the Pursuit of Happiness
2010	Nurturing Compassionate Communities: Connecting Faith and Service
2011	Loving God, Loving Neighbor, Living in Harmony

CIVILIZATION	$\Rightarrow$	RELIGION	$\Rightarrow$	FAITH
outside		border		within
distant/other		near/contact		immanent/self
Islam		Abrahamic		American civil religion

* "Diversity" here refers to the internal diversity of Muslims (i.e., the range of ethnicities and denominations).

(i.e., to make "sense" of). Faces turned toward each other share a common sense. Common sense makes each face "a familiar face."

Here I offer two examples of how this entry into common sense, or cultivation of solidarity with the host culture, takes place. As will become clear, Muslims as citizens of America grow strong faith and generate good humor.

As the chapter on Muslim interfaith dialogue illustrates, Muslims seek kinship through Abraham. Equally noteworthy, however, is the transition from the God of Abraham to an American God. Like Abraham's own story of searching for a progressively higher power (looking for the most potent protector, he venerates first the moon, then the sun, and finally God alone), here we have Muslims repositioning their faith from Muslim to Abrahamic and from Abrahamic to American civil religion. This transition can be traced through the ways Muslim organizations define their religious identity. A good example is the series of titles chosen as convention themes by the Islamic Society of North America (ISNA) over the past decade (table C.1).

In the initial moment of anxiety, Muslims talk about Islam as a separate and self-centered civilization, if not a countercivilization. With respect to the religion and culture of America, Islam is seen as a distinct and distant entity. Such an identification is deployed against an exterior world—American culture—that is in part threatening. Both Islam and America are religiously "distinct." The interest is in self-celebration for the sake of self-preservation. The dominant feeling is concern and anxiety.

Then engagement with other religions imposes itself more seriously. A language of challenge (a demand for receptivity and attunement), balance, and reaching out emerges. Distances are diminished and Islam becomes a "religion" in neighborly contact with other "religions," primarily Christianity and Judaism. Nearness establishes the equivalence of Islam, Christianity, and Judaism as "religions." Here Abraham, the father of all three, presides over the rapprochement of the alienated family members (call them Ishmael and Isaac). The dominant feeling is closeness and familiarity.

In the third stage, Islam disappears from sight. The language of "religion" gives way to that of "faith," which makes Muslimness a part of the unity of American civil religion. The dominant feeling is love and dissolution. It comes as no surprise that one of the most "naturalized" Muslim authors, Eboo Patel, has written a book with the very generic title *Acts of Faith* (2007). To the extent that Islam is seen as domestic to America, it is referred to as a faith rather than a religion. This overall pattern is clear to see in the gradual disappearance of Islam from ISNA's convention themes. It may seem that the later titles betake of a Christian vocabulary, but in truth they are part of the language of generic American religion. Islam becomes an American faith when the aura of otherness that surrounds it is extinguished.

The same logic comes into play in the seemingly less serious work of the Muslim comedian. The task of this frontier figure and second-generation athlete in the race toward a homeland is to make the Muslim body disappear as an obscure object. Like the airplane ride that Azhar Usman takes, the immigrant's marathon starts with unpredictability and leads eventually to enjoyment. When the comedian enters the plane, he inspires terror; faces fall. Idle talk is abandoned and truths are told. A passenger calls his wife, "Honey, I am going to die." The passenger has discovered that he, too, is diasporic, a being-toward-death with no ground under his feet. There is no other sentence he can construct as truthful as this one. Facing his reality, he suddenly becomes authentic: "Honey, I love you."

The plane is full of passengers awaiting, in fear and trembling, their destination (or destiny). All are fully conscious. When the plane lands and the gap of separation is bridged, habitus and habitat shake hands. The peace of at-homeness fills the air as ontological complicity is achieved between Muslim (Usman) and American (the passenger). From the temporal and orientational direction of the Muslim, Usman represents the will (subjective culture) and the American passenger (objective culture) represents destiny. From the viewpoint of the American passenger, the passenger is will and Usman is his destiny (unpredictable, dangerous). When at the end it turns out that they are just two travelers and there is no terrorist, they discover themselves to be "in sync" as fellow passengers. Now the suspense is over and the passengers are released from their diasporic condition: as they land, they burst into laughter. The passengers are happy; they come up to Usman: "I was all ready to kill you, but see, you are just like us." Usman's face—which had struck them as uncanny, marked by the elusiveness of treachery—finally gives itself to familiarity: "He's just another passenger, after all." The anxiety that held them apart is eliminated and they collapse into one another. *Asabiyya* is achieved: the bonds of unity branch out in all directions, and sameness penetrates to the core of the object, leaving no room for opacity and otherness. We are the same, we are all human: Muslimness dissolves into Americanness. This is the journey of Azhar Usman's stand-up comedy.

After this alchemical performance, the American audience, too, begins to see Muslims as American. Someone walks up to Usman at the end of the show and tells him that he now sees him not as a Muslim but as a human being. The object that had threatened and resisted the subject has now been transcended, sublated. In the end Usman really has killed something: he has killed his own otherness. The distance between Muslim and American is erased—or at least whittled down to a hyphen. Here the genius of the Muslim comedian lies in embodying the meeting point of Muslim and American, will and destiny, subject and object. For in the moment of "enjoyment" such oppositions are effaced (Simmel 1997, 63). After the performance, Americans and Muslims have gained a degree of certainty; as they drive home, they feel more at home with one another.

Islam and America: An Entanglement

As Muslims culturally settle in the American environment, Islam and America find themselves increasingly entangled. At first glance, this entanglement might seem purely conflictual. We see a constant discovery and rejection of Islam by the likes of Obama "birthers," entrenched opponents of neighborhood Muslim institutions (Parc51 is just one), states like Oklahoma making heroic preemptive strikes against creeping sharia, publicity-seeking congressmen (such as Peter King) digging for potential radicalization among domestic Muslims (aka American citizens), obscure pastors popping up from the middle of nowhere and threatening to burn the Qur'an, Republican candidates competing to show the depth of their disdain for Islam, and opportunist Muslims from all over the world jumping in to claim their fifteen minutes of fame as native experts in the Western cottage industry of Islam bashing (e.g., Ayaan Hirsi Ali).

Islam has become a resource for domestic consumption. Its very amorphousness at this stage of America's mental digestion allows it to be used for a variety of purposes. It is red meat for certain electoral constituencies. It can be held up as a monster to mobilize the patriotic base. While immigrant Muslims who used to flaunt their Islam are today at pains to make it disappear from public view, it seems that a big chunk of America wants to keep emphasizing Islam and putting it on public display, as if sensing that this is the last chance to catch something rapidly sinking into invisibility. In short, Islam is now more American than ever before. The decade of foreign Islam—the 2000s, the decade of 9/11, characterized by the discourse of jihad—is giving way to a new decade of domestic Islam, characterized by sharia law. No longer sharp or shocking enough, jihad talk is being replaced by concern over sharia as the new tool of Islamophobia. Jihad was *looming* but sharia is *creeping*. Not only is Islam an imminent danger, but it is dangerously close to becoming immanent.

Yet at the same time, Islam is being domesticated. We already see the signs of this trajectory in the diversification of Muslim presence in America. We see a more frequent discovery and acceptance of Islam—in the White House, with its Muslim advisers; in Congress, with its two Muslim members; in the rise of an American-born Muslim leadership and clergy; in the form of *hijabi* weight lifters joining in national competitions, country singers with Muslim backgrounds, mainstream pundits who proudly proclaim their Muslim roots, and even a Muslim Miss USA.

In this trickling of Islam into the interior of American space (cultural, political, economic, and psychic), it becomes increasingly difficult to make judgments that assume the externality of Islam to American society. Islam and America have become enmeshed. It is becoming impossible to objectify Islam in America without mutilating America itself. The fact that this object of attention has become part of the subject shows that Muslim life has started taking on American forms. Ironically, the choice of the adjective "creeping" by Islamophobes captures precisely the ongoing routinization of Islam in America. Islam is sinking into familiarity and common sense. Its edginess and strangeness are melting away as a result of an unintentional collaboration between the Islamophobes who attack Muslims on a regular basis and the Muslims working relentlessly to prove their Americanness.

In this final chapter I close the journey of the book with two themes: the process of appropriation between Islam and America and a general theory of inhabitation. The first offers a series of interpretive judgments about the venture of Islam in its American habitat. The second attempts to articulate a broader understanding of inhabitation and clarifies a potential vocabulary for future approaches to inhabitation and home.

The Diasporic: Traversing an Absent Ground

Social scientists love to study and talk about exile, immigration, mobility, and the public sphere, but they are mostly silent about home and what it means to feel at home (Duyvendak 2011, 26). The concept of diaspora has been used intensively in cultural, postcolonial, and immigration studies (Braziel and Mannur 2003). Diaspora means "having been spread out." The two core characteristics of diaspora are dispersion in space and continuing orientation toward a distant homeland (Brubaker 2005, 5). My usage here is slightly different. Though the two ultimately converge, I believe it is more fruitful to think of diaspora as a condition not so much of being away from where home is but of not being at home where one is. Most of the literature on immigrant experience relies on a backward-looking conception of diaspora (i.e., focusing on the movement from home to diaspora). In this book, I worked with a forward-looking conception of diaspora (the movement from diaspora to new home). While the former is encapsulated in the notion of "nostalgia," the latter is a matter of hope and fear.

Diaspora can make sense only in relation to a home and exists only as a separation from it. But at the same time, home is not just a past place; it is an object of desire. It is the separation itself that creates the object and the desiring subject. If we do not impose our chronological definition of home on the immigrant, we will see that home is not exclusively what is left behind but also *what is always ahead*: home is a destination, even a destiny. Home is that toward which one walks to close the wound of separation. Home need not be narrowly conceived as the place of origination but rather can be viewed as the destination of longing: "Ultimately all of our paths are determined by whether we are going away from home by them or coming home upon them" (Simmel 2010, 171).

The diasporic lives in a place that is not home—yet. His home is not where he finds himself standing. The emptiness beneath his feet causes panic and anxiety. He casts about for firmer footing. But this requires building a ground that is not readily present. He has to make the ground on which to stand. This is inhabitation.

Inhabitation is something we have to cultivate. All the forms of artifacts and relations that we humans generate are expressions of this necessary cultivation. We have culture as cultivation because it closes a gap we are born with. We are born as immigrants. That is what makes us ethical beings.

The idea that every human being is born prematurely (Lacan 1977, 3; Simmel 2010, 165; Nietzsche 1999, 56) acquires a second meaning in the case of the immigrant. Unlike the citizen, the immigrant is born into the community prematurely (though he perceives it as "too late" rather than "too early"): his birth is premature because he is only partly present. He needs to be brought into full presence. If the citizen is a virtuoso of his native culture, the immigrant is an apprentice. His language is incomplete, his loyalty suspect, his sense of direction unsteady; his tastes and constitution are peculiar. He is a stranger. As soon as he discovers his condition, he wants to overcome it. To dissolve into community, the immigrant must make himself into an athlete and run a marathon. The distance he is covering in this marathon is less a spatial one than a temporal and cultural one—he has to make up the time he has been absent, running to catch up with the community in which he technically already lives. He subjects himself to exercises to become "fit"—a fitness that is less about shape of body or quality of mind than about the manner of their uses. As the newcomer closes the gap with the community, he becomes established: "familiar" (no longer strange) and "familial" (no longer a stranger). And the space that he crosses becomes home or an extension of home—a place of intensified familiarity. Things at home with each other rely and rest upon one another. Inhabitation creates solidarity through solidity: it requires the elimination of gaps in the way of full presence. The certainty it gives is achieved by the removal of the islands of doubt that stand in the way of unity.

A Digression on Nativism

The immigrant is the product of a rift. He feels it as a pain, a burden in the form of consciousness, restlessness. He wants to become a citizen (the citizen being the one who participates in the body of the city). If the immigrant is a stranger (Simmel 1971, 143), then the citizen is a host. Put differently, the citizen is immanent in that to which the stranger is near or far. The citizen is a subject who comes into being as a result of subjection (he "is already in himself the effect of a subjection much more profound than himself" [Foucault 1977, 30]). The citizen enjoys amnesia about his origin. He is born into submission and thus does not need to initiate the ritual of submission (the oath the immigrant takes to become a citizen). The immigrant experiences citizenship as a *Gestell* (Heidegger 1977, 19), an iron law that ethically cuts through his world, forcing him into an ascesis of shape and ergonomic fitness. He becomes a project for himself. He has to internalize customs and become accustomed to his new place. He has to prove his fitness in a Hegelian war of self against consciousness.

In acts both of love and of war one kills alterity. The mysterious and fearful image of "love as murder" reflects the nature of the act: two become one. Both war and love are negations of duality—liftings of consciousness and erasures of anxiety. Inclusive gestures of liberal humanism (love) and exclusive acts of nativism (war) are equally aimed at securing unity. Both of these reactions are directed at the immigrant when he appears on the horizon as an alterity. As reactions to the alien or immigrant, one of these seems *conscious* and the other *naïve*. The liberal finds in the immigrant her own history, while the nativist, a restful subject, wakes up to the immigrant as to a violation of his dream. Being native, he has no memory of himself as an immigrant and wants only to return to sleep.

Nativism is the alienation of the native from his peaceful immanence. It is the intrusion of the immigrant's otherness, which, like a crack, introduces a limit, a border to the limitless native self. In other words, the emergence of otherness on the horizon unsettles the enjoyers of common sense. Nativism is the ideology of common sense ("this is our home," "no immigration"), and liberal humanist inclusivism is the common sense of ideology ("we are all immigrants," "we are all human"). Faced with the immigrant, the native feels himself alienated and out of place (practically diasporic)—hence all the sound and fury. Nativism is a reaction to the disruption of at-homeness. Once the source of anxiety is arrested, either through love (included among the rest of us) or war (excluded from the rest of us), common sense is restored and unity is won. Then the nativist falls silent.

A dramatic and emblematic story in this regard was reported by the *New York Times* on July 19, 2011) under the headline "The Hated and the Hater, Both Touched by Crime":

Mark Stroman, 41, a stonecutter from Dallas, shot people he believed were Arabs, saying he was enraged by the terrorist attacks of Sept. 11, 2001. He killed at least two: Vasudev Patel, an Indian immigrant who was Hindu, and Waqar Hasan, a Muslim born in Pakistan. A third shooting victim, Rais Bhuiyan, 37, from Bangladesh, survived after Mr. Stroman shot him in the face at close range. Mr. Stroman admitted to the shootings. He is scheduled to be executed on Wednesday [July 20, 2011]. Mr. Bhuiyan, despite being partly blinded in his right eye, has spent the past several months creating a Web site with a petition and meeting with officials in Texas to try to persuade the state to spare Mr. Stroman.

The *Times* interviewed both the victim, who came very close to death, and the perpetrator, who was sitting on death row. They asked the Muslim victim, Mr. Bhuiyan, what he would say to Mr. Stroman if he had a chance to meet him. He said,

I would talk about love and compassion. We all make mistakes. He's another human being, like me. Hate the sin, not the sinner. It's very important that I meet him to tell him I feel for him and I strongly believe he should get a second chance. That I never hated the U.S. He could educate a lot of people. Thinking about what is going to happen makes me very emotional. I can't sleep. Once I go to bed I feel there is another person that I know who is in his bed thinking about what is going to happen to him—that he is going to be tied to a bed and killed.

A few weeks before his scheduled execution, the *Times* asked Mr. Stroman what he thought. Here is an excerpt from his written response (the ellipses are his own):

Not only do I have all My friends and supporters trying to Save my Life, but now I have The Islamic Community joining in . . . Spearheaded by one Very Remarkable man Named Rais Bhuiyan, Who is a Survivor of My Hate. His deep Islamic Beliefs Have gave him the strength to Forgive the Un-forgivable . . . that is truly Inspiring to me, and should be an Example for us all. The Hate, has to stop, we are all in this world together.

Appropriation: A Requisite of Inhabitation

Inhabitation is a broad process and largely taken for granted. At its heart lies the mechanism of appropriation, which consists of three steps. The first is *ethical inclusion*. You relate to the other through the spread of smell, taste, voice, sight. This is the price of exposure. The second step is *binding and ratiocination.* You get *entangled* with the other through the establishment of a series of bonds that hold, arrest, tame, and liberate. This is the hermeneutical work of digestion. The third step is *routinization and rectification.* You have reached *beyond* yourself to arrive at a new self; that which binds and that which is bound become indistinguishable from one another. Alterity is transformed into identity.

The process of inhabitation can be traced through and illustrated by the unfolding of mutual appropriation between Islam and America in the aftermath of 9/11. The initial phase, *encounter,* is characterized by anxiety. First we have an event: the towers fell. Then this event is interpreted, absorbed: we were attacked. The event clears the space in which the Muslim appears as an object of concern and fear.[2] As not-yet-property, the Muslim is a source of unpredictability and insecurity. He becomes charismatic and emanates terror. Both America and the terrorists (and unfortunately, by extension, nonterrorist Muslims) are present-at-hand with respect to one another. They appear to one another as resistant, obstinate. The parties are in a state of heightened wariness, if not actual war. The War on Terror abroad has its domestic counterpart in homeland insecurity and public suspicion toward American Muslims. Encounter first and foremost puts the two parties in the same space. They are becoming involved with one another.

As an inevitable consequence of this anxious encounter, *attunement* develops. The parties learn words from each other's language. After all, the enemy is an attentive partner in conversation. "Jihad" becomes an American buzzword, and the terrorists begin to release statements in English. Attunement leads to sensory overflow: sights, smells, flavors pass between the two parties. Sharing the same space leads to the same *mood.* They challenge and provoke one another. Locked in conflict with the terrorists, America feels compelled to distinguish between bad Muslims and good Muslims. American Muslims take the opportunity to express themselves and prove their normality. But the prolonged tension is tiring, and both parties begin to show signs of fatigue.[3]

Prolonged attunement leads to *coordination and adjustment.* One sees early attempts at a "reduction of contrasts" (Elias 1994a, 454) between the Muslim and the American. This is evident in increasing calls for outreach, dialogue, and mutual understanding. Adjustment increases recognition and the opening of space for each other. By choosing the path of "talking to the enemy" (Atran 2010), each comes under the "sway" of the other. A war president is followed by a president who shyly extends his hand in mutuality and calls for peace (e.g., President Obama's Cairo speech).

The small gestures of adjustment facilitate mutual *appropriation.*

Distances are further reduced. Neutral conversation leads to sympathy, and sympathy to love. Common bodies (channels of dialogue, interfaith partners, etc.) form more readily. By now most government institutions are well attuned to Muslims. For example, the State Department, Department of Homeland Security, FBI, and US Navy (all of whom have maintained booths at ISNA's annual convention in recent years) recognize the existence of Muslims and want to engage them more closely. The aim is to bring people "near" and "in." When such reaching out is coming not from one side but both, we have a perfect match, even the beginning of a love affair. Unification through marriage results in a "family" (children of Abraham, American citizens, ultimately "a more perfect union"). Thanks to the time spent together, their venture toward *indistinguishability* begins. They explain and expose themselves to each other so much that they begin to cultivate a common language.

At this stage the parties become *property* to one another. The Muslim becomes American (i.e., Americanness becomes a normal property of being Muslim) and America becomes Muslim (so, e.g., President Obama declares that "the U.S. could be seen as a Muslim country too").[4] The initial anxiety has been erased. That which is property is pacified, the owned becomes an extension of the self, and the subject and its property are courteous and hospitable to each other. Things that are mutually appropriated act not as burdens or impediments but as relief tools of convenience. They synchronize their sway so that it all radiates in the same direction in the form of laws, morals, and manners. They become ready-to-hand to one another. Violence disappears as together they make room for dwelling.[5]

Of course all this is formulated in the language of "being" but should be understood in that of "becoming." All these stages and achievements are historical and fragile. There is never absolute repose, containment of violence, or pure monodirectionality of sway. But what matters more here is the nature of the process: how foreign pieces come together as one.

A Vocabulary of Inhabitation

One cannot truly grasp the meaning of home without understanding inhabitation. Inhabitation takes place through appropriation, a mechanism that brings far things near. In this part of the discussion, I would like to introduce a series of interrelated concepts that underpin the notion of inhabitation. Some are already familiar to sociologists and some are not.

Habitus is the ethical form one has taken or been given in the course of being in the world. Habitus is another name for the imprints of inhabitation. According to Bourdieu (1990, 9, 13), it is a system of dispositions acquired through experience. Here is my own take on this notion: ethical beings have no fixed nature; habitus is the closest thing to what could be called human nature. Habitus (1) is constituted by the totality of past symbolic violence/s (the subject's exposure to the world, the accumulated traces of the social and physical environment on the subject) and (2) is constantly transformed and revised by new practices, forms of life that bring newness into the world. Habitus is nature not-yet-established. History does not allow the ethical being to fully settle. Being historical in the sense of history making (hence the need for the ethical as decision making), the human being lacks an inherent nature. But he needs a familiar blanket to rest and feel at home in. He is given that blanket through habitualization: the sense of "in-ness." "'In' is derived from '*innan*'—'to reside,' 'habitare,' 'to dwell.' . . . 'Being-in' is thus the formal existential expression for the Being of *Dasein*, which has Being-in-the-world as its essential state" (Heidegger 1962, 79).

Our habit(u)s conceal from us our groundlessness. Habitus releases us into the world. From this shore we swim into the Open (which is the meaning of *practice*) but we do so conservatively.

Inhabitation is the process of flowing on to a (new) surface that is punctuated by nonhuman nature and human culture (including architecture, taste, language, etc., a totality of sway in the form of society, the world of the given—what Bourdieu calls the field). It is the process of acquiring dispositions. Inhabitation generates habitus. There can be no habitus without inhabitation. We inhabit because we are thrown into the world, and we need habitus (a second nature) to stand on. Inhabitation is our being-in-the-world (Heidegger 1962, 78), and habitus is the world in our being (Bourdieu 2000, 141–42). Therefore, the understanding of one sheds light on the other.

Attunement is openness, receptivity to an environment or a specific object. Attunement links the subject to an object or to other subjects. It reflects the desire for reducing distances—overcoming gaps and discordances. Attunement is a thirst, an eidetic desire turned toward an object (sublime or otherwise). Attunement allows things to matter to us. It is an oriented openness. Attunement is the medium of solidarity—the invisible conveyor belt that draws people and objects closer together.

Mood is the key, or tuning, we find ourselves in. We do not have moods, they have us: "the dispositions have man and consequently determine him in various ways, even in his corporeality" (Heidegger 1994, 133).

Property is that which is held. As an object, it can be a thing you own, but it can also be a quality of the self—a thing, in essence, that owns and defines you. Property is sticky; it seeks solidarity with its possessor. As an object, it disappears into its owner; as a quality, it reveals him.

The appropriate is that which fits. It is what belongs or should belong in a given setting (a situation or a person). It is neither too tight nor too loose. The appropriate is to property what skin is to the body. Only those who are born with a lack are moral/ethical beings; they have to appropriate and thus one can speak of virtue for them.

The world we inhabit (when lived and experienced "properly") is an extended skin (equipment, as Heidegger would have it, or, for Simmel, a tool). It is thicker, softer, and more transparent. But it is not a dispensable luxury, an additional aura worn over a free body. A true skin is more than worn—it disappears on the body, as does a true body on a soul: "Just as the hand is a tool of the soul, so too the tool is a hand of the soul" (Simmel 1959, 269). And a tool worthy of its function becomes inseparable from its owner.

Conductance is the ability to transmit a signal or mood. Its opposite is resistance. Both objects and subjects have some form of conductance, but what distinguishes the subject is its ability to resist conductance. It can choose not to do it. The human body cannot resist electricity, because it is an object. But the human mind can resist a certain emotion or idea and choose to stay outside it or against it. Only human beings can choose to disallow or avoid conductance. Conductance turns the human being into a vessel for transmission. It undoes the subject status. In submitting, the subject becomes an object. Attunement is what the subject does to facilitate conductance. Attunement and conductance open the space for *asabiyya* and effervescence.

Asabiyya, a term introduced into social thought by Ibn Khaldun, is the wiredness, the "nerviness," that makes it possible for pieces to have a common attunement, to share the same "feeling." A group that has nerves that run through it has *asabiyya*. Individuals or a group that function as a strong conductor have a better solidarity and a stronger *asabiyya*. They become strong conductors by harmonizing their orientations, habits, and interests—in short, by having the same attunement. By submitting to a common cause (in the multiple senses of the word) they achieve full attunement and become receptacles of a common spirit.

Effervescence is the undoing of consciousness, the disappearance of diasporic distance. In ecstatic moments of solidarity, feelings can traverse multiple bodies (subjects) because those bodies are attuned to the same thing or share the same *asabiyya*. Durkheim (1994) conceptualized collective effervescence as a form of solidarity with society, because for him society was the only source of effervescence. This, of course, is a limitation of his science and does not reflect the reality of effervescence. Collective effervescence (the kind we find at sporting events or concerts, to give just two examples) is a situation where subjects are unburdened of themselves. They submit to each other and collectively become vessels of a certain emotion as it spreads through and across them.

Inspiration comes to you. You are only a recipient of it. You accept it as it is because it is about something of which you know nothing. Notice that we do not label as inspiration thoughts that are routine or already owned. Inspiration comes from nowhere (it does not have a dwelling place yet, it is a stranger), and as it comes we move into it (we dwell in it as it begins to dwell in us). The subject's relationship to inspiration is both temporal and expansive. It is a frontier experience. Inspiration comes at the edges and on the frontiers (of thought, practice, etc.). An inspired person does not know why he does something, he just does it. It feels right. How does he know that it is appropriate? He does not know. But it is appropriate. It appropriates.

Ascesis is the shaping of body or soul (depending on the culture or religion) toward "fitness." A bodily ascetic seeks fitness in body and resorts to exercise and diet (or steroids); a spiritual ascetic seeks fitness in soul (however he may imagine it) and resorts to exercise or contemplation. The ascetic process is a process of *sharpening*: it eliminates extras and fills in gaps. It loosens the tight and tightens the loose. In its search for appropriateness, an ascetic entity pushes itself toward frontiers as though running a marathon. A saint is an athlete as much as an athlete is an ascetic. Their notions of fitness might differ, but their practices of "getting near the source" are the same. As Foucault notes, "the sage is an athlete of the event" (2005, 322). By repeating certain practices, the athlete/ascetic develops habits, but what makes him an athlete or an ascetic is that those practices prepare him for the "event."

The **event** is always an appropriating event. It can be a vision, a thought, a calamity—but it is always an inspiration. It can be found at the frontiers. Repeated exercises (hence the notion of "improvisation") serve the function of carrying one to the frontiers in anticipation of the event, which comes out of nowhere. As it comes, it appropriates the subject, making him its property by owning him. Refinement and the achievement of transparency prepare the subject. When he gains lucidity through the ascetic practice of attunement and openness, the event enters him. It flows through him without any resistance. He becomes the vessel of the event and achieves singularity (genius). He looks appropriate, right, perfect, without knowing why. This is where the genius, the heroism, and the naïveté of submission meet. (The subway hero always says, when asked why he did it: "I just did it. It was the right thing to do.") It comes as *natural* (animalistic or angelic) but not rational (human). He becomes what he does. As though when what he does is removed from him, he will have no residue. That is virtue.

Virtue is bestowed, but only upon those who have done the work of ascesis in preparation to receive it. It is not that an athlete reaches virtue (*arete*, excellence) because he practices so much that he has *control over what he does*; rather, because he practices so much, he reaches the degree of purity that allows him to *lose control over himself*. A virtuoso is a product of purification and submission. He has traveled "from the work of eyes, to the work of the heart" (Heidegger 1971, 136). Because the virtuoso submits to his fate and, upon reaching the frontier, surrenders to the beyond, he renders himself receptive to the bestowal of virtue. That virtue reveals itself in the form of creativity, originality, charisma. It appropriates the person as a vessel, who in turn cannot explain or cognitively teach what he has received. He is possessed. As a subject he is indistinguishable from his object (Simmel 1997, 63). A virtuoso understands without thinking. No Cartesian "I think" interferes. Urgency, necessity close all distances. Such a solidarity leaves no room for thinking about rules and procedures. As Bourdieu notes, only a virtuoso can "produce the actions appropriate in each case, at the right moment, that of which people will say, 'There was nothing else to be done.' [Here] we are a long way, too, from the norms and rules" (1990: 107). A virtuoso possesses *excellence*, which is "the art of the necessary improvisation" (1990: 107). Improvisation happens at the frontier of reason and the threshold of the given. Beyond the domain of reason, one is inspired by the given.[6]

Here we reach a point where we can discuss the implications of this process for morality and virtue ethics. Neo-Kantianism in sociology (Durkheim, obediently, and Weber, reluctantly) confronts a challenge from what can be called the ethics of the hero. Heroic ethics is always amoral. It is formulated explicitly in both Nietzsche and Simmel. Except for Weber's half-repressed notion of charisma, the objective science of sociology denies us the language for grasping such an ethics. To understand heroic ethics, we need to contrast ethics with morality.

Ethics versus morality: A hero is very ethical but lacks morality.

Morality comes from outside and resides somewhere above the individual, whereas ethos comes from inside and is the impression the individual leaves upon outside objects and observers through his behaviors. Morality subdues the individual, while ethos represents the freedom of the individual. Ethos is the way one lives, a style of being, doing, and the like. A hermit might have no morality but a rich ethics. When the ethos of different individuals merges through sociation and civility, ethics becomes morality in the form of an average, an expectation. A category that forms through averaging, it is then forced upon all. As a universal obligation, morality is the ethics of the collective. Unlike morality, ethos is not normative; it is *expressive*. It is not pushed upon the individual person as an imposition but pulled by a sense of necessity within the individual. Morality is disciplinary, chastising. And when one imposes one's ethos on another person, it becomes naked domination. When the source of an ethos that demands obedience becomes anonymous, emanating instead from a community, then the domination becomes invisible, and the norm appears ownerless. Because it is not personal and presumably applies to everyone, morality triumphs (as a leveling superego)—but it remains the wrong-size jacket for many bodies, who are forced to live in bad conscience.

The hero is the ethos that rises above morality; heroic ethics is a nonmoral ethics. It is the authentic ethics of the *lifeworld* before it is arrested and processed by the *system* of morality.[7] As Simmel (1991, 160) noted, the "ought" of heroic ethics (expressed by Nietzsche) is even more forceful than the "imperative" of categorical morality (imposed by Kant). What this whole digression on ethics and morality has been driving toward is this: one feels at home where morality is a seamless extension of ethics.

What Is Home?

The human being is an ethical being (i.e., one compelled to appropriate and inhabit). In the figure of the immigrant the human being is withdrawn from his habitat. In my discussion so far I have characterized the immigrant as a "becoming" in relation to the citizen, who has in turn been assumed to be a "being." But the truth of the citizen is that he is also a becoming. Here is one of the reasons why humans find nowhere an absolute rest or perfect feeling of at-homeness. The world is in constant flux, never entirely habitable. The difference between the immigrant and the citizen is that the former's reality (his uncanniness, his groundlessness) has become explicit, whereas the latter's remains implicit. An animal has its innate nature to ground it, but a human being's nature is his culture, which he creates as he moves along. While the animal fulfills its nature, the human being can only come to himself. He has to achieve what has not been given or what has been lost in the dispersal.

Thus, inhabitation is the achievement of givenness and common sense. It is the articulation of habitus and the attainment of nativity, at-homeness. Feeling at home means the disappearance of consciousness, vigilance, and anxiety. One feels at home in the things one takes for granted.

There is no such thing as "a bare subject without a world" (Heidegger 1962, 152). We are born into givenness and we dwell in common sense. We want to restore them only because we have lost them. Bourdieu defines common sense as "undisputed, pre-reflexive, naïve, native compliance with the fundamental presuppositions of the field" (1990, 68). The doxic condition of being-in-the-world is "beyond the opposition of subject-object, and this has a psychological counterpart in the simple, primitive condition of being possessed by the content of a perception, like a child who does not yet speak of himself as 'I'" (Simmel 2004, 63). If inhabitation is the cultivation of common sense, then it must require the cultivation of naïveté. And such naïveté assumes a perfect match between the subject and the external world. As poet Wallace Stevens says in his poem "An Ordinary Evening in New Haven,"

. . . We seek,

The poem of pure reality, untouched
By trope or deviation, straight to the word,
Straight to the transfixing object, to the object

At the exactest point at which it is itself,
Transfixing by being purely what it is,
View of New Haven, say, through the certain eye,

The eye made clear of uncertainty, with the sight
Of simple seeing, without reflection.

While the native is fluent in his world, the stranger must struggle with it, for he is not yet *in* it. He is coming at it from outside. The stranger can become native only when he comes to partake naïvely of the common sense of the natives. He has to learn ignorance and make their sense his own. He has to become fluent in the city and its culture, so much so that he dissolves in it. He must become unaware of his own self.

Home is the place where objective space is made purely subjective. We like our homes because they are as we want them to be. We cannot confidently call a place home unless we can pour ourselves out and let ourselves dissolve there. The physical expression of this is the fact that when we arrive home, we release our bodies from all physical strictures and pressures: ties are untied, clothes are removed, shoes taken off. They are the shackles and terrors of the *habitat* (street, public), gladly left behind as the subject returns to himself in his *habitus* (home, privacy). At home, not only are these objects that cling to the self cast aside, but the self that clings to the self (in the form of self-consciousness, uncomfortable self-awareness) is removed. We arrive at a self that is perfectly unselfconscious. What a relief!

There is no place like home, because when at home, I return my self to myself—or, better, I forget myself. Only when there is a countercurrent (a mouse, an intruder) is my self delivered back to me and I find myself again in anxiety. The subject's relationship to his home almost looks like self-deception: of course you like your home; you decorated it. It smells homely because it smells like you. What does that mean? It means two things. First, as an ethical being, man is a dweller, an openness, the maker of his own laws. Man has no fixed nature but grows habitus around himself like a cocoon. Second, it means that home is a space transparent to us. It shows us ourselves. It releases us from the resistance we face in the form of anxiety. Home is a place of no opacity and no resistance. Its objects are oriented toward us and are in our service. Home as a whole is a kind of Heideggerian workshop, a zone of comfort whose objects are attuned to us.

For those thrown and destined to fall, the homeward path is crossed by the labor of appropriation and inhabitation. The stranger must be a man of courtesy and cultivation. He has to wear his environment like a pair of shoes or gloves. He has to transform the objects around him from present-at-hand to ready-to-hand. The stranger's marathon of ascesis gives transparency, conductance, and lightness to the objects that surround and threaten him, hemming him in like the walls of the grave. By purifying the objective culture between himself and the horizon, he arrives at the frontier of his new—extended—self and reaches immediacy. He arrives at peace because he is now fully present. Truly, "for those who bear the burden of alienation, there is paradise."

Notes

1. The surge of nativism and securitization of American society is not unique to 9/11 and Muslims. Rather it represents a recurring pattern in American political history. The most obvious moments include detention of German immigrants and citizens during World War I and the internment of Americans of Japanese origin during World War II. To this wartime mass discrimination based on ethnicity one can add specifically religious and ideological instances: the anti-Catholicism that greeted the arrival of non-Protestant immigrants, the anti-Semitism that persisted up until the Cold War and beyond, and recurrent bouts of anticommunism (e.g., the Palmer Raids and McCarthyism). For more on this I refer readers to Bakalian and Bozorgmehr 2009, 32–65, a comprehensive chapter contextualizing the post-9/11 backlash in comparative and historical perspective.

2. *New York Times*, August 17, 2006.

3. The notion of *asabiyya* was introduced by Ibn Khaldun, a fourteenth-century Muslim thinker from North Africa—and the great theorist of inhabitation. The word is often translated as "solidarity" but it has a richer meaning. Unlike the modern concept of solidarity, *asabiyya* has the connotation of a solidarity that is not only a work of consciousness among individuals who choose to come together but a deeper sense of oneness within a collective individuality.

4. In response to growing controversies about immigration across the globalized world, scholars of citizenship are increasingly turning their attention to the mutually constitutive nature of the notions of "citizen" and "alien" (Benhabib 2004; Bosniak 2006).

5. This is where the universalism of liberalism and the exclusivity of democracy (what Habermas calls "public autonomy") come into conflict.

6. For an in-depth history of Islam in Detroit, see Howell 2009.

7. Sunni and Shia are the two sects in Islam. The difference goes back to the question of the succession of Prophet Muhammad. Sunnis, who constitute the majority sect, believe that there was not a designated caliph and that the successors of the Prophet were his companions. Shia, on the other hand, believe that the fourth caliph, Ali, was the designated successor and that the family of the Prophet (Ahl ul Bait) has priority over his companions.

8. More information can be found at http://biid.lsa.umich.edu/.

9. In this study, I use the word "Muslim" to refer to individuals whose primary identification is with Islam. The experience of nonobservant Muslims is not covered in this work, although their experience might not be very different from that of religious Muslims as far as the impact of 9/11 is concerned.

10. The percentages on a national level are South Asians, 32 percent; Arabs, 26 percent; African Americans, 20 percent; and other, 22 percent (Bukhari et al. 2003, 9).

11. Ever since a *New York Times* article (February 21, 1989) cited 6 million as the number of Muslims in the United States, the Muslim population figures have been subject to contestation. Ihsan Bagby et al.'s study *The Mosque in America: A National Portrait* (2001), based on a sample of 416 mosques, estimated the Muslim population in the United States to be somewhere between 6 and 7 million. Another study put the estimate at 5.7 million (Ba-Yunus and Kone 2003, 314). The most commonly cited number of 6 million has recently been severely undercut by the Pew Research Center's study *Muslim Americans: Middle Class and Mostly Mainstream* (2007). This Pew report estimated 2.35 million Muslims in the United States. In his famous Cairo speech in 2009, President Obama said that there are "7 million" Muslims in America.

12. Some noteworthy recent examples of phenomenological sociology are found in the works of Andreas Glaeser (1999), Jack Katz (1990), Robert Garot (2010), and Iddo Tavory (2010). Patrik Aspers recently drew my attention to an essay of his where he aptly calls for a second, Heideggerian, road to phenomenology (Aspers 2010).

13. What does one mean when one says that human beings are moral agents? Human beings are moral agents not because they have a conception of right and wrong but because they make decisions. Decisions are what make us moral beings. Their rightness or wrongness (hence, their compatibility with a certain conception of good) is irrelevant to our being moral. While the everyday understanding of the term is not wrong, it is not entirely correct either. The source of our being moral lies not in the morality that we have but in the fact that we can have a morality.

14. This non-Cartesian truth finds its poetic expression in the lines of American poet Wallace Stevens:

> The man bent over his guitar,
> A shearsman of sorts. The day was green.
> They said, "You have a blue guitar,
> You do not play things as they are."
> The man replied, "Things as they are
> Are changed upon the blue guitar."

15. This is another expression of the same critique of Kantian "disinterestedness" (i.e., objectivity) that one finds in Nietzsche's perspectivalism, in Dilthey's methodological insights, in Gadamer's positive take on "prejudice" as a necessary component of understanding, and in Bourdieu's critique of Kantian judgment of taste.

CHAPTER ONE

1. José Casanova has kindly drawn my attention to the fact that, while Muslim directionality toward Mecca is somehow unique, the task of reorienting oneself in American space is not unique to Muslims. For many immigrant groups the experience of settlement in America was an ambiguous, if not dangerous, "errand into the wilderness."
2. The perception of America as an open space is not unique to Muslims. The discovery of America also resulted in a change in the orientation of Europeans who "considered Rome or Jerusalem to be the center of the earth." But "in 1492, when a 'new world' actually emerged," it "did not appear as a new enemy, but as *free space*" (Schmitt 2003, 87).
3. Imam Karoub is buried in Roseland Park Cemetery. When I later visited the cemetery, I read on his gravestone: "Rev. Imam Hussien Karoub— Leader of Islam in North America—born 1893 died 1973."
4. The five pillars are (1) testimony of faith, (2) five daily prayers, (3) fasting during the month of Ramadan, (4) almsgiving, and (5) pilgrimage to Mecca.
5. Mecca and the experience of hajj loom large in many convert narratives. One of the most famous Western converts is Muhammad Asad (formerly Leopold Weiss), who wrote about his conversion and experience in Mecca in *The Road to Mecca* (2000; originally published in 1954). For a more recent book on the conversion and hajj experiences of Westerners, including Muhammad Asad and Malcolm X, written by an American convert, see Michael Wolfe's *One Thousand Roads to Mecca* (1997).
6. There are many ways in which groups such as the Abrahamic religions of Judaism, Christianity, and Islam stress their distinctiveness with respect to one another. A list of the boundary work in which those monotheistic religions engage would include such practices as dietary laws (kosher and halal) and dress codes, including head covering for women and men.

7. "Anecdote of the Jar"

    > I placed a jar in Tennessee,
    > And round it was, upon a hill.
    > It made the slovenly wilderness
    > Surround that hill.
    >
    > The wilderness rose up to it,
    > And sprawled around, no longer wild.
    > The jar was round upon the ground
    > And tall and of a port in air.
    >
    > It took dominion everywhere.
    > The jar was gray and bare.
    > It did not give of bird or bush,
    > Like nothing else in Tennessee.

8. "Charisma" in its pre-Weberian religious use means a "gift of grace," and it refers to an incursion of the divine into everyday life. A spring of singularity and miracles, charisma therefore recognizes no established rule (Rieff 2007).

9. Durkheim used the concept of anomie primarily to refer to a condition of inadequate procedural rules or to a failure of rule development to keep pace with social change. This means that at the margins (frontiers) of social change we come across anomic space, where rules are absent. On closer inspection, Durkheim's two concepts of anomie refer to inadequacy or absence of nomos whether they are procedural rules (in *Division of Labor in Society*) or moral norms (in *Suicide*) (Olsen 1965).

10. Before Islam, the Kaaba was a sacred temple controlled by the pagan tribes of Arabia and the building was full of the idols they worshiped. Those idols were later removed by Prophet Muhammad after he took control of Mecca. The emptiness of the Kaaba is thus in itself a symbol of Islamic monotheism.

11. According to Heidegger, contemplation "is derived from *templum*, i.e., from [the name of] the place which can be seen from any point, and from which any point can be seen. The ancients called this place a *templum*" (1977, 166). Heidegger's insight was later developed by Henry Corbin in *Temple and Contemplation* (1986).

12. Samory Rashid argues against this common conclusion (Rashid 2004, 55).

13. Two organizations often referred to as representatives of proto-Islam in America are the Moorish Science Temple of Noble Drew Ali (1913) and the Nation of Islam (1930) led by Elijah Muhammad. Both organizations relied on a genealogical discourse and linked themselves to Muslim slaves and the history of Islam in Africa.

14. In Sunni tradition, the Prophet's companions have semisacred status as bearers of religious knowledge.

15. A recent commentary on the intersection of black and Muslim identities is Zaid Shakir's *Scattered Pictures: Reflections of an American Muslim* (2005, 63–76).

16. When Dawud Walid, the executive director of Council on American-Islamic Relations–Michigan, gave a lecture to the members of the Muslim Student Association on the University of Michigan campus in Ann Arbor (February 2, 2006), he structured his narrative about the Muslim *ummah* (community, nation) around the figure of Bilal as a way of bridging the divide between African American and immigrant Muslim communities.

17. Another parallel movement is the Rastafarian movement. For the competition between the Bilalian and the Rastafarian movements, see Mazrui 2004, 121.

18. Many Muslims have difficulties getting days off for holidays because they themselves do not know exactly when the holiday starts. They are torn between two calendars, two ways of partitioning time: solar and lunar. The lunar calendar, which has been marginalized in practical life by the hegemony of the solar calendar in the Christian era, resurfaces on special religious days. Although both solar and lunar calendars are ways of partitioning time, they slice time differently. As a consequence, there is always a certain disjuncture between the two. The debate over moon sighting among American Muslims constitutes another interesting avenue of exploration.

CHAPTER TWO

1. The only exception I am aware of is a two-page note in Metcalf 1994, xv.

2. Symbolic violence is not necessarily violence by other means. For example, what is symbolic violence in the act of name-calling? That the person is called a name that she does not want to be called is certainly a symbolic "violence." But the concept of symbolic violence refers not only to schoolyard taunts and racial name-calling but also to parental name-giving. Therefore, it may not be and usually is not perceived as something negative or harmful.

3. Bourdieu himself does not distinguish between the two types of symbolic violence presented here. The distinction between "constitutive" and "restrictive" types of symbolic violence is mine.

4. Durkheim used the concept to refer to the weakening or absence of normative standards in modern society (1951, 241). A narrowly understood concept in sociology, anomie etymologically means the absence of nomos.

5. I use the term "historical" here to draw attention to the historicity, contingency, and constructedness of these experiences rather than the obvious fact that they happened in the past, are in the way of becoming past, or both.

6. Abul Ala Mawdudi (1903–79) is the founder of Jamaat-e-Islami, a Muslim political party, in British India. Mawdudi's works are often to be found in

American Muslim mosque libraries. This holds true for African American mosques as well.

7. In a recent visit to the Muslim Center of Detroit, a predominantly African American mosque with a vibrant community and leadership, while checking the books on display and for sale after the Friday prayer I was not surprised to see Mawdudi's book *Toward Understanding Islam*.

8. As noted by Barbara Metcalf, "Islamic bookshops in Washington DC, Durban, London and Karachi will likely carry the same range of English books produced by English-speaking Muslims throughout the world" (1994, xv).

9. For an extended discussion of CAIR, see chapter 4. An extended profile of Walid is in chapter 5.

10. A. James, interview with Dawud Walid, *Muslim Observer*, January 6–12, 2006.

11. For example, English has been receiving particular attention from the US government. In an effort to combat Islamic extremism, the Bush administration seems to have engaged in promoting the English language. In 2003 the *Washington Post* reported the recent change in school curricula in Qatar as "more English, less Islam" (Susan Glasser, "Qatar Reshapes Its Schools, Putting English over Islam," *Washington Post*, February 2, 2003).

12. According to the British daily *The Independent*, within ten years half of the world will be speaking English (James Burleigh, "English to Be Spoken by Half of the World's Population within 10 Years," *The Independent*, December 9, 2004).

13. Many Muslims would object to the distinction between center and periphery for Islam since theologically the religion is not tied to any location. Nevertheless, the geographies where Islam has a recent presence despite its historical presence elsewhere can be defined as the periphery of Islam.

14. *Dawah* is the Arabic word for service and propagation of Islam. It is an important idiom in the discourse of English-speaking Muslims and an essential element in the repertoire of diasporic Islam.

15. Malaysian Muslim scholar Sayyid Muhammad Naquib al-Attas, along with many other Muslim scholars before him, classifies the learning of other languages as *fard kifayah* (a communal obligation), "which means that there has to be a certain number of educated Muslims who should master certain languages so that they can acquire the knowledge that could be obtained through those languages" (Mohd-Asraf 2005, 115).

16. A list of American-based Muslim thinkers who have influenced overseas Muslim intellectual life would include important scholars such as Seyyed Hossein Nasr and Fazlur Rahman.

17. Suhail Karmani, the editor of *TESOL Islamia*, an online journal, parodies this problem of "future tense" in an interesting essay, "Future Im-perfect" (2003a).

18. Most Muslims would object to the translation of *jihad* as "holy war." Similarly, Muslims would also prefer the use of the word mecca/Mecca only in a religious context.

19. Muslims initially used the labels and titles present in the mainstream culture. For example, the first Muslim mosque in Michigan (1921) was advertised as the "Muhammadan Prayer Hall." In other instances, mosques were called Moorish or Moslem "temples." Such titles were gradually replaced with "Islamic Center" or *masjid*, the Arabic word meaning "mosque." The evolution of names and titles provides an interesting illustration of the shift from the labels applied by someone else to one's own designation.

20. Credit for the successful codification of some Islamic vocabulary should go to the Nation of Islam (led by Elijah Muhammad and Malcolm X) and its successor, the American Muslim Mission (led by Warith Deen Mohammed). They successfully corrected the spelling and hence pronunciation of some major terms in the media. Old British uses such as "Moslem" and "Koran" were replaced by "Muslim" and "Qur'an." The latter are increasingly becoming the norm even while the former remain in use.

21. SoundVision's mission statement notes that "the attitudes and behavior of men and women today are shaped and molded by the media whose ideals and images, by and large, are non-Islamic. SoundVision aims to produce content with Islamic ideals and images for all current and future media. SoundVision would like to lead the *Ummah* in the field of communication, *Insha Allah*."

22. Laurie Goodstein, "U.S. Muslim Clerics Seek a Modern Middle Ground," *New York Times*, June 18, 2006.

23. For more on African American Muslims and their relationship to Christianity, see chapter 5.

24. Abdullah Yusuf Ali, *The Holy Qur'an* (1934); Muhammad Marmaduke Pickthall, *The Meaning of the Glorious Qur'an* (1938).

CHAPTER THREE

1. Home is a special kind of space: it is carved out of a general space and marked as exclusive; it is the surface upon which subjective construction of a world takes place. Our selves are anchored in the things around us. It is because of the intensity of this anchoredness that we often say "there's no place like home." Home is the place where the subjective (self) pours itself out in things (Levinas 1969, 153). Unlike the street (or city square), which is a public space presumably accessible to all citizens, home is not open to all. It is a topographically opaque spot on the surface of public space. On closer inspection, of course, we notice that the street is not open to everyone either: it is open only to citizens (similar to Habermasian public autonomy [Habermas 1996, 34] and the boundaries of nation). Yet it remains an intersubjective realm. By contrast, home is a subjective realm, an exclusive space corresponding to the private autonomy of the individual in liberal political philosophy (Arendt 1998). The private and public spheres are, respectively, subjective and intersubjective—that is, the domains of individuation and de-individuation.

2. An extreme case would be the situation of individuals kidnapped into slavery, which results in social death (Patterson 2005).

3. Islamic law is not necessarily state law. It is produced by jurists who are often outside the control of the state.

4. The Jewish religious idea of *eruv* stands between the Muslim idea of qibla and the notion of *dar al Islam*. An *eruv* is a symbolically appropriated place where space is codified and made—literally—navigable during the Sabbath. The single most important social function of the *eruv* is the creation of a communal domain through a religious marking of the public sphere. The *eruv* sets aside a portion of the public sphere and symbolically transforms it into a communal sphere (Rosen Zvi 2004; Cooper 1998).

5. American Muslim scholar Nuh Ha Mim Keller describes *darura* as vital interest: "How is it possible that the ruling of Allah could vary from place to place? One scholarly answer is found in the Islamic legal concept of *darura* or 'vital interest' that sometimes affects the *shari'a* rulings otherwise normally in force. Although the fundamental basis of Islamic law is that it is valid for all times and places, Allah Most High, in His divine wisdom, stipulates in Surat al-Hajj that *'He has not placed any hardship upon you in religion'*" (Qur'an 22:78) (Keller 1995).

6. Here is an illustration of a prosaic case of *darura*: if a Muslim is marooned on a desert island with nothing to eat but a ham sandwich, he or she may eat it.

7. A Shia handbook that I obtained from the Islamic Center of America in Dearborn, where it is used as a textbook for English-speaking youth and converts, addresses the issues of Muslim minorities in the West: "A believer is allowed to travel to non-Muslim countries provided that he is sure or feels confident that the journey would not have a negative impact on his faith. Similarly a believer is allowed to reside in non-Muslim countries provided that his residing there does not become a hurdle in the fulfillment of his or her religious obligations" (al-Hakim 1999, 42).

8. "During the early days of Islam, a number of Muslims took refuge in the non-Muslim land of Abyssinia in order to preserve their faith. This episode bears particular significance [to the situation of Muslim minorities today] because it occurred at a time when the foundations of Islamic law and *fiqh* [jurisprudence] were still being established" (al-Alwani 2003, 30–31).

9. Chapter 2, on qibla, also reveals the starting point of the canopy and its end point. Perhaps nowhere else do we have mosques with two qiblas but in Medina and Detroit.

10. In *Being and Time*, a phenomenological critique of the Cartesian division of the world, Heidegger argues that modern rationalism assumes "a worldless subject" (1962, 144) and ignores the idea of *worldhood*. As human beings, we are not self-contained subjects but entities in an existential state of Being-in (1962, 84). Unlike objects, we are always oriented; we are in the

world and we have a world. Our being in the world is quite different from a chair's being in the room (1962, 81). Our residence in the world is made possible by our involvement with it. While our relationship to our environment is one of encounter, that of two objects is not. They are in that sense worldless. Our practical experience of being-in-the-world is

> such that [our] Being-in-the-world has always dispersed itself or even split itself up into definite ways of Being-in. The multiplicity of these is indicated by the following examples: having to do with something, producing something, attending to something and looking after it, making use of something, giving something up and letting it go, undertaking, accomplishing, evincing, interrogating, considering, discussing, determining. . . . All these ways of Being-in have *concern* as their kind of Being. . . . Leaving undone, neglecting, renouncing, taking a rest—these too are ways of concern; but these are all *deficient* modes, in which the possibilities of concern are kept to a "bare minimum." (1962, 83)

In Heidegger's later thought, the idea of being-in-the world evolves into the concept of "dwelling." Once anchored, the subject can produce sustained interaction, which leads to habitualization and the construction of the world (Berger and Luckmann 1966). Heidegger's paragraph quoted above makes clear that there is an intimate link between dwelling and ethics. For being-in-the-world or dwelling is understood in terms of *care*, involvement, the disposition that allows something to matter to us. Dwelling situates us in a world, not in the sense in which a chair is *in* a room, but rather in the sense in which someone is *in* a family or *in* love with someone else (Foltz 1995, 156). To put it in more familiar sociological terms, Bourdieu's notion of habitus is a simple inversion of Heidegger's notion of dwelling. Dwelling is *us in the world* and habitus is *the world in us*. Thus, as a term that captures both habit and ethos, "habitus" has dwelling as its history. Ethics develops through involvement with the environment. In that sense, there is a homology between the degree of involvement and the nature of the ethics (or ideology) one has toward that environment. This will be further illustrated in the case of Muslims in America, where different degrees of involvement with American habitat are linked to different conceptions of America, ranging from the abode of war (*dar al harb*) to the abode of Islam (*dar al Islam*).

11. A note on transliteration: Except for *jihad*, these terms have no standard transliterations. The reason we have a standard transliteration for *jihad* is that, thanks to mass media and global terrorism, it has "settled," or sedimented, in the English language, albeit—Muslims believe—with some distortion. The same cannot be said for the other words, which can be spelled *hijrah*, *umma*, or *daawah* (or *da'wah*), respectively. I am using the most common spellings. For an extended discussion of the fate of Islamic terms in relation to English, see chapter 2.

12. *Medina* is both the Arabic word for "city" and the root of *madaniyyah*, "civilization."

13. The author of *Jihad vs. McWorld*, for example, notes that "while for many Muslims it may signify only ardor in the name of a religion that can properly be regarded as universalizing, I borrow its meaning from those militants who make the slaughter of the 'other' a higher duty" (Barber 1996, 17).

14. The list of Muslim immigrant topoi can be extended to include tropes like *ijtihad*, which refers to the mechanism for new codification and extension of the Islamic juridical canopy so that it includes new legal cases. Put more simply, *ijtihad* is the seeking of the reasonable ruling in the face of new situations.

15. Recent Muslim perspectives on this subject include calls for a generalized *darura* and reclamation of alternative juridical concepts. "Perhaps, in modern times, it is more precise to speak of '*asr al-darura*' (time of necessity) instead of *dar al-darura*, since for Muslims, to a great extent, living under *darura* conditions has become the norm in the global village and is more associated with the *Zeitgeist* rather than the geographical locality of one's residence" (Yilmaz 2002, 39).

16. It would be interesting to compare early American frontier discourse with the Muslim discourse depicting America as frontier. My intuition tells me that the association of the frontier with chaos, the devil, and risk is a common thread in both cases. A topic not much discussed and yet worthy of noting here is that certain threads in the discussion of Muslim presence in America portray Islam and Muslims as a "frontier within" that needs to be (re)moved and pushed back. The calls for internment of Muslims and the alarmist idea of an "enemy within" espoused by some conservative pundits illustrate the persistence of frontier discourse in its postterritorial forms.

17. The same can be said for the perspective of some of the Muslims in Europe. In Tariq Ramadan's words, such Muslims are "living in Europe out of Europe. To avoid being absorbed into Western societies, they have found a refuge within community life. . . . The aim is to be 'at home,' *in Europe but at home*" (2002, 186; italics in original).

18. Oil-producing countries like Saudi Arabia had disproportionate ideological influence during the early decades of Muslim immigration to the United States.

19. Sayyid Qutb, chief ideologue of the Muslim Brotherhood, visited and spent two years in the United States in 1948–50. Upon his return to Egypt he wrote an essay, "The America I Have Seen," in which America represented everything that Islam was not (Qutb 2000). One section of the piece bears the title "America: The Peak of Advancement and the Depth of Primitiveness."

20. I have chosen to suppress the name of the mosque and refer to its imam by a pseudonym in deference to his concerns about publicity. He also

expressed reluctance at the idea of recording the interview. The dialogue is based on my notes taken during our conversation.

21. A movement in Sunni Islam, Salafism seeks to restore the golden age of Islam by purging what it perceives to be later cultural influences and innovations. This simplistic conception of Islam is a modern form of Puritanism.

22. Although the imam and his mosque identify themselves as *salafi*, not all *salafi* imams would hold these ideas. The development of diplomatic language among immigrant imams and community leaders is an interesting thread for further research.

23. This Qur'anic injunction charges Muslims with the responsibility of changing their environment in a positive way. It lends itself to multiple interpretations. Some groups use it as a justification for interventionist, authoritarian practices, while others (e.g., many African American Muslim groups) consider it an Islamic basis for social justice work.

24. As a matter of fact, the transformation that Shakir has personally experienced and that partly represents the trend in the Muslim community can be observed clearly in two interviews that Shakir gave to Bill Moyers of PBS on January 18, 2002, and on June 22, 2007.

25. In my discussion, while talking about the cultural settlement of Islam in the United States, I take the liberty of drawing on the European perspective. This is not because I treat both cases under the general rubric of Western Islam—although that would be fully justified—but because intellectual discourses circulate back and forth across the Atlantic and need to be analyzed in conversation with each other. A simple illustration of this is the attempt on the part of Notre Dame University to hire Tariq Ramadan, which created enthusiasm among the new generation of American Muslims and stirred a debate on academic freedom when the State Department revoked Ramadan's visa on obscure grounds and denied him entry to the United States in 2004.

26. "Wherever a Muslim, saying 'I testify that there is no god but God and that Muhammad is His Messenger' is in security and able to perform his/her fundamental religious duties, he/she is *at home* for the prophet taught us that the whole world is a mosque" (Ramadan 2002, 144; italics in original).

27. I should note that the change of political orientation is still ongoing. There has been a shift in the American Muslim "political qibla" from Jerusalem to Washington, from the question of Palestine to domestic American Muslim issues.

28. A Danish newspaper, the *Jyllands-Posten*, published twelve highly unflattering cartoons of Prophet Muhammad, which provoked responses in the Muslim world that ranged from a boycott of Danish goods to violent street protests, including the torching of the Danish embassy in Syria.

29. For more on Muslim comedians, see chapter 6.

CHAPTER FOUR

1. Iqbal's testimony was also distributed to the audience as a handout.

CHAPTER FIVE

1. Along the same lines, conservative talk radio hosts have echoed Ann Coulter's call to "invade their countries, kill their leaders, and convert them to Christianity."

2. Muslims themselves are increasingly becoming aware of the negative consequences of the confusion over the equivalence between Allah and God. Community leaders frequently lecture on how to present the community to the larger public. At an event with the theme "Presenting Islam to Fellow Americans" held on February 23, 2008, at the Islamic Center of America (organized by CAIR–Michigan and the Young Muslim Association, the youth organization of the Islamic Center of America), Dawud Walid recommended that his audience "keep Islamic nomenclature to the bare minimum. Don't use too many Islamic terms. Say 'God' instead of 'Allah.'"

3. "War of Words," *ABC News*, June 5, 2002.

4. "But It's Thomas Jefferson's Koran," *Washington Post*, January 3, 2007.

5. The diversity of the Muslim community is bewildering. Muslims in the Detroit area are divided along ethnic, sectarian, racial, and temporal lines. Some of these mosques are predominantly Iraqi, Lebanese, Yemeni, Bangladeshi, Bosnian, Albanian, Indo-Pakistani, African American, or immigrant African. Some of them are well-established communities, while others are not-yet-settled, diasporic communities (e.g., the Senegalese Mourids). Some of them are proud to be American and display their pride through flags and critique of Muslim cultures overseas; others are too new to know whether they should be proud or how to show it. While immigrant mosques and imams authenticate themselves through the English language and American flags, some African American mosques and imams authenticate themselves through conspicuous use of Arabic vocabulary and displays of green flags with crescent and star. Some mosques are interested in interfaith activities; some are not. Some can afford to do such work; others cannot.

6. In some of my visits, I was with colleagues from the Building Islam in Detroit Project, a program initiated by Andrew Shryock and Sally Howell to document various aspects of Detroit mosque cultures. The program has produced a traveling exhibition; information is available at http://biid.lsa.umich.edu.

7. In addition to the usual Sunday school and other religious courses, the center offers various recreational activities, including women's aerobics classes and a Ladies Badminton Club.

8. See http://ca.cair.com/losangeles/news/calif._muslims_launch_eid_radio _ads (last accessed in 2007).

9. At a talk given to a predominantly non-Muslim audience on a college campus, Najah Bazzy (borrowing the language of cell phone ads, which were cluttering the airwaves at the time) compared the Sunni and Shia schools of Islam to the "friends" and "family" plans. During my interview, I told her that I liked this distinction and asked whether one could apply it to the two options available to Muslims for accommodation in American society. I asked which plan she would prefer, Abrahamic (family plan) or liberal pluralism (friends plan). She replied:

> Well, I would say that I would prefer the family plan of Abrahamic faith with an invitation to friends, a true invitation to friends. I think if it's just the family plan it's not good, it's almost coercion in faith. If it's just the friends plan, I think we're in serious trouble. Very serious trouble because then you lose moral authority. Core values that our society needs. So I do think the foundation needs to be belief in one God and then even, really, a closer examination of Hinduism and of Sikhism; . . . they're still rooted in the concept of one God. They really are. You know, they might have different variations of how to worship that God, but you know for the most part they're all tied to one Creator, the Divine Creator.

CHAPTER SIX

1. There is an interesting connection between earthquakes and laughter. "One study reported that survivors of the San Francisco earthquake laughed at the slightest provocation" (Brottman 2004, 76).

2. "Sometimes on the street," says Azhar Usman, "I say to people, 'Relax. I am Muslim but I am an American Muslim. I consider myself a very patriotic American Muslim, which means I would die for this country—by blowing myself up—inside a Dunkin' Donuts.'"

3. It is important to remember the well-known distinction between an accent or a dialect and a language. An accent is an accent only in relation to a language. What is crucial here is that the language itself is just another accent: the official, standard accent. Bourdieu (1991, 45) has aptly drawn attention to the relationship between linguistic and political unifications. An accent is imperfect and thus funny only from the point of view of the official accent (language).

4. Neil MacFarquhar, "Sitcom's Precarious Premise: Being Muslim over Here," *New York Times*, December 7, 2006.

5. The series premiere attracted 2.09 million viewers, an impressive number for Canada, where a show with an audience of 1 million is considered a

runaway hit. The CBC reported that it had not had a show draw an audience of that size in a decade (*"Little Mosque* Defuses Hate with Humor," *New York Times*, January 16, 2007).

6. Nawaz's first short film bears the title *BBQ Muslims* (1996) and is inspired by her anger at the finger-pointing at Muslims in the aftermath of the Oklahoma City bombing in 1995. In this short film, two Muslim brothers are suspected of being Middle Eastern terrorists after their backyard barbecue explodes. A radio news announcer says, at the start of the film, "This bombing has all the markings of Muslim fundamentalists: a large hole in the ground, charred grass and dead animals."

7. A dimension of the emergence of Muslim comedy that we cannot neglect is the creation of various Muslim media where a dispersed community finds a common public sphere. Of particular note is the launch of Bridges TV in 2004, the first Muslim American television channel in English. Muslim comedians are a staple of Bridges TV. In addition to Bridges TV, the Muslim community is experiencing a proliferation of online and print magazines and weeklies such as the *Muslim Observer* (published in Detroit, Michigan). Muslim comedians, and the Muslim minority in general, are also taking advantage of the revolutionary opportunities offered by new media such as YouTube. Most rising comedians are still local and they use venues like YouTube to reach audiences. Both AMMF and AOE also have pages on virtual networking sites like Facebook and MySpace and during live performances make a point of inviting their fans to visit their pages.

8. *Allah Made Me Funny: The Official Muslim Comedy Tour 2008 Program*, February 15, 2008, p. 5.

9. There is a growing literature on "racialization" of Arab and Muslim Americans after 9/11. For a notable example, see Jamal and Naber 2008.

10. Elsewhere, Azhar Usman complains about such uncles' tendency to brag about the number of Muslims in the United States: "We have these uncles in the community who are always bragging about it. [*He puts on an Indian accent*] 'We have seven million Muslims in America. Can you imagine, Bob?'" Azhar continues: "Right! The funny thing is that he is bragging about it to his friend at work: 'Can you believe it, Bob? Seven million Muslims in America?' He thinks Bob is impressed. Bob is not impressed. Bob is scared!!"

11. Here is Victor Turner's definition of antistructure: "Liminality, the optimal setting of communitas relations, and communitas, a spontaneously generated relationship between leveled and equal total and individuated human beings, stripped of structural attributes, together constitute what one might call 'anti-structure'" (1973, 216).

12. Maysoon Zayid, a Palestinian American comedian from New Jersey, describes how she hates flying out of Newark airport. "I have cerebral palsy," says Zayid, "so when I walk in, security doesn't just see an Arab. They see

a shaking Arab. 'She's nervous!' And I'm afraid of flying so I'm crying. So now, I'm a crying, shaking Arab. 'She's guilty!'"

13. According to a statement released on March 11, 2004, by the Transportation Security Agency, "in January (2004) a 21-year-old woman was jailed for joking about bombs in her luggage." The TSA Press Office website sternly reminds passengers not to joke at the airport (http://www.tsa.gov /press/releases/2004/press_release_0401.shtm).

14. For the purposes of this chapter, I do not distinguish between comedy, humor, and laughter. Although there are some nuances in usage, I will not engage in a terminological discussion here due to my special focus on "ethnic comedy" and limitations of space.

15. It is worth noting that the theoretical affinities between Simmel and Elias are not accidental. Elias (together with Kurt H. Wolff) studied under Karl Mannheim, who in turn was a student of Simmel's.

16. As Randall Collins points out, "Sociological theory does not pay enough attention to the dynamics of processes over time. We tend to be stuck in a meta-theoretical dichotomy between static comparisons of how structures hang together and an actor-centered view of fluid action. But processes have shapes in time, patterns of intensity, rapid shifts, and gradual declines, which sweep people up at one moment and bring them down at another" (2004, 53).

17. Bourdieu, in his *The Weight of the World*, for example, shows how people of different class and location backgrounds have incongruent views of the world (Bourdieu et al. 2000).

18. Heidegger argues that "the word *techne* denotes rather a mode of knowing. To know means to have seen, in the widest sense of seeing, which means to apprehend what is present, as such. For Greek thought the nature of knowing consists in *aletheia*, that is, in the uncovering of beings. *Techne*, as knowledge experienced in the Greek manner, is a bringing forth of beings in that it *brings forth* present beings as such beings *out of* concealedness" (1971, 75).

19. Alfred Schutz (1962) also pays particular attention to the importance of *relevance* in the constitution of our (multiple) worlds.

20. Azhar Usman describes this experience with an almost existentialist punch line: "The worst thing is that they constantly repeat: 'Please report any suspicious activity; please report any suspicious individuals.' Well, I am at the airport at this corner. I thought I saw this guy. He looks shady. I called the security guy; he said, 'Sir, you are looking at the mirror.'" Here Usman takes on the gaze/vision of the majority (the objective culture, that is to say, the subjective culture of the majority) and sees himself as an other. As himself (Usman-in-himself) he sees the anxiety and gaze of the others, but when he participates in the act of seeing like the majority, he turns himself into an object. Reflection in the mirror reflects the objectified subject.

Usman's joke is also Lacanian in pointing to a mirror stage for Muslim ethnic selfhood in America.

21. We can appropriate the notion of "fusion of horizons" (Gadamer 2004) here as "fusion of visions." The fusion of visions happens when the "events" (i.e., the facticity generated by 9/11) are given meaning through interpretation.

22. What remains is actually mainstream comedy still labeled as ethnic, as in the case of Jewish and African American comedy in the United States, where the ideas of mainstream and ethnic become hard to disentangle.

23. As forms of return to immediacy, both laughing and crying are underappreciated phenomena that give access to our existential nature (Plessner 1970).

CONCLUSION

1. Direction involves bodily disposition, but the turning of the heart toward Mecca is not just about the body. Similarly, the determination of qibla, arrived at via an agonistic process, is a struggle that cannot be reduced to a competition for power (symbolic or otherwise), as Bourdieu's analysis asks us to believe. In addition to this reduction of all struggles to competition, Bourdieu's approach is being undermined by another recent problem: today there is a body overload in the social sciences. The body is burdened with too much work.

The body is neither a corpse to be dragged to and fro in the service of the mind, nor is it the autonomous source and surface of practices. The corporeal turn in the social sciences needs to be freed from these two extremes. In part, the problem stems from a misunderstanding of Bourdieu's notion of habitus. Its anti-Cartesian quality—that is, its not being cognitive—is frequently understood to mean that it is simply about the body. Not being cognitive is reduced to corporeality or carnality. While metaphorically the contrast between body and mind invites such an emphasis, the non-Cartesian conception of habitus is not simply a reference to the body but includes mental presuppositions and anything mind-related that is not intentional, deliberate. It should also include things beyond both mind and body such as inspiration (about which more later). Too much emphasis on the body shows that we are still stuck on the Cartesian subject.

Interest in the body as an object of social scientific inquiry is thus valuable but also misguided. The impression is that, with the discovery of the body, the ground on which mental activity takes place has been revealed and the excavation of the so-called subject is complete. On the contrary, we are still vacillating between the Cartesian angel and the Cartesian animal. We have still not fully arrived at the human, which is not only "both" but "more than" both. Should we not instead be looking into the Pascalian "heart"?

2. The human being is the terrible one (*deinon*), the uncanny. He terrorizes, for he holds sway over other beings (Heidegger 2000, 161; Nietzsche 1967, 43). Terrorism is only one manifestation of human character. Sociologists have known since Durkheim that crime exists only against the background of law. We noncriminals remain terrorizers in that we exert terror, but we do it in directions approved by the law: in work (as builders and demolishers), in the army (as killers of the enemy), in speech (as generators of symbolic violence), at the dinner table (as consumers of animals), and so on. The terrorist is merely our naked and criminal form—the same wind blowing in the wrong direction. Most of our actions (and all action is violence) are not perceived as violent or terroristic because they blow in the direction of the law.

3. Here external constraint is on the path to becoming an internal self-constraint where the self will be released into new boundaries (Elias 1994a, 493, 468). And here too lies the origin of "responsibility," whether it is Freud's famous superego or Nietzsche's infamous "bad conscience" (1967, 59).

4. *New York Times*, June 2, 2009.

5. This is how Germany was brought into Europe after the terror of World War II by the strong embrace of France and others in the form of the European Coal and Steel Community. The resistant object (Germany) was appropriated and transcended in the form of a supranational organization. Europeans who were terrorized by Germany now could feel relief from the prospects of another war. Eventually they weakened their borders and dissolved into each other (creating the European Union, adopting the euro, etc.).

6. "And in what way then have I attained this knowledge, which I have this dim remembrance of acquiring? Have I, impelled by a burning desire of knowledge, toiled on through uncertainty, doubt and contradiction?—have I, when any belief was presented to me, withheld my assent until I had examined and reexamined, sifted and compared it,—until an inward voice proclaimed to me, irresistibly and without the possibility of doubt—'Thus it is—thus only—as surely as thou livest and art!'—No! I remember no such state of mind. Those instructions were bestowed on me before I sought them, the answers were given before I had put the questions. I heard, for I could not avoid doing so, and what was taught me remained in my memory just as chance had disposed it;—without examination and without interest I allowed everything to take its place in my mind" (Fichte 1910, 2).

7. In her extraordinary book, Saba Mahmood (2005) criticizes the presumed universalism of certain ethics in liberal feminism. The problem of moral universalism can be found even in theorists of practice who oppose the egoism in moralistic universalism (Bourdieu 2000, 65). Bourdieu, to whom the discipline of sociology owes a great deal for historicizing reason, fails to question a recently universalized modern obsession: power.

Bibliography

Abdali, S. Kamal. 1978. *Prayer Schedules for North America*. Indianapolis: American Trust Publications.
———. 1997. "The Correct Qibla." www.patriot.net/users/abdali
/ftp/qibla.pdf (last accessed on August 15, 2006).
Abdallah, Umar Faruq. 2004. "One God, Many Names." Working
paper, Nawawi Foundation, Chicago.
———. 2006. *A Muslim in Victorian America: The Life of Alexander
Russell Webb*. Oxford: Oxford University Press.
Abdo, Geneive. 2006. *Mecca and Main Street: Muslim Life in America
after 9/11*. Oxford: Oxford University Press.
Abraham, Nabeel. 2000. "Arab Detroit's 'American' Mosque." In
Arab Detroit: From Margin to Mainstream, edited by Nabeel
Abraham and Andrew Shryock. Detroit: Wayne State Univer-
sity Press.
Abraham, Nabeel, and Andrew Shryock, eds. 2000. *Arab Detroit:
From Margin to Mainstream*. Detroit: Wayne State University
Press.
Agamben, Giorgio. 1998. *Homo Sacer: Sovereign Power and Bare Life*.
Translated by D. Heller-Roazen. Stanford, CA: Stanford Uni-
versity Press.
———. 2005. *State of Exception*. Translated by K. Attell. Chicago:
University of Chicago Press.
———. 2009. *What Is an Apparatus? And Other Essays*. Palo Alto,
CA: Stanford University Press.
Ahmed, Akbar. 2010. *Journey into America: The Challenge of Islam*.
Washington, DC: Brookings Institution Press.
Alexander, Jeffrey C. 2004. "Toward a Theory of Cultural Trauma."
In *Cultural Trauma and Collective Identity*, by Jeffrey C. Alex-
ander et al. Berkeley and Los Angeles: University of California
Press.

Ali, Abdullah Yusuf. 1987. *The Holy Qur'an*. Elmhurst, NY: Tahrike Tarsile Qur'an.

Allah Made Me Funny: The Official Muslim Comedy Tour. 2005. Produced by Francisco Aguilar and Jaime Valdonado. DVD.

Alwani, Taha Jabir al-. 2003. *Towards a* Fiqh *for Minorities: Some Basic Reflections*. London: International Institute of Islamic Thought.

Anderson, Benedict. 1991. *Imagined Communities*. Rev. ed. London: Verso.

———. 1998. *The Spectre of Comparisons: Nationalism, Southeast Asia and the World*. London: Verso Press.

Arendt, Hannah. 1973. *The Origins of Totalitarianism*. New ed. with added prefaces. San Diego: Harcourt, Brace.

———. 1998. *The Human Condition*. 1958. Reprint, Chicago: University of Chicago Press.

Argungu, Dahiru M. 1996. "English, Muslims and Islamization: Between Needs and Deeds." In *English and Islam: Creative Encounters '96*, edited by Jalal Uddin Khan and Adrian Hare. Kuala Lumpur, Malaysia: Research Center, IIUM.

Armstrong, Karen. 2006. *Muhammad: A Prophet for Our Time*. New York: HarperCollins.

Asad, Muhammad. 2000. *The Road to Mecca*. Louisville, KY: Fons Vitae.

Aspers, Patrik. 2010. "The Second Road to Phenomenological Sociology: Socio-ontology and the Question of Order." *Society* 3 (47): 214–19.

Atran, Scott. 2010. *Talking to the Enemy*. New York: HarperCollins.

Austin, Allan D. 1997. *African Muslims in Antebellum America: Transatlantic Stories and Spiritual Struggles*. New York: Routledge.

The Axis of Evil Comedy Tour. 2007. Image Entertainment. DVD.

Badiou, Alain. 2006. *Being and Event*. New York: Continuum.

Bagby, Ihsan, et al. 2001. *The Mosque in America: A National Portrait*. Washington, DC: Council on American Islamic Relations.

Bail, Christopher. 2008. "The Configuration of Symbolic Boundaries against Immigrants in Europe." *American Sociological Review* 73 (1): 37–59.

Bakalian, Anny P., and Mehdi Bozorgmehr. 2009. *Backlash 9/11: Middle Eastern and Muslim Americans Respond*. Berkeley and Los Angeles: University of California Press.

Baker, Wayne, and Andrew Shryock. 2009. "Citizenship and Crisis." In *Citizenship and Crisis: Arab Detroit after 9/11*. New York: Russell Sage Foundation.

Bakhtin, Mikhail. 1968. *Rabelais and His World*. Cambridge, MA: MIT Press.

Balibar, Etienne. 2004. *We, the People of Europe? Reflections on Transnational Citizenship*. Princeton, NJ: Princeton University Press.

Barber, Benjamin R. 1996. *Jihad vs. McWorld*. New York: Ballantine Books.

Barrett, Paul M. 2007. *American Islam: The Struggle for the Soul of a Religion*. New York: Farrar, Straus and Giroux.

Bashear, Suliman. 1991. "*Qibla Musharriqa* and Early Muslim Prayer in Churches." *Muslim World* 81 (3–4): 267–82.

Ba-Yunus, Ilyas, and Kassim Kone. 2003. "Muslim Americans: A Demographic Report." In *Muslims' Place in the American Public Square: Hope, Fears, and*

Aspirations, edited by Zahid H. Bukhari et al. Walnut Creek, CA: AltaMira Press.

Beg, Mirza A. 2008. "America Is Our Home." www.americanmuslimforum.org (last accessed on April 10, 2008).

Bellah, Robert, et al. 1985. *Habits of the Heart: Middle America Observed*. London: Hutchinson.

Benhabib, Seyla. 2004. *The Rights of Others: Aliens, Residents, and Citizens*. Cambridge: Cambridge University Press.

Berger, Peter L. 1969. *The Sacred Canopy: Elements of a Sociological Theory of Religion*. New York: Anchor Books.

———. 1997. *Redeeming Laughter: The Comic Dimension of Human Experience*. Berlin: Walter de Gruyter.

Berger, Peter L., Brigitte Berger, and Hansfried Kellner. 1974. *The Homeless Mind: Modernization and Consciousness*. New York: Vintage Press.

Berger, Peter L., and Thomas Luckmann. 1966. *The Social Construction of Reality: A Treatise in the Sociology of Knowledge*. New York: Anchor Books.

Bergmann, Martin. 1999. "The Psychoanalysis of Humor and Humor in Psychoanalysis." In *Humor and Psyche: Psychoanalytic Perspectives*, edited by James W. Barron. Hillsdale, NJ: Analytic Press.

Bilici, Mucahit. 2010. "Being Targeted, Being Recognized: The Impact of 9/11 on Arab and Muslim Americans." *Contemporary Sociology* 40 (2): 133–37.

Bin Bayyah, Abdullah. 1999. "Muslims Living in Non-Muslim Lands." Speech delivered in Santa Clara, CA, July 31. www.zaytuna.org.

Bosniak, Linda. 2006. *The Citizen and the Alien: Dilemmas of Contemporary Membership*. Princeton, NJ: Princeton University Press.

Bourdieu, Pierre. 1984. *Distinction: A Social Critique of the Judgement of Taste*. Cambridge, MA: Harvard University Press.

———. 1986. "The Forms of Capital." In *Handbook of Theory and Research for the Sociology of Education*, edited by John G. Richardson. New York: Greenwood Press.

———. 1990. *The Logic of Practice*. Stanford, CA: Stanford University Press.

———. 1991. *Language and Symbolic Power*. Cambridge, MA: Harvard University Press.

———. 1998. *Practical Reason*. Palo Alto, CA: Stanford University Press.

———. 2000. *Pascalian Meditations*. Translated by R. Nice. Stanford, CA: Stanford University Press.

———. 2004. "The Peasant and His Body." *Ethnography* 5(4): 579–99.

Bourdieu, Pierre, et al. 2000. *The Weight of the World: Social Suffering in Contemporary Society*. Stanford, CA: Stanford University Press.

Braziel, Jana E., and Anita Mannur. 2003. *Theorizing Diaspora: A Reader*. Malden, MA: Wiley-Blackwell.

Brottman, Mikita. 2004. *Funny Peculiar: Gershon Legman and the Psychopathology of Humor*. Hillsdale, NJ: Analytic Press.

Brown, Adam. 1996. "The Treatment of Religious Terminology in English

Dictionaries." In *English and Islam: Creative Encounters '96*, edited by Jalal Uddin Khan and Adrian Hare. Kuala Lumpur, Malaysia: Research Center, IIUM.

Brubaker, Rogers. 2004. *Ethnicity without Groups*. Cambridge, MA: Harvard University Press.

———. 2005. "The 'Diaspora' Diaspora." *Ethnic and Racial Studies* 28 (1): 1–19.

Bukhari, Zahid H., et al, eds. 2003. *Muslims' Place in the American Public Square: Hope, Fears, and Aspirations*. Walnut Creek, CA: AltaMira Press.

Cainkar, Louise. 2009. *Homeland Insecurity: The Arab American and Muslim American Experience after 9/11*. New York: Russell Sage Foundation.

Casanova, José. 1994. *Public Religions in the Modern World*. Chicago: University of Chicago Press.

———. 2007. "Immigration and the New Religious Pluralism: An EU/U.S. Comparison." In *Democracy and the New Religious Pluralism*, edited by Thomas Banchoff. Oxford: Oxford University Press.

Cesari, Jocelyne. 2004. *When Islam and Democracy Meet: Muslims in Europe and in the United States*. New York: Palgrave Macmillan.

Chittick, William C. 2007. *Ibn 'Arabi: Heir to the Prophets*. Oxford: Oneworld Publications.

Cole, David. 2005. *Enemy Aliens: Double Standards and Constitutional Freedoms in the War on Terrorism*. New York: New Press.

Collins, Randall. 2004. "Rituals of Solidarity and Security in the Wake of Terrorist Attack." *Sociological Theory* 22 (1): 53–87.

cooke, miriam, and Bruce Lawrence. 2005. *Muslim Networks from Hajj to Hip Hop*. Chapel Hill: University of North Carolina Press.

Cooper, Davina. 1998. *Governing Out of Order: Space, Law and the Politics of Belonging*. London: Rivers Oram.

Corbin, Henry. 1986. *Temple and Contemplation*. N.p.: Kegan Paul.

Crane, Robert Dickson. 1997. *Shaping the Future: Challenge and Response*. N.p.: Tapestry.

Curtis, Edward E. 2009. *Muslims in America: A Short History*. New York: Oxford University Press.

Dannin, Robert. 2002a. *Black Pilgrimage to Islam*. Oxford: Oxford University Press.

———. 2002b. "The Greatest Migration?" In *Muslim Minorities in the West: Visible and Invisible*, edited by Yvonne Yazbeck Haddad and Jane I. Smith. Walnut Creek, CA: AltaMira Press.

"A Decade of Growth." 2004. CAIR Tenth Anniversary Report, 1994–2004. Washington, DC.

de Certeau, Michel. 1984. *The Practice of Everyday Life*. Translated by Steven Rendall. Berkeley and Los Angeles: University of California Press.

Deleuze, Gilles. 1992. "Postscript on the Societies of Control." *OCTOBER* 59:3–7.

Delgado-Moreira, Juan M. 1997. "Cultural Citizenship and the Creation of European Identity." *Electronic Journal of Sociology*, vol. 002.003.

Denny, Frederick Mathewson. 1994. "Islamic Theology in the New World: Some

Issues and Prospects." *Journal of the American Academy of Religion* 62 (4): 1069–84.

Derrida, Jacques. 1980. "Structure, Sign, and Play in the Discourse of Human Sciences." In *Writing and Difference*, translated by Alan Bass. Chicago: University of Chicago Press.

Dilthey, Wilhelm. 1962. *Pattern and Meaning in History.* New York: Harper Torchbooks.

Diouf, Sylviane A. 1998. *Servants of Allah: African Muslims Enslaved in the Americas.* New York: New York University Press.

Douglas, Mary. 1966. *Purity and Danger: An Analysis of Concepts of Pollution and Taboo.* New York: Praeger.

———. 1975. *Implicit Meanings: Essays in Anthropology.* London: Routledge.

Dreyfus, Hubert L. 1984. "Beyond Hermeneutics: Interpretation in Later Heidegger and Recent Foucault." In *Hermeneutics: Questions and Prospects*, edited by Gary Shapiro and Alan Sica. Amherst: University of Massachusetts Press.

———. 1991. *Being-in-the-World: A Commentary on Heidegger's "Being and Time, Division I."* Cambridge, MA: MIT Press.

Durkheim, Emile. 1951. *Suicide.* New York: Free Press.

———. 1995. *The Elementary Forms of Religious Life.* New York: Free Press.

———. 1997. *The Division of Labor in Society.* New York: Free Press.

Duyvendak, Jan Willem. 2011. *The Politics of Home: Belonging and Nostalgia in Western Europe and the United States.* New York: Palgrave Macmillan.

El Fadl, Khaled Abou. 2005. *The Great Theft: Wrestling Islam from the Extremists.* New York: HarperOne.

Elias, Norbert. 1994a. *The Civilizing Process: The Sociogenetic and Psychogenetic Investigations.* Oxford: Blackwell.

———. 1994b. *The Established and the Outsiders: A Sociological Enquiry into Community Problems.* 2nd ed. London: Sage Publications.

Elkholy, Abdo A. 1966. *The Arab Moslems in the United States: Religion and Assimilation.* New Haven, CT: College and University Press.

Fanon, Frantz. 1967. *Black Skin, White Masks.* New York: Grove Press.

Faruqi, Ismail Raji al-. 1962. *Urubah and Religion: A Study of the Fundamental Ideas of Arabism and of Islam as Its Highest Moment of Consciousness.* Amsterdam: Djambatan.

———, ed. 1982. *Trialogue of the Abrahamic Faiths.* Beltsville, MD: Amana Publications.

———. 1986. *Toward Islamic English.* Ann Arbor, MI: New Era Publications.

Fichte, Johann Gottlieb. 1910. *The Vocation of Man.* 1800. Translated by William Smith. Chicago: Open Court.

Fine, Gary A. 1998. Review of *Redeeming Laughter: The Comic Dimension of Human Experience*, by Peter L. Berger. *Contemporary Sociology* 27 (4): 383–85.

Foltz, Bruce. 1995. *Inhabiting the Earth: Heidegger, Environmental Ethics, and the Metaphysics of Nature.* Atlantic Highlands, NJ: Humanities Press.

Foner, Nancy. 2005. *Wounded City: The Social Impact of 9/11*. New York: Russell Sage Foundation.

Foucault, Michel. 1977. *Discipline and Punish: The Birth of the Prison*. Translated by Alan Sheridan. London: Penguin Books.

———. 1980. *Power/Knowledge: Selected Interviews and Other Writings, 1972–1977*. Edited by Colin Gordon. New York: Pantheon Books.

———. 1991. "Governmentality." In *The Foucault Effect: Studies in Governmentality*, edited by Colin Gordon, Graham Burchell, and Peter Miller. Chicago: University of Chicago Press.

———. 2003. *The Essential Foucault*. Edited by P. Rabinow and N. Rose. New York: The New Press.

———. 2005. *The Hermeneutics of the Subject: Lectures at the College de France, 1981–1982*. Translated by Graham Burchell. New York: Palgrave Macmillan.

Freud, Sigmund. 1961. *Civilization and Its Discontents*. Standard ed. New York: Norton.

———. 2003. *The Uncanny*. London: Penguin Books.

Frisby, David, and Mike Featherstone, eds. 1997. *Simmel on Culture: Selected Writings*. London: Sage Publications.

Fuchs, Stephan. 2001. *Against Essentialism: A Network Theory of Culture and Society*. Cambridge, MA: Harvard University Press.

Gadamer, Hans-Georg. 2004. *Truth and Method*. Translated by J. Weinsheimer and D. Marshall. New York: Continuum.

Garot, Robert. 2010. *Who You Claim: Performing Gang Identity in School and on the Streets*. New York: New York University Press.

Ghamari-Tabrizi, Behrooz. 2004. "Loving America and Longing for Home: Ismail al-Faruqi and the Emergence of the Muslim Diaspora in North America." *International Migration* 42:61–86.

GhaneaBassiri, Kambiz. 2010. *A History of Islam in America*. Cambridge: Cambridge University Press.

Glaeser, Andreas. 1999. *Divided in Unity: Identity, Germany, and the Berlin Police*. Chicago: University of Chicago Press.

Gordon, Colin. 1987. "The Soul of the Citizen." In *Max Weber, Rationality and Modernity*, edited by Scott Lash and Sam Whimster. London: Allen and Unwin, 1987.

Gottdiener, Mark. 2001. *Life in the Air: Surviving the New Culture of Air Travel*. Lanham, MD: Rowman and Littlefield.

Habermas, Jurgen. 1987. *The Theory of Communicative Action*. Vol. 2, *The Critique of Functionalist Reason*. Translated by T. McCarthy. Cambridge: Polity.

———. 1989. *The Structural Transformation of the Public Sphere: An Enquiry into a Category of Bourgeois Society*. Cambridge, MA: MIT Press.

———. 1996. *Between Facts and Norms: Contributions to a Discourse Theory of Law and Democracy*. Cambridge, MA: MIT Press.

———. 1998. *The Inclusion of the Other: Studies in Political Theory*. Edited by C. Cronin and P. DeGreiff. Cambridge, MA: MIT Press.

———. 2001. *The Postnational Constellation: Political Essays*. Cambridge, MA: MIT Press.

Haddad, Yvonne Yazbeck. 2002. *Muslims in the West: From Sojourners to Citizens*. New York: Oxford University Press.

———. 2004. *Not Quite American? The Shaping of Arab and Muslim Identity in the United States*. Waco, TX: Baylor University Press.

Haddad, Yvonne Yazbeck, and John L. Esposito, eds. 2000. *Muslims on the Americanization Path?* Oxford: Oxford University Press.

Haddad, Yvonne Y., and Adair T. Lummis. 1987. *Islamic Values in the United States: A Comparative Study*. Oxford: Oxford University Press.

Haddad, Yvonne Yazbeck, and Jane I. Smith, eds. 2002. *Muslim Minorities in the West: Visible and Invisible*. Walnut Creek, CA: AltaMira Press.

Hakim, Abdul Hadi al-. 1999. *A Code of Practice for Muslims in the West*. London: Imam Ali Foundation.

Haley, Alex. 1976. *Roots: The Saga of an American Family*. New York: Doubleday.

Haley, Alex, and Malcolm X. 1964. *The Autobiography of Malcolm X*. New York: Ballantine Books.

Hegel, Georg W. F. 1956. *The Philosophy of History*. Translated by J. Sibree. New York: Dover Books.

Heidegger, Martin. 1962. *Being and Time*. Translated by J. Macquirre and E. Robinson. New York: HarperCollins.

———. 1971. *Poetry, Language, Thought*. Translated by A. Hofstadter. New York: Perennial Classics.

———. 1977. *The Question concerning Technology, and Other Essays*. Translated and with an introduction by William Lovitt. New York: Harper and Row.

———. 1994. *Basic Questions of Philosophy*. Bloomington: Indiana University Press.

———. 2000. *Introduction to Metaphysics*. New Haven, CT: Yale University Press.

Herberg, Will. 1983. *Protestant-Catholic-Jew: An Essay in American Religious Sociology*. Chicago: University of Chicago Press.

Hermansen, Marcia. 2004. "Muslims in the Performative Mode: A Reflection on Muslim-Christian Dialogue." *Muslim World* 94:387–97.

Herzfeld, Michael. 1997. *Cultural Intimacy: Social Poetics in the Nation State*. New York: Routledge.

Hindess, Barry. 1993. "Citizenship in the Modern World." In *Citizenship and Social Theory*, edited by Bryan Turner. London: Sage Publications.

Howell, Sally, and Andrew Shryock. 2003. "Cracking Down on Diaspora: Arab Detroit and America's War on Terror." *Anthropological Quarterly* 76 (3): 443–62.

Howell, Sarah. 2009. "Inventing the American Mosque: Early Muslims and Their Institutions in Detroit, 1910–1980." PhD diss., University of Michigan.

Hussain, Altaf. 2001. "Interfaith Dialogue: Are We Up to the Challenge?" www.islam-online.net/English/Society/2001/02/article18.shtml (last accessed on November 23, 2005).

Isin, Engin F. 2004. "The Neurotic Citizen." *Citizenship Studies* 8 (3): 217–35.

Isin, Engin F., and Bryan S. Turner. 2002. *Handbook of Citizenship Studies*. London: Sage Publications.

Isin, Engin F., and Patricia K. Wood. 1999. *Citizenship and Identity*. London: Sage Publications.

Jackson, Sherman A. 2003. "Black Orientalism: Its Genesis, Aims and Significance for American Islam." In *Muslims in the United States*, edited by Philippa Strum and Danielle Tarantolo. Washington, DC: Woodrow Wilson Center.

———. 2005. *Islam and the Blackamerican: Looking Toward the Third Resurrection*. Oxford: Oxford University Press.

Jamal, Amaney, and Nadine Naber. 2008. *Race and Arab Americans before and after 9/11: From Invisible Citizens to Visible Subjects*. Syracuse, NY: Syracuse University Press.

Joas, Hans. 1997. *The Creativity of Action*. Chicago: University of Chicago Press.

———. 2000. *The Genesis of Values*. Chicago: University of Chicago Press.

Juwayriyah, Umm. 2009. *The Size of a Mustard Seed*. Tempe, AZ: Muslim Writers Publishing.

Kahera, Akel Ismail. 2002. *Deconstructing the American Mosque: Space, Gender, and Aesthetics*. Austin: University of Texas Press.

Kant, Immanuel. 1987. *Critique of Judgment*. Indianapolis: Hackett Publishing.

Karmani, Sohail. 2003a. "Future Im-perfect." www.tesolislamia.org (last accessed on February 20, 2006).

———. 2003b. "Islam, English and 9/11." www.tesolislamia.org (last accessed in February 2006).

Katz, Jack. 1990. *Seductions of Crime*. New York: Basic Books.

Kearney, John. 2004. "My God Is Your God." *New York Times*, January 28.

Keller, Nuh Ha Mim. 1995. "Which of the Four Orthodox *Madhhab*s Has the Most Developed Fiqh for Muslims Living as Minorities?" www.masud.co.uk/ISLAM/nuh/fiqh.htm (last accessed on May 10, 2008).

———. 2001. *Port in a Storm: A Fiqh Solution to the Qibla of North America*. Amman: Wakeel Books.

Khalidi, Omar. 2000. "Approaches to Mosque Design in North America." In *Muslims on the Americanization Path?*, edited by Y. Y. Haddad and J. L. Esposito. Oxford: Oxford University Press.

Khan, Jalal Uddin, and Adrian Hare, eds. 1996. *English and Islam: Creative Encounters '96*. Proceedings of the international conference organized by International Islamic University Malaysia, December 20–22, 1996. Kuala Lumpur, Malaysia: Research Center, IIUM.

Khan, M. A. Muqtedar. 2002. *American Muslims: Bridging Faith and Freedom*. Beltsville, MD: Amana Publications.

Kierkegaard, Søren. 1982. *Concluding Unscientific Postscript*. Princeton, NJ: Princeton University Press.

Klein, Naomi. 2007. *Shock Doctrine: The Rise of Disaster Capitalism*. New York: Metropolitan Books.

Koller, Marvin R. 1988. *Humor and Society: Explorations in the Sociology of Humor*. Houston: Cap and Gown Press.

Kymlicka, Will. 1998. "Multicultural Citizenship." In *The Citizenship Debates: A Reader*, edited by Gershon Shafir. Minneapolis: University of Minnesota Press.

Lacan, Jacques. 1977. *Écrits: A Selection*. Translated by Alan Sheridan. New York: W. W. Norton.

Lamont, Michel. 1992. *Money, Morals, Manners: The Culture of the French and American Upper-Middle Class*. Chicago: University of Chicago Press.

Lefebvre, Henri. 1991. *The Production of Space*. Oxford: Blackwell Publishing.

Leonard, Karen. 2003a. "American Muslim Politics: Discourse and Practices." *Ethnicities* 3(2): 147–81.

———. 2003b. *Muslims in the United States: The State of Research*. New York: Russell Sage Foundation Publications.

Levinas, Emmanuel. 1969. *Totality and Infinity: An Essay on Exteriority*. Pittsburgh, PA: Duquesne University Press.

Levitt, Peggy. 2007. *God Needs No Passport: Immigrants and the Changing American Religious Landscape*. New York: New Press.

Looking for Comedy in the Muslim World. 2005. Written and directed by Albert Brooks. Warner Independent Pictures. DVD.

Lowe, John. 1986. "Theories of Ethnic Humor: How to Enter, Laughing." *American Quarterly* 38 (3): 439–60.

Lyon, David. 2003. *Surveillance after September 11*. Cambridge: Polity Press.

———. 2008. "Filtering Flows, Friends, and Foes: Global Surveillance." In *Politics of the Airport*, ed. Mark Salter. Minneapolis: University of Minnesota Press.

Mahmood, Saba. 2005. *Politics of Piety: The Islamic Revival and the Feminist Subject*. Princeton, NJ: Princeton University Press.

Malak, Amin. 2005. *Muslim Narratives and the Discourse of English*. Albany: State University of New York Press.

Mamdani, Mahmood. 2004. *Good Muslim, Bad Muslim: America, the Cold War, and the Roots of Terror*. New York: Pantheon.

Mamiya, Lawrence A. 1982. "From Black Muslim to Bilalian: The Evolution of a Movement." *Journal for the Scientific Study of Religion* 21 (2): 138–52.

Mandaville, Peter G. 2003. *Transnational Muslim Politics: Reimagining the Umma*. London: Routledge.

Marshall, T. H. 1964. "Citizenship and Social Class." 1950. In *Class, Citizenship, and Social Development*, by T. H. Marshall. Garden City, NY: Doubleday.

Mart, Michelle. 2004. "The 'Christianization' of Israel and the Jews in 1950s America." *Religion and American Culture* 14 (1): 109–46.

Mattson, Ingrid. 2003. "How Muslims Use Islamic Paradigms to Define America." In *Religion and Immigration: Christian, Jewish, and Muslim Experiences in the United States*, edited by Yvonne Y. Haddad, Jane I. Smith, and John L. Esposito. Walnut Creek, CA: AltaMira Press.

Mawdudi, Abul Ala. 1992. *Towards Understanding Islam*. Chicago: Kazi Publications.

Mazrui, Ali A. 1971. *Islam and the English Language in East and West Africa*. London: Oxford University Press.

———. 2004. "Muslims between the Jewish Example and the Black Experience: American Policy Implications." In *Muslims' Place in the American Public Square: Hope, Fears, and Aspirations*, edited by Zahid H. Bukhari et al. Walnut Creek, CA: AltaMira Press.

Metcalf, Barbara Daly. 1994. *Making Muslim Space in North America and Europe*. Berkeley and Los Angeles: University of California Press.

Mintz, Lawrence E. 1985. "Standup Comedy as Social and Cultural Mediation." *American Quarterly* 37(1): 71–80.

Mohd-Asraf, Ratnawati. 1996. "Teaching English as a Second or Foreign Language: The Place of Culture." In *English and Islam: Creative Encounters '96*. Edited by Jalal Uddin Khan and Adrian Hare. Kuala Lumpur, Malaysia: Research Center, IIUM.

———. 2005. "English and Islam: A Clash of Civilizations?" *Journal of Language, Identity and Education* 4 (2): 103–18.

Moore, Kathleen M. 1995. *Al-Mughtaribun: American Law and the Transformation of Muslim Life in the United States*. Albany: State University of New York Press.

Moran, Dermot. 2000. *Introduction to Phenomenology*. London: Routledge.

Morreal, John. 1983. *Taking Laughter Seriously*. Albany: State University of New York Press.

Muhammad, Amir N. A. 1998. *Muslims in America: Seven Centuries of History, 1312–2000*. Beltsville, MD: Amana Publications.

Mujahid, Abdul Malik. 2006. "Can There Be a Muslim English? A *SoundVision* Guide for Common Arabic Usage in the English Language." www.sound vision.com/Info/education/muslimenglish.asp (last accessed in February 2006).

Naber, Nadine. 2005. "Muslim First, Arab Second: A Strategic Politics of Race and Gender." *Muslim World* 95 (4): 479–95.

Nachef, Riad, and Samir Kadi. 1990. *The Substantiation of the People of Truth That the Direction of al-Qibla in the United States and Canada Is to the Southeast*. Philadelphia: Association of Islamic Charitable Project.

New Beginnings: The Story of the Islamic Center of America. 2005. Directed by Raad Alawan. Live Camera Productions. DVD.

Nietzsche, Friedrich W. 1967. *On the Genealogy of Morals and Ecce Homo*. Edited by W. Kaufman. New York: Vintage Books.

———. 1999. *Beyond Good and Evil*. Oxford: Oxford University Press.

———. 2006. *The Nietzsche Reader*. Edited by K. A. Pearson and D. Large. Malden, MA: Blackwell.

Nyers, Peter. 2006. "The Accidental Citizen: Acts of Sovereignty and (Un)making Citizenship." *Economy and Society* 53 (1): 22–41.

Olsen, Marvin E. 1965. "Durkheim's Two Concepts of Anomie." *Sociological Quarterly* 6 (1): 37–44.

Ong, Aihwa. 1996. "Cultural Citizenship as Subject-Making: Immigrants Negotiate Racial and Cultural Boundaries in the United States." *Current Anthropology* 37 (5): 737–62.

Pakulski, Jan. 1997. "Cultural Citizenship." *Citizenship Studies* 1 (1): 73–86.

Patel, Eboo. 2007. *Acts of Faith: The Story of an American Muslim, the Struggle for the Soul of a Generation*. Boston: Beacon Press.

Patterson, Orlando. 2005. *Slavery and Social Death*. Cambridge, MA: Harvard University Press.

Peirce, Charles S. 1935. *The Collected Papers (1931–1935)*. Vols. 1–6. Edited by C. Hartshorne and P. Weiss. Cambridge, MA: Harvard University Press.

Pennycook, Alastair. 1994. *The Cultural Politics of English as an International Language*. Oxford: Oxford University Press.

Pew Forum on Religion and Public Life. 2003. *Religion and Politics: Contention and Consensus*. www.pewforum.org/Politics-and-Elections/Religion-and-Politics-Contention-and-Consensus.aspx.

Pew Research Center for the People and the Press. 2007. *Muslim Americans: Middle Class and Mostly Mainstream*. Washington, DC: Pew Research Center for the People and the Press.

Pickthall, Muhammad Marmaduke. 1938. *The Meaning of the Glorious Qur'an*. Hyderabad-Deccan: Government Central Press.

Plessner, Helmuth. 1970. *Laughing and Crying: A Study of the Limits of Human Behavior*. Evanston, IL: Northwestern University Press.

Prager, Dennis. "America, Not Keith Ellison, Decides What Book a Congressman Takes His Oath On." *Townhall Magazine*, November 28, 2006.

Qutb, Sayyid. 2000. "The America I Have Seen: In the Scale of Human Values." 1951. In *America in an Arab Mirror: Images of America in Arabic Travel Literature—an Anthology*, edited by Kamal Abdel-Malek. New York: Palgrave Macmillan.

Ramadan, Tariq. 2002. *To Be a European Muslim*. Leicester, UK: Islamic Foundation.

Rappoport, Leon. 2005. *Punchlines: The Case for Racial, Ethnic, and Gender Humor*. Westport, CT: Praeger.

Rashid, Samory. 2004. "Blacks, the WOI Theory, and Hidden Transcripts." *American Journal of Islamic Social Sciences* 21 (2): 55–76.

Rieff, Philip. 2007. *Charisma: The Gift of Grace, and How It Has Been Taken from Us*. New York: Vintage Books.

Rorty, Richard. 1982. *Consequences of Pragmatism*. Minneapolis: University of Minnesota Press.

Rosaldo, Renato. 1997. "Cultural Citizenship, Inequality, and Multiculturalism." In *Latino Cultural Citizenship: Claiming Identity, Space, and Rights*, edited by William V. Flores and Rina Benmayor. Boston: Beacon Press.

Rosen-Zvi, Issachar. 2004. *Taking Space Seriously: Law, Space and Society in Contemporary Israel*. London: Ashgate.

Roy, Olivier. 2004. *Globalized Islam: The Search for a New Ummah*. New York: Columbia University Press.

Saeed, Agha. 2002. "The American Muslim Paradox." In *Muslim Minorities in the*

West: Visible and Invisible, edited by Yvonne Yazbeck Haddad and Jane I. Smith. Walnut Creek, CA: AltaMira Press.

Safi, Omid, ed. 2003. *Progressive Muslims: On Justice, Gender, and Pluralism.* Oxford: Oneworld Publications.

Salter, Mark B. 2007. "Governmentalities of an Airport: Heterotopia and Confession." *International Political Sociology* 1:49–66.

Saussure, Ferdinand de. 1959. *Course in General Linguistics.* New York: McGraw-Hill.

Schimmel, Annemarie. 1994. *Deciphering the Signs of God: A Phenomenological Approach to Islam.* Albany: State University of New York Press.

Schmidt, Garbi. 2004. *Islam in Urban America: Sunni Muslims in Chicago.* Philadelphia: Temple University Press.

———. 2005. "The Transnational Umma—Myth or Reality? Examples from the Western Diaspora." *Muslim World* 95 (4): 575–86.

Schmitt, Carl. 1976. *The Concept of the Political.* New Brunswick, NJ: Rutgers University Press.

———. 1988. *Political Theology: Four Chapters on the Concept of Sovereignty.* Translated by G. Schwab. Cambridge, MA: MIT Press.

———. 2003. *The Nomos of the Earth.* Translated by G. L. Ulmen. 1950. Reprint, New York: Telos Press.

Schopenhauer, Arthur. 1966. *The World as Will and Representation.* 2 vols. New York: Dover Books.

Schumann, Christoph. 2007. "A Muslim 'Diaspora' in the United States?" *Muslim World* 97 (1): 11–32.

Schutz, Alfred. 1962. *Collected Papers.* Vol. 1, *The Problem of Social Reality.* The Hague: Martinus Nijhoff.

———. 1967. *The Phenomenology of the Social World.* Evanston, IL: Northwestern University Press.

Shafir, Gershon. 1998. *The Citizenship Debates: A Reader.* Minneapolis: University of Minnesota Press.

Shakir, Zaid. 2005. *Scattered Pictures: Reflections of an American Muslim.* Hayward, CA: Zaytuna Institute.

———. 2006. "Clash of the Uncivilized: Insights into the Cartoon Controversy." www.zaytuna.org/articleDetails.asp?articleID=92 (last accessed on May 9, 2008).

Shapiro, Gary, and Alan Sica. 1984. *Hermeneutics: Questions and Prospects.* Amherst: University of Massachusetts Press.

Shaukat, Khalid. N.d. "The Islamic Calendar Development in North America." www.moonsighting.com/icdna.html (last accessed in August 2006).

Shils, Edward. 1972. *The Constitution of Society.* Chicago: University of Chicago Press.

Shklar, Judith. 1991. *American Citizenship: The Quest for Inclusion.* Cambridge, MA: Harvard University Press.

Shryock, Andrew, ed. 2004a. "In the Double Remoteness of Arab Detroit: Reflections on Ethnography, Culture Work, and the Intimate Disciplines of Americanization." In *Off Stage, on Display: Intimacy and Ethnography in the Age of Public Culture*, edited by Andrew Shryock. Stanford, CA: Stanford University Press.

———. 2004b. *Off Stage, on Display: Intimacy and Ethnography in the Age of Public Culture*. Stanford, CA: Stanford University Press.

———. 2007. "Finding Islam in Detroit: The Multiple Histories, Identities, and Locations of a City and Its Muslims." http://stanford.edu/dept/fren-ital /institute/Conferences/Papers/Shryock.pdf.

Simmel, Georg. 1950. *The Sociology of Georg Simmel*. Translated, edited, and with an introduction by Kurt H. Wolff. Glencoe, IL: Free Press.

———. 1959. *Essays on Sociology, Philosophy, and Aesthetics*. Edited by Kurt H. Wolff. Columbus: Ohio State University Press.

———. 1971. *On Individuality and Social Forms*. Chicago: University of Chicago Press.

———. 1991. *Schopenhauer and Nietzsche*. Urbana: University of Illinois Press.

———. 1997. *Simmel on Culture: Selected Writings*. Edited by D. Frisby and M. Featherstone. London: Sage Publications.

———. 2004. *The Philosophy of Money*. London: Routledge.

———. 2010. *The View of Life: Four Metaphysical Essays with Journal Aphorisms*. Chicago: University of Chicago Press.

Smelser, Neil. 2004. "September 11, 2001, as Cultural Trauma." In *Cultural Trauma and Collective Identity*, by Jeffrey C. Alexander et al. Berkeley and Los Angeles: University of California Press.

Smith, Christian. 2010. *What Is a Person?* Chicago: University of Chicago Press.

Smith, Jane I. 1999. *Islam in America*. New York: Columbia University Press.

———. 2004. "Muslims as Partners in Interfaith Encounter." In *Muslims' Place in the American Public Square: Hope, Fears, and Aspirations*, edited by Zahid H. Bukhari et al. Walnut Creek, CA: AltaMira Press.

Smith, Rogers. 1997. *Civic Ideals: Conflicting Visions of Citizenship in U.S. History*. New Haven, CT: Yale University Press.

Somers, Margaret. 2006. "Citizenship, Statelessness and Market Fundamentalism: Arendtian Right to Have Rights." In *Migration, Citizenship, Ethnos*, edited by Y. Michal Bodemann and Gokce Yurdakul. New York: Palgrave Macmillan.

———. 2008. *Genealogies of Citizenship: Markets, Statelessness, and the Right to Have Rights*. Cambridge: Cambridge University Press.

Stevens, Wallace. 2009. *Selected Poems*. New York: Alfred A. Knopf.

Strauss, Leo. 1989. *The Rebirth of Classical Political Rationalism: An Introduction to the Thought of Leo Strauss*. Selected by Thomas L. Pangle. Chicago: University of Chicago Press.

Swidler, Ann. 1986. "Culture in Action: Symbols and Strategies." *American Sociological Review* 51 (2): 273–86.

Takim, Liyakatali. 2004. "From Conversion to Conversation: Interfaith Dialogue in Post 9-11 America." *Muslim World* 94:343–55.

Tavory, Iddo. 2010. "Of Yarmulkes and Categories: Delegating Boundaries and the Phenomenology of Interactional Expectation." *Theory and Society* 39 (1): 49–68.

Taylor, Charles. 1994. "The Politics of Recognition." In *Multiculturalism: Examining the Politics of Recognition*, edited by Charles Taylor and Amy Gutman. Princeton, NJ: Princeton University Press.

Torpey, John. 2000. *The Invention of the Passport: Surveillance, Citizenship, and the State*. Cambridge: Cambridge University Press.

Turner, Lorenzo D. 1949. *Africanisms in the Gullah Dialect*. Chicago: University of Chicago Press.

Turner, Victor. 1969. *The Ritual Process: Structure and Anti-structure*. Chicago: Aldine.

———. 1973. "The Center Out There: Pilgrim's Goal." *History of Religions* 12 (1): 191–230.

———. 1974. *Dramas, Fields, and Metaphors: Symbolic Action in Human Society*. Ithaca, NY: Cornell University Press.

Warner, Stephen, and J. Wittner, eds. 1998. *Gatherings in Diaspora: Religious Communities and the New Immigration*. Philadelphia: Temple University Press.

Weber, Max. 1946. *From Max Weber: Essays in Sociology*. Translated, edited, and with an introduction by H. H. Gerth and C. Wright Mills. New York: Oxford University Press.

———. 1968. *Economy and Society*. Edited by Günther Roth and Claus Wittich. Translated by Ephraim Fischoff et al. 3 vols. New York: Bedminster Press.

———. 1992. *The Protestant Ethic and the Spirit of Capitalism*. Translated by Talcott Parsons. 1930. Reprint, London: Routledge.

Weingartner, Rudolph H. 1960. *Experience and Culture: The Philosophy of Georg Simmel*. Middletown, CT: Wesleyan University Press.

Wiktorowicz, Quintan. 2005. *Radical Islam Rising: Muslim Extremism in the West*. Lanham, MD: Rowman and Littlefield.

Wittgenstein, Ludwig. 1997. *Philosophical Investigations*. 2nd ed. Oxford: Blackwell.

Wolfe, Michael. 1997. *One Thousand Roads to Mecca*. New York: Grove Press.

Wolff, Kurt H. 1991. *Survival and Sociology*. New Brunswick, NJ: Transaction.

Wuthnow, Robert. 2005. *America and the Challenges of Religious Diversity*. Princeton, NJ: Princeton University Press.

Yasin, Zayed. 2002. "Of Faith and Citizenship: My American Jihad." www.people .fas.harvard.edu/~yasin/speech.html (last accessed on August 22, 2003).

Yee, James. 2005. *For God and Country: Faith and Patriotism under Fire*. New York: PublicAffairs.

Yilmaz, Ihsan. 2002. *Muslim Laws, Politics and Society in Modern Nation States: Dynamic Legal Pluralism in England, Turkey and Pakistan*. London: Ashgate Press.

Younis, Waheed. 2006. "*Qibla* in North America." http://moonsighting.com /qibla-wy.pdf (last accessed on August 15, 2006).

Yusuf, Irfan. 2003. "The Islaam of Double Vowels." www.muslimwakeup.com /main/archives/2003/02/the_islaam_of_d.php (last accessed in February 2006).

Zaidi, Ali Hassan. 2011. *Islam, Modernity, and the Human Sciences*. New York: Palgrave Macmillan.

Zerubavel, Eviatar. 1982. "Easter and Passover: On Calendars and Group Identity." *American Sociological Review* 47:284–89.

———. 1991. *The Fine Line: Making Distinctions in Everyday Life*. New York: Free Press.

Zolberg, Aristide, and Long Litt Woon. 1999. "Why Islam Is Like Spanish: Cultural Incorporation in Europe and the United States." *Politics and Society* 27 (1): 5–38.

Zubrzycki, Geneviève. 2006. *The Crosses of Auschwitz: Nationalism and Religion in Post-Communist Poland*. Chicago: University of Chicago Press.

Index

Abdali, S. Kamal, 54–55
Abdallah, Umar Faruq, 148–49
abode: of Islam/peace (see *dar al Islam*); of mission (see *dar al dawah*); of treaty (see *dar al ahd*); of war (see *dar al harb*)
Abrahamic discourse, 32, 146; in CAIR radio ad, 162–63; vs. liberal pluralism, 164, 231n9; and Muslim Unity Center rock, 156–57; in National Day of Prayer address, 166; as personal appeal, 169–70; reservations about, 164–65; as response to Islamophobia, 163; transition to American civil religion, 201. *See also* Children of Abraham Project
Abyssinia, 98, 226n8
advocacy groups, Muslim: early successes, 126; Gulf War impact on, 127. *See also* Council on American-Islamic Relations (CAIR)
African American Muslims: in CAIR ads, 140; comfort with Christianity, 86; divide with immigrant Muslims, 155, 223n16; English and, 86–88; *hijra* likened to Great Migration, 98; and *qibla*, 57–61; teaching immigrant Muslims, 138
Ahmed, Ahmed, 176, 182–83
airport, 7–9; ban on jokes at, 184, 233n13; Muslim jokes about, 181; visibility of Muslims at, 172–73, 193. *See also* No-Fly List

Alawan, Eide, 55, 145, 152–53, 158–59, 162, 165–67
Albanian Islamic Center, 43–44, 55, 84
aletheia, 25, 193, 233n18. *See also* Heidegger, Martin
alienation, 1, 7–8, 33, 92, 207, 217
Allah: not biblical God, 147–48, 163; used interchangeably with "God," 82, 148–49, 177, 230n2
Allah Made Me Funny (AMMF), 33, 176–78, 195
Alper, Rabbi Bob, 184, 196
Alwani, Taha Jabir al-, 61
Amer, Mohammed, 176–79
American Civil Liberties Union (ACLU), 129, 131
American civil religion. *See* religion, American civil
American Moslem Society (Dix Mosque), 41–43
American Muslim Center, 41
Amin, Imam Abdullah El-, 60, 146, 153–55, 157, 161–62, 166–68
anomie, 21; as absence of nomos, 222n9, 223n4; and America, 49; linguistic, 67, 88; temporally limited, 100–101; and the uncanny, 93
anthropology, philosophical, 29
Anti-Defamation League, 136, 151
appropriation, 10, 26, 33, 94, 120; of English, 65–69; stages of, 208–10
Arendt, Hannah, 6, 92, 123–25, 174
asabiyya, 10, 15, 143, 203, 212; distinguished from solidarity, 219n3